The Old Country Cookbook

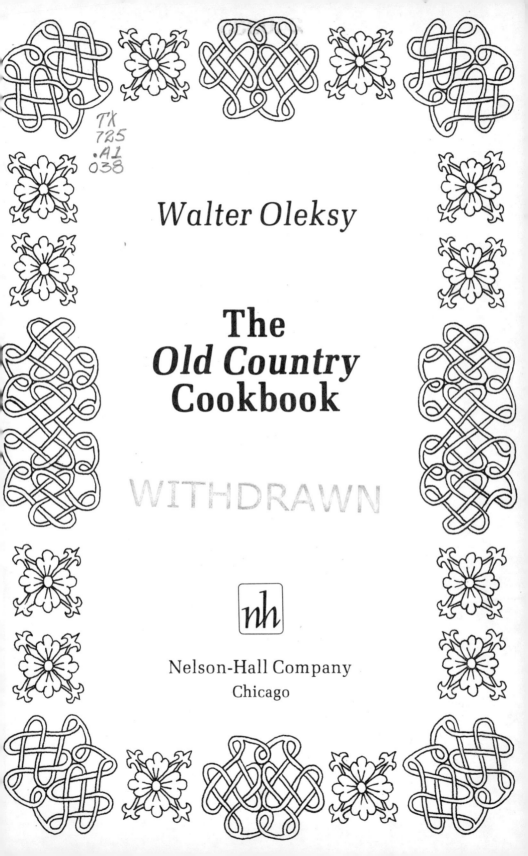

Walter Oleksy

The
Old Country
Cookbook

nh

Nelson-Hall Company
Chicago

ISBN: 0–88229–105–X

Library of Congress Catalog Card No.: 73–81082

Copyright © 1974 by Walter Oleksy

Manufactured in the United States of America

To Mom
And all the other lovely ladies
who contributed their recipes

CONTENTS

INTRODUCTION

The reasons for traveling in Europe are numerous, but one that everyone shares is the experience of dining there. Sampling the dishes of different cultures, in elaborate or quaint atmospheres, is a strong attraction and among the delights we remember most.

The custom of eating out is much more developed in Europe, and is a major reason why you will find many more restaurants and cafes abroad than you will at home.

In the early days of our own country, people dining out often had to depend on inns, sometimes located in terms of the time it took a carriage or horse to travel from one point to another. Restaurants and cafes did develop in our cities, but they were slow to come to other areas until the appearance of the automobile. Unfortunately, our restaurants often served food of institutional quality, mass produced for mass serving.

The tradition of eating at home is strong in this country, primarily because of the needs and dining habits of generations of immigrants, who came mainly from Europe and the British Isles. The majority were peasants or laborers and, back in the "Old Country," ate most of their meals at home, mainly for economic reasons.

When they came to this country, the new arrivals faced many adjustments. Their custom of eating at home was reinforced as an expedient to avoid one additional adjustment, though of course they patronized their local ethnic restaurant on special occasions. As a result of families having most of their meals at home, ethnic recipes have been preserved, handed down from generation to generation.

Since the turn of the century, Americans have begun to travel in greater numbers, and most of this tourism abroad is still focused on Europe. This influence is strongly reflected here in ethnic restaurants, patronized not only by more affluent descendants of the immigrants, but also by those who have traveled to Europe, bringing back with them memories of food they ate abroad, and anxious to relive the experience this side of the ocean.

But whether food interest can be traced to ethnic influences or to travel experiences, the results are the same, if the bent is to enjoy authentic Old Country food.

In my own case, interest in and love for Old Country cooking came to me at an early age. I grew up in two of the best possible culinary worlds: my mother is Austrian and my father Polish-Ukrainian.

When my sister and brother and I were born, my parents made a bargain: he would not speak Polish around our house in Chicago, if she would not speak German. This was a move to further Americanize the family. Happy to say, the ethnic embargo did not apply to cooking. My mother brought to our table many of her mother's favorite Austrian, German, Dutch, Bavarian, Hungarian, and Bohemian dishes. And, from my father's mother, and from old Polish and Slavic ladies in the heavily immigrant-populated neighborhoods we lived in, she also brought to our table Polish, Ukrainian, Russian, Latvian, and Czechoslovakian dishes.

When I was a boy in Chicago, the corner butcher shop, on any Saturday morning, was as close to a farm as any of us city kids got. We would get up early and watch the old ladies do their shopping. Stacked out on the sidewalk in front of the butcher shop would be wooden crates containing live chickens, turkeys, ducks, geese, and even pigs. The ladies would thrust their hands inside and move the poultry around, in order to make their selection.

A goose would be picked by a very particular housewife, the

butcher would kill it for her, drain and save the blood which would be used for *Czarnina* (a dark, sweet-sour soup), and even the feathers were kept—washed and dried and stuffed into featherbed quilts for a warm winter's sleep.

In summertime, when the kitchen windows were open, an incredible variety of aromas told you what neighbors were having for dinner that night—chicken paprikash, Caucasian lamb shashlik, Esterhazy beef stew, Bavarian pork chops, oxtail ragout, veal stroganoff, or Lombardy pot roast. Often, of course, the aromas were from less glamorous-sounding dishes —goulash, corned beef and cabbage, or pig's knuckles and sauerkraut.

More often than not, one of the old ladies on our block would come over to our house with a bowl of steaming-hot vegetable soup with *knadles* (Austrian bacon dumplings), Hunter's stew, or half an almond coffee cake she wanted us to sample. And my mother, naturally, asked for the recipe.

Later, when I grew up and traveled abroad, my experiences in Old Country dining were broadened and my love for ethnic cooking was intensified. I recall the hours spent in restaurants and cafes of Europe as keenly as I can those spent wandering through museums and castles.

At Rotensturmstrasse 12, not far from St. Stephen's cathedral, in the heart of Vienna, there is a small garden cafe called the Linde. Lantern lights shine on the rose arbors at night, a string quartet plays Mozart, and the *Lindenschnitte schnitzel* is so thin and tender and the apple strudle so plump and juicy that you wonder if it isn't all a dream.

And there is the Goldener Hecht, a student inn at Heidelberg, where the songs and *gemütlichkeit* flow like wine, and the Hussars' roast is so spicy and succulent—or the small family-run hotel near the university in Brussels where the brown beef soup is so thick, yet so smooth—and the frescoed, white marble Buca Lapi basement restaurant in Florence where everything from the lasagna to the strawberry torte contains brandy or rum.

You know the places, or ones like them, either from having traveled abroad or from dining in some of the good ethnic restaurants in this country. If you have ever wanted to bring some of their gastronomical wonders back home with you, to try out in your own kitchen, this book is for you.

Most cookbooks are written by great cooks, chefs, home economists, or gourmets who gallop around the kitchen. I am an amateur cook; a venturesome one, I might add, as well as discriminating. But I walk, not gallop, around my apple-green kitchen in a suburb north of Chicago.

The real authors of this book are dozens of excellent cooks, but none is famous, except in their families and neighborhoods. When I talked about my dining experiences in the great capitals of Europe to relatives and friends from the old ethnic neighborhoods of Chicago, they insisted they have recipes better than those used in the fancy restaurants. Their recipes, they proudly maintain, are of the authentic, country-kitchen variety that have been handed down from their mother and their mother's mother.

Most of the recipes come from plump, jolly old ladies who emigrated here half a century ago, who cook and keep house to make their men and children happy. They serve dishes that are hearty, tasty, and plentiful, which fill the men who fire the furnaces, drive the trucks, and pour the concrete that build this country.

We can't get to Europe every day, and we can't bring Vienna or Heidelberg or those other charming cities of Europe back home with us, except in memories. But we can bring back the *schnitzel* and *strudle* and other dishes, in the form of recipes. Thanks to the generosity of the Old Country housewives who share their recipes with us, we can be in Vienna, Berlin, Prague, Warsaw, Paris, or London anytime we wish. Europe, in this sense, is only as far away as our kitchen.

The culinary treasures of the Old Country will be covered by country, with a preface to acquaint you with some of the traditions and history behind the cooking.

The recipes in this book are not necessarily difficult or expensive to prepare for family or guests. Often, the difference in recreating a favorite Old Country dish lies in the use of herbs, spices, sauces, or other flavoring ingredients that are the individual nationality's specialty and give the dish its distinction.

The only ingredient some of the recipes call for that American cooks may not use often in their cooking is wine. Much of foreign cooking calls for wine to be used in the meat or seafood dishes. The wine need not be expensive, and if you keep on hand two bottles, one white and one red, and keep them well-corked between uses, they will last for some time.

As for how many new dishes you should attempt for any one meal, it is best to concentrate on one unfamiliar dish at a time, both in preparation demands and the capability to enjoy the results. And, of course, never plan more than one dish that requires last-minute attention. No matter how good your meal will taste, guests won't enjoy it if you come to the table exhausted or, worse, can't join them for each course because you're off in the kitchen, working on the next one.

None of the dishes in this book are beyond the skill of an amateur cook. It's time and concentration that will see you through. I once tackled a three-layered Viennese *schaumtorte* that even two fine old cooks said they wouldn't have the courage to attempt. Mine took four hours to make, but Wow! It was a sensation.

Finally, a word on the Old Country itself. Where *is* the "Old Country"? It is the homeland from which peoples of many nationalities emigrated. You hear the term used mainly by Central Europeans who came to America around the turn of the century and up to the first two or three decades of this century: the Austrians, Czechs, Germans, Hungarians, and Swiss; and the Poles, Estonians, Latvians, and Lithuanians of the Baltic.

But the Old Country is also "The Old Sod" to the sons of Erin and those who came from elsewhere in the British Isles. It is home for Danes, Finns, Norwegians, and Swedes from Scandinavia; for Belgians and Dutch of the North Sea; for Frenchmen, Italians, Spaniards, and Portuguese of the Latin countries; for Albanians, Bulgarians, Greeks, Rumanians, and Slavs of the Balkans; for Russians of Eastern Europe; and for Armenians, Serbs, Syrians, and Turks of the Near East.

Some of these nations no longer enjoy the political freedom they enjoyed before World Wars I and II. The land still exists, however, no matter what it is called, and the people who live in what once was called Estonia but now is called the Estonian

Soviet Socialist Republic, or in Serbia, which is now a part of Yugoslavia, are really not Russian or Yugoslavian; they are still Estonians and Serbs. The same is true of the Poles, Latvians, Lithuanians, Czechoslovakians, and Armenians.

What makes the peoples of the Old Country remain what they were, despite the loss of their sovereign independence, is the land, their national customs, their religions, their inbred character traits, their dress and, not lastly, their food.

Europe, and Europeans, has changed greatly since the end of World War II. Now, more than 25 years later, many of the nations of Europe live under the Common Market, a system of agreement in sharing trade and economics that is tending to bring peoples of countries together at last who once wouldn't think of sitting down together at the same conference table.

I like to think that there is another Common Market at work in the world, not only in Europe. It is the marketplace of the breadbasket; the *dining* table at which men of all national origins can sit in brotherhood and share the land's bounty.

The Old Country Cookbook aspires to share the best of that bounty with present and future generations.

Leave the doors of our homes closed, if we must. But let's open up the kitchen windows.

1

Central Europe

Austria, Germany, Czechoslovakia, Hungary, Switzerland

Sit down to dinner in Austria, Germany, Czechoslovakia, Hungary, or Switzerland, and you may never want to get up again. The food is substantial and hearty, but most of all, it tastes *so* good.

Perhaps it's because you have been hiking up and down mountains all day, exploring the birthplaces of emperors or composers, or simply because you are dining by candlelight with an orchestra playing soothing music. Whatever the reasons, the food will taste different, and delicious.

The distinctive flavor comes from the

seemingly little things the cooks of these countries add: rich beef stock for gravy, sometimes with sour cream; sweet-sour flavoring in meats and vegetables; the addition of peppercorns, paprika, caraway seeds, garlic, juniper berries, and other ingredients to spice up a dish.

Desserts are rich and filling: coffee cakes with sugar toppings and filled with fresh fruits or nuts; tortes with layers of whipped cream; strudles with fruits and raisins wrapped inside.

The food is substantial because, traditionally, the people needed good, solid nourishment to work the land.

Situated geographically in the middle of Europe, the people grew to know about the foods of other countries, primarily because of wars. The Italians and French from the West, and Tartars and Turks from the East all left something behind when they left: their recipes. You might not like an invading army, but you never hold their food against them; not if it tastes good.

Some of the meals eaten around campfires by invading armies, and later taught to cooks in the inns of the conquered villages, later became absorbed into the eating habits of the country when it again became liberated.

The culinary heritage of the Central European countries is among the finest in the world. You may be familiar with some of the dishes, from eating in ethnic restaurants. It's more fun to try them out in your own kitchen.

Chapter 1

AUSTRIA

At the mention of Austria you're bound to think of storybook villages with houses of gingerbread, castles high up in the Alps, Viennese ballrooms where orchestras are playing Strauss waltzes, and palatial hotel restaurants or quaint Tyrolean inns where the goose and strudle are absolutely out of this world.

Some things change or, worse, never were. Austria *was* and still *is,* and not the least wonderful thing that has not changed is its food.

You come away from Austria with incredible memories and a deep, warm love for the country. What you may have seen in *The Sound of Music* might have seemed like a bit too much whipped cream for you, but there are two things about Austria that even Hollywood cannot exaggerate, and they are the Alpine scenery and the food.

Travel from Vienna to the Tyrol by car, bus, or train, and you will pass through some of the most beautiful mountain country in the world. Hike in the mountains, walk barefoot in the grass, skip stones across a stream, and sit down to a meal and you will know you are living the good life.

My favorite of all places in Austria, even surpassing the magnificence of Vienna, is Landeck, a village on the Inn river in the Tyrol, which you'll have to look closely to find on a map. The Arlberg Alps seem to come right down to the village streets, and there is a hotel built beside the rushing river. I looked out my bedroom window one August morning and couldn't believe anything I saw. The sun was causing the ice to glisten high up on the mountains, the cattle were grazing pastorally on the verdant slopes, and just below, along a dirt road, Heidi and Peter were actually pulling a small wooden cart that contained their books and dolls.

It is impossible to forget the roast duck and three-layered schaumtorte filled with fresh peaches and strawberries that were served in the garden of the inn by a pretty young hostess in a colorful dirndl and immaculate white apron, her blonde hair braided in pigtails, while half a dozen musicians in lederhosen played some bouncy landlers.

In a setting such as that, even the townsfolk sitting at nearby tables with glasses of wine (red for the men, white for the ladies), seemed to forget that it wasn't always like this in Austria. Innumerable partitions and two World Wars have changed its borders, but not its people.

Today, Austria is a republic with a population of about ten million, covering about 33,000 square miles, most of it towered over by the great Alps.

When the Hapsburg dynasty ruled in Europe during most of the last five centuries, all or part of Germany, The Netherlands, Poland, Czechoslovakia, Hungary, Yugoslavia, Rumania, Italy, and even Spain belonged to the Austrian Empire.

From this treasurehouse of cultures, Austria inherited not only considerable monetary tribute, but a great wealth of recipes. They learned of goulash from the Hungarians, dumplings from the Bavarians, pot cheese and clabber from the Slavs, sturdy yeast pastries from the Bohemians, sweet-sour carp from the Poles, and even *Wiener Schnitzel,* which means "Vienna slice," is an adaptation of Italy's Veal Milanese.

Austria itself invented chicken stuffed with goose liver and Madeira, the Sacher Torte (chocolate cake with apricot jam), the Dobosh (ten thin layers of cake with chocolate filling), the Pischinger Torte (wafers of crystallized sugar), egg dumplings, smoked pork with sauerkraut in wine, and last but not least, the hot dog.

The hot dog is, in Austria, a sausage. It is called a "wiener" because it was born in Vienna, which in Austrian is called "Wien," but pronounced with a "v."

Coffee and cake is a staple of Austrian dining, but neither can be considered of Austrian origin. It was what the Austrians did with them that matters. Coffee became known to the Austrians as a result of two invasions by the Turks, in 1529 and 1683. Strudles and tortes the Austrians invented and made even more tasty by adding "Schlag," the German name for whipped cream. Today, "kaffe mit schlag," whether the whipped cream is in the coffee or the pastry or on the side, is a typically Austrian dining custom.

Another is the *Heuriger.* It means "this year's" new wine, and a new vintage is a better reason than most to celebrate. Originally, the custom was to set up tables in the vineyards, for peasants to sample the new wine. A buffet of sausages and pickles would be served. Later, festivals were held to celebrate more elaborately. The most famous were held, and still are, in Grinzing, a Vienna suburb where in spring the garden cafes are filled with wine, women, song, and delicious food.

Naturally, you can't celebrate a wine festival for long unless you eat something. And, in Austria, the eating is about as good as it gets anywhere: hearty soups, zesty sausages, dark breads, sauerkraut, sauerbraten, rabbit, roast goose and duckling, apple pancakes, and those pastries for which the country is perhaps more famous than anything else except the waltz.

Suffice it to say that from Vienna and Austria's storybook provinces come some of the world's most beautiful scenery, charming traditions, and delicious foods. Therefore we'll bypass the opera houses, palaces, museums, royal gardens, and move directly to the sidewalk cafes, hotel restaurants, and, best of all, the kitchens, for some of the best of the dishes of Austria.

Appetizers

Österreichische Eier
(Austrian eggs)

Hard-boil a dozen eggs. Remove shells and cut them in half and remove the yolks. Mash yolks in a bowl and add small quantities of finely-chopped cooked mushrooms, chopped anchovies, smoked tongue, lean cooked ham, a little oil, vinegar, salt, and pepper. Fill egg whites with this mixture. Yield: 2 dozen halves.

Hühnerleber auf Apfelscheiben
(chicken livers on sliced apples)

6 chicken livers
3 tablespoons butter
2 tablespoons Madeira wine

½ teaspoon salt
6 apple slices, ¼ inch thick
sliced truffles or black olives

Clean livers and saute in butter. Pour flaming Madeira wine over them. Salt lightly. Cool. Simmer apple slices in water until almost tender. Cool. Place one liver on each apple slice. Garnish with sliced truffles or black olives. Yield: 6 servings.

Soup

Erbsensuppe
(split pea soup)

1½ quarts stock from boiling smoked pork
1½ cups dried split peas
1 cup cooked smoked pork butt, diced

1 small carrot, sliced thin
1 tablespoon chopped onion
2 tablespoons chopped parsley
2 tablespoons fat
2 tablespoons flour

For smoked pork stock, cook 2 pounds of smoked pork butt in three quarts of unsalted water, covered, for 1¼ hours. Remove smoked pork and dice enough to make 1 cup. Add split peas, smoked pork, and carrot to liquid and cook, covered, for half an hour. Saute onions and parsley in fat. Add flour to onion and parsley mixture. Stir until well blended. Add this mixture to soup. Cook a few minutes until soup thickens. Yield: 6 servings.

Salads

Kartoffel Salat
(potato salad)

4 to 6 potatoes, boiled in their
   jackets
1 tablespoon onion, chopped
1 clove garlic, crushed
salt and pepper

2 tablespoons olive oil
3 tablespoons wine vinegar
¾ teaspoon French mustard
1 tablespoon parsley

Peel and slice potatoes while still warm. Put in salad bowl with onions, garlic, and seasoning. Bring the oil, vinegar, and mustard slowly to a boil. Pour over the potatoes. Mix carefully. Serve cold, garnished with parsley. Yield: 4 to 6 servings.

Österreichischer Salat
(Austrian salad)

Dice equal quantities of cooked potatoes and peeled and cored apples. Mix with a dressing of equal parts oil and vinegar. Season with salt and pepper. Garnish with slices of hard-boiled eggs. You can also add beets cut in cubes and uncooked filleted herrings, cut in strips.

Fisolensalat
(green bean salad)

3 cups cooked Frenched green
   beans (2 packages frozen)
¼ cup olive oil
¼ cup wine vinegar

1 teaspoon salt
⅛ teaspoon pepper
2 tablespoons chopped onion

Cook beans in salted water until barely tender. Drain, then run under cold water to cool, and drain thoroughly. Mix oil, vinegar, salt, and pepper. Add beans and mix. Sprinkle with onion. Chill half an hour before serving. Yield: 6 servings.

Vegetables

Österreichischers Kraut
(Austrian cabbage)

1 small head of cabbage
butter or bacon fat
½ teaspoon salt
1 teaspoon paprika

1 tablespoon minced onion or
    crushed garlic clove
½ pint sour cream

Shred and wash cabbage. Saute lightly in butter or bacon fat. Add salt, paprika, and onion or garlic. Put into baking dish and pour on sour cream. Bake in 350 degree oven for 20 minutes. Yield: 6 servings.

Sauerkraut
(sour cabbage)

2 tablespoons butter or
    equivalent bacon fat
2 small or 1 large onion, sliced
1 quart sauerkraut
1 medium sized potato or 1

large tart apple
stock to cover kraut
1 or 2 tablespoons brown sugar
1 teaspoon caraway seed

Melt butter in large skillet and saute sliced onion until transparent. Rinse sauerkraut and drain. Add to onion and butter and saute 5 minutes. Peel and grate potato or apple and add to kraut. Cover with stock (water and beef bouillon will do). Cook, uncovered, 30 minutes, then cover and cook in 350 degree oven another 30 minutes. Season with brown sugar and caraway seeds if desired. Yield: 4 servings.

Potatoes and Dumplings

Tirolerspeckknödel
(Tyrolean bacon dumplings)

4 slices bacon, diced
8 slices bread, diced

1 teaspoon salt
1 cup flour

1 small onion, diced
2 eggs
1 cup milk

½ teaspoon baking powder
¼ teaspoon pepper
dash garlic powder

Saute diced bacon, bread, and onion in skillet until bread is firm but not crisp and bacon is still transparent. In a bowl, beat eggs, milk, and salt until frothy. Blend gradually with sifted flour and baking powder. Add bread, bacon, and onion mixture, pepper and garlic powder. Sprinkle flour on your hands and shape the mixture, moist but not soggy, into dumplings the size of golf balls. Cook gently, covered, in salted water about 15 minutes. Drain dumplings and serve with soup or meat and gravy dishes. Yield: 10 dumplings.

Erdapfelknödel
(potato dumplings)

3 large potatoes
¼ cup butter, creamed
2 eggs

2 teaspoons salt
⅛ teaspoon nutmeg
2 cups flour

Boil potatoes with jackets; peel and rice them while hot. Combine with butter, eggs, salt, nutmeg, and flour. Form into dumplings the size of plums. Cook gently in salted water, covered, 15 minutes. Drain and serve with gravy. Yield: 6 servings.

Fish

Fisch Paprikash
(fish with paprika)

¼ pound margarine
1 pound onions, sliced
2 pounds carp, haddock, bass,
    or mackerel

¾ pint sour cream
2 teaspoons paprika
salt and pepper

Saute onions lightly in margarine. Clean fish and put whole on the onions and add cream mixed with paprika, salt and pepper.

Bake until tender. Strain sauce over the fish. Yield: 4 to 6 servings.

Poultry

Paprikahendl
(paprika chicken)

2 fryers, 2½ pounds each
½ cup margarine, melted
¾ cup flour, sifted
2 tablespoons paprika

1 tablespoon minced onion
1 tablespoon salt
¼ tablespoon pepper
1 cup sour cream

Cut chickens into serving pieces. Pour melted margarine into a pie plate. In another pie plate, mix flour, paprika, onion, salt, and pepper. Dip chicken parts into butter, then into flour mixture. Save left-over flour mixture for gravy. Place chicken parts in shallow baking pan. Pour remaining butter over chicken. Bake at 400 degrees for 1 hour, or until tender. Remove chicken from pan. Pour butter drippings and flour into saucepan, stir in 1 cup water. Cook, stirring until gravy thickens, and boil for 1 minute. Blend in sour cream but do not boil. Pour gravy over chicken and serve. Yield: 4 to 6 servings.

Mandel Hendl
(almond chicken)

3-pound fryer, cut up
½ cup flour
1 tablespoon salt
1 tablespoon paprika
¼ teaspoon pepper
½ cup almonds, slivered
½ cup salad oil

2 chicken bouillon cubes
2 cups boiling water
1 cup ketchup
1 cup sour cream
½ cup sharp cheddar cheese,
    grated

Shake chicken parts in paper bag containing flour and seasonings. Brown chicken in salad oil. Place chicken in a 2-quart casserole. Saute almonds in salad oil left in skillet. Blend in flour mixture remaining in bag. Stir in bouillon stock (2 chicken bouillon cubes dissolved in boiling water). Cook, stirring constantly until mixture begins to thicken. Stir in ketchup and sour cream. Pour over chicken in casserole. Cover and bake in 375 degree oven for 50 minutes or until tender. Uncover and sprinkle cheese over chicken. Return to oven and bake 10 more minutes until cheese melts. Yield: 6 servings.

Gebratene Ente mit Sauerkraut
(roast duck with sauerkraut)

1 duckling, 4 to 5 pounds	1 teaspoon caraway seeds
½ cup oil	3 cups sauerkraut
1 medium onion, chopped	salt and pepper to taste
1 apple, peeled, cored, and chopped	1 tablespoon cornstarch

Quarter the duckling and brown in oil in skillet. Drain all but 2 or 3 tablespoons fat and saute onion and apple for a few minutes. Add caraway seeds and sauerkraut, mixing lightly. Arrange duckling on top of sauerkraut, season, and cover. Cook on top of stove over low flame about 1½ hours or in a 325 degree oven. Remove duck and place in broiler under moderate heat about 5 to 10 minutes before serving. Combine cornstarch and 2 tablespoons water, add to sauerkraut. Simmer, stirring constantly, until thickened. Serve around duck. Yield: 6 to 8 servings.

Meat

Wiener Schnitzel
(Vienna breaded veal cutlets)

2 pounds veal	1 cup bread crumbs
⅜ cup flour	½ cup cooking oil
2 eggs, beaten	½ cup shortening
milk	

Select milk-fed veal, soft pink in color. Trim off all fat, and pound each slice as thin as possible (about ⅛ inch). Make small cuts around meat edge so slices do not curl when cooked.

Sprinkle flour over both sides of veal. Beat eggs with a little milk, and dip veal into mixture. Press bread crumbs firmly on the veal and shake off excess. Combine cooking oil and fat and heat until it smokes. Fry veal about 2 to 3 minutes on each side, or until golden brown. Yield: 4 servings.

Variations and garnishes for schnitzels:

A popular Austrian garnish for schnitzel consists of a thin slice of lemon on each slice of veal, with an olive on top, and a boned anchovy around the olive. The dish is further garnished with capers, finely chopped yolks of hard-boiled eggs, chopped egg whites, and a sprig of parsley.

Two teaspoons of paprika and 1 medium-sized onion, minced, also can be added to the flour-and-egg mixture, for a Hungarian touch.

Two teaspoons grated Parmesan cheese also can be added to the eggs when beaten in milk, for an Italian touch.

Schnitzel a la Holstein consists of a fried egg placed on top the schnitzel just before serving, with or without a slice of lemon and caper.

Schnitzel also can be served smothered in sliced mushrooms sauted in butter, with sweet or sour cream poured over the veal just before serving.

Gefüllter Kalbsbraten
(stuffed veal)

1 leg of veal	1 calf's kidney
4 or 5 onions	a little fat
6 anchovies	salt and pepper
1 or 2 egg yolks	butter
2 or 3 slices bread soaked in milk	1 cup sour cream

The leg of veal should be boned, then flattened and stuffed with finely chopped onions, boned anchovies, eggs yolks, bread, kidney, all of which were previously browned in a little hot fat and seasoned moderately. Baste veal with butter and roast. Heat sour cream in top of double boiler and pour over veal before serving. Yield: 4 servings.

Schwein mit Kraut
(pork with cabbage)

3 large onions
¼ pound margarine
paprika
2 pounds pork

salt and pepper
1 head cabbage
4 tablespoons sour cream or
    milk

Slice onions and brown in margarine and sprinkle with 1 tablespoon paprika. Add 1 cup warm water and the pork, cut in 1-inch lengths. Season to taste and simmer gently for 1 hour or until tender. Shred cabbage and put in a deep skillet with ¼ pound margarine and 4 tablespoons sour cream or milk. Simmer 1 hour, covering pan with lid or a plate. Season with salt and pepper. At end of hour, add cabbage to pork and onion, mix, and cook together another 30 minutes. Yield: 4 servings.

Eisbein mit Sauerkraut
(pig's knuckles with sauerkraut)

3 pounds pig's knuckles
1 tablespoon salt
½ teaspoon pepper
1 bay leaf
2 carrots
1 stalk celery
1 parsnip

2 large onions
2 pounds sauerkraut
2 apples, peeled and diced
2 tablespoons flour
¼ cup dry white wine
2 tablespoons parsley, minced

Wash pig's knuckles and place in large saucepan. Cover with cold water. Add salt, pepper, bay leaf, carrots, celery, parsnip, and one onion. Bring to boil, cover, and cook over low heat 3 hours. While knuckles are cooking, chop remaining onion and add to undrained sauerkraut and apples. Cook over low heat in separate pan for 1½ hours, mixing often. Drain knuckles and place on heated serving dish. Strain and measure 2 cups stock from knuckles in a saucepan. Mix flour and wine until smooth and add to the stock. Cook, stirring steadily, and bring to boiling point. Cook over low heat 5 more minutes. Stir in parsley. To serve, spread sauerkraut around the knuckles, put gravy in a gravy boat. Serve with boiled potatoes. Yield: 4 to 5 servings.

Pastries, Desserts

Linzer Torte

1½ cups sifted flour
½ teaspoon baking powder
¼ teaspoon salt
1 teaspoon cinnamon
¼ teaspoon ground cloves
1½ cups fine, dry bread crumbs

¾ cup butter
1 cup sugar
1 teaspoon grated lemon rind
2 eggs
1½ cups walnuts, ground
1 12-ounce jar plum jam

Sift flour, baking powder, salt, and spices together. Stir in walnuts and bread crumbs. Cream butter and sugar until light. Add lemon rind. Beat in eggs. Stir in walnuts. Pat a layer of dough ¾ inch thick over the bottom of a greased and floured 8-inch spring form pan. Build up the edge one-inch thick and one-inch wide. Spoon jam in center of dough. Pat out remaining dough on a floured surface and cut into fancy designs and place on top of jam. Bake in moderate oven at 375 degrees for 45 minutes or until dough is firmly set. Torte can be eaten immediately or covered and allowed to stand in a cool place and mellow for a few days.

Innsbrucker Torte

1¾ cups unsifted flour
1¾ cups sugar
½ teaspoon salt
1¼ teaspoons baking soda
¼ teaspoon baking powder
⅔ cup margarine
4 squares unsweetened
    chocolate, melted and
    cooled
1¼ cups water

1 teaspoon vanilla
3 eggs
2 packages (4 ounces each)
    sweet cooking chocolate
¾ cup margarine
½ cup toasted almonds,
    chopped
2 cups (1 pint) heavy cream
1 teaspoon vanilla
1 tablespoon sugar

Combine flour, 1¾ cups sugar, salt, baking soda, baking powder, ⅔ cup margarine, melted unsweetened chocolate, water, and one teaspoon vanilla, in large mixing bowl. Beat at low speed to blend, then beat 2 minutes at medium speed, then add eggs and beat 2 more minutes at medium speed. Pour batter into four

9-inch layer pans lined with wax paper. Layers should be thin. Bake all layers at once in middle of oven at 350 degrees for 17 to 20 minutes or until cake tester in center comes out clean. Cool slightly in pans, then remove and cool on racks.

In a saucepan, melt 1½ packages sweet cooking chocolate over a pan of hot water. Allow to cool, then blend in ¾ cup margarine and the almonds.

Whip the cream with one tablespoon sugar and one teaspoon vanilla.

Place one layer of cake on a serving plate and spread with half the chocolate frosting mixture. Top with next layer and spread with half of the whipped cream. Repeat layers spreading whipped cream on top. Do not frost sides.

Using a vegetable peeler, make chocolate curls from the remaining half package of sweet cooking chocolate, and place on top final layer of whipped cream to decorate. Cover torte with a lid or plastic wrap and refrigerate until ready to serve.

Kuchen
(butter cream rolls)

1 ounce compressed yeast	½ teaspoon vanilla
1 tablespoon sugar	3 cups flour
⅓ cup soft butter	*Butter cream* (combine
¼ cup granulated sugar	and beat well):
2 eggs, beaten	1 cup powdered sugar
¾ cup scalded milk	1 teaspoon vanilla
½ teaspoon salt	½ cup margarine or butter

Whip yeast and one tablespoon sugar until liquified. Cream butter and sugar, add beaten eggs, milk, salt, yeast mixture, and vanilla. Mix well. Add sifted flour and beat until smooth and shiny. Allow to rise twice. Divide dough in half and roll each half into a long, thin rectangular sheet. Spread each sheet of dough with the butter cream mixture, reserving enough butter cream to grease cup cake form. Roll each section of dough in jelly roll shape. Cut each roll into 12 slices. Place one slice into each section of a cupcake pan. Let rise for 10 minutes and bake at 350 degrees for 20 minutes. Frost rolls with icing.

Schaum Torte

6 egg whites   2 teaspoons vinegar
2 cups sugar   2 teaspoons vanilla

Beat egg whites until stiff. Gradually add sugar and beat until all required sugar is added. Then add vinegar and vanilla. Cover a cookie sheet with brown paper and place a cardboard cake band in the center of the paper, to hold the meringue. Drop meringue by tablespoonsful inside the cake band. Bake in 300 degree oven for 50 minutes. Remove immediately from pan. Cool and cut a layer off the top of the torte. Spread whipped cream and drained, crushed pineapple and sliced bananas, or fresh strawberries and bananas between the two layers.

Garprobe
(risen yeast, used for buns and cakes)

1 cake yeast   1 tablespoon sugar
¼ cup flour

Dissolve yeast in ¼ cup lukewarm water, then add flour and sugar. Stir until mixture is smooth. Cover with warm cloth and set in warm but not hot place until mixture rises to double its size (in about ¾ hour). Use in making *Gugelhupf* and yeast fruit buns.

Gugelhupf
(lemon, raisin cake)

⅔ cup butter   3 cups flour
½ cup sugar   ½ teaspoon salt
4 egg yolks   ⅔ cup raisins
grated rind of ½ lemon   2 egg whites, stiffly beaten
1 cup milk, warm   ½ cup slivered almonds
risen yeast (see above)

Cream butter and sugar until light and fluffy, then beat in egg yolks. Add lemon rind, milk, and risen yeast. Sift in flour and salt. Work all together with wooden spoon until dough no longer sticks. Add raisins; fold in egg whites. Sprinkle almonds over bottom of buttered, floured 10-inch cake form. Pour in dough and cover with warmed cloth. Leave in warm place until dough rises to one or two inches from top of form (about 1½ hours). Bake in 350 degree oven 1 hour or until cake is done. Invert onto a board or rack and gently ease cake out. Sprinkle top with powdered sugar.

Buchteln
(yeast fruit buns)

½ cup milk, warm
1 egg at room temperature
¼ cup sugar
grated rind of 1 lemon
3 tablespoons butter, melted
risen yeast (as above)

¼ teaspoon salt
2½ cups flour
⅜ cup apricot or prune jam or
   jam of your choice
¼ cup melted butter
powdered sugar

Add milk, egg, sugar, lemon rind, butter to risen yeast and mix until smooth. Sift salt and all but 1 tablespoon of the flour in a warm bowl. Make a well and pour yeast mixture into the center. Work all together with wooden spoon until dough no longer sticks. Sift 1 tablespoon flour over surface and cover with warmed cloth. Leave in warm place until dough rises to double its size (about 1½ hours). Roll out dough ¼ inch thick on floured board. Cut into rectangles about 3 by 4 inches. Put 1 teaspoon jam at center of each rectangle and fold. Pinch all sides closed. Brush bottom with melted butter. Cover with warmed cloth and leave in warm place until buns rise to double their size (about ½ hour). Bake in 350 degree oven for half an hour. Place on rack and separate buns when cool enough to handle. Sprinkle with powdered sugar. Yield: 20 buns.

Strudel Teig
(strudle dough)

1 cup flour
1 teaspoon salt

1 egg yolk, beaten
1 tablespoon melted butter

Sift flour and sprinkle salt into a warmed bowl. Make a well in center and add beaten egg yolk, butter, and enough warm water (about 1 cup) to make a soft dough. Knead on a warmed, floured board. When smooth, cover with a warm bowl and a cloth. Cover a large dough board or table with a clean cloth. Sprinkle flour on the cloth and place dough in center and roll out as thin as possible with a warmed, floured rolling pin. Put your hands under the dough and gently pull it out thinner from the middle.

Apfel Strudel
(apple strudle)

strudle dough (as above)	grated peel of ½ lemon
1½ pounds cooking apples	½ cup powdered sugar
¼ cup currants	½ teaspoon ground cinnamon
⅓ cup dry bread crumbs fried in butter	½ cup butter, melted

Prepare strudle dough and while it is resting before being pulled out and rolled, prepare filling. Peel, core, and slice apples thinly, then without breaking them, mix with other ingredients. When dough is ready, trim off thick edges and spread with the apple mixture, leaving an inch uncovered around all the edges. Roll dough very gently and pinch edges together and place on a buttered baking sheet. Brush with melted butter or margarine and bake at 350 degrees for 20 minutes, then lower to 250 degrees and bake another 30 minutes. Brush with melted butter, 2 or 3 times during baking. Serve sliced hot or cold. Yield: 4 to 6 servings.

Pfeffernusse
(pepper nuts)

4 cups sifted flour	1 teaspoon mace
1 teaspoon baking powder	¾ cup unsulphered molasses
1 teaspoon soda	¾ cup honey
1 teaspoon salt	¾ cup butter, margarine, or shortening
½ teaspoon black pepper	

1 teaspoon allspice
¼ teaspoon powdered anise or
   anise seed

1 egg
powdered sugar

Sift all dry ingredients together. Place molasses and honey in saucepan and heat, but do not boil. Add butter (or margarine or shortening), and stir. Let melt in the warm liquid. Cool. Then add the beaten egg. Stir in dry ingredients, careful not to overmix the dough. Let mixture stand 15 minutes, then form into nut size balls and place on greased baking sheet. Bake 12 to 15 minutes at 350 degrees. Roll in powdered sugar while still warm. (They can be made a week in advance of serving and kept covered in a cool place.) Yield: 2 dozen pepper nuts.

Chapter 2

GERMANY

How can any of us who love to waltz and polka and enjoy a crisp *schnitzel* or fat sausage dipped in hot mustard washed down by some heady beer not be accused of being a Germanophile?

My favorite memories of Germany are those hours I sat in the gardens of the Kaiserkeller hotel in Frankfurt, listening to three alternating string orchestras play Strauss waltzes and Mozart symphonies while I cut into succulent *Hasenpfeffer* (rabbit) or a "swallow's nest" (veal rolled in bacon), with some dry white Riesling wine followed by a *blitz torte* or cheese *strudle.* Then a short walk to the opera to hear Annie Schlem in *The Tales of Hoffman* shout-sing to the hero, *Hoff-man, ich liebe dich!"*

Germany is Berchtesgaden covered with freshly fallen snow at Christmastime, and the candlemaker's tiny shop with shelves lined with delicately carved candles containing miniature Nativity scenes. And the corner table at the neighborhood inn where two white-mustached old men in their green Bavarian country squire coats puffed their furnace-covered pipes while they drank from tankards of beer and played checkers.

In springtime it is the weekend wine festivals, like the fantastic champagnefest in Eltville on the Main river near Wiesbaden where polka bands played in coves along grape arbors and the *frauleins* all said yes when you asked them to dance.

It is also an idyllic summer day spent in a boat trip down the Rhine to the Lorelei, via Assmannshausen and the Watch on the Rhine, and an afternoon in the beer and wine gardens of Rüdesheim, on the way back counting castles high up on the vineyards and not counting steins of beer refilled.

At Oktoberfest time, it is the Haufbrau Haus in Munich where the local revelers squeezed together on their benches to make room at their table for my party and we drank and sang "Ein Prosit" and the bosomy blonde carnival queen on stage with a goat consented to polka with me, tying the goat to a post first.

Back in Chicago I search out German cafes and restaurants the way I searched out wine festivals along the Rhine. Friends asked how I knew of so many festivals. I told them to look at any *kiosk,* the round outdoor billboards found on most street corners throughout Germany. Look for a poster with a picture of a clump of grapes and some glasses, I told them. Then take down the name of the town and the date and go there!

Chicago, as most American cities, has places where you can relive some of those happy hours in Bavarian villages and under Alpine towers. Places like the Schwaben Stube and the Golden Ox where the goulash is magnificent and the *apfelkuchen* is no less, where I hear the man in lederhosen at the bar pluck the strings of his zither to "Village Swallows" and I am transformed back to Heidelberg at the student inn.

It's all a dream, mixed with nightmare and dream; the wars dating back to Caesar's time, the horror of two world wars, the partitioning of Germany into East and West, the incredible recovery of West Germany since the war that makes it the most affluent partner of the Free European Alliance.

The city of Germany remains Berlin, an island of western freedom in East Germany that, let's face it, is made that much more exciting simply because it *is* in the Soviet zone of Germany. After a *Sauerbraten* (sweet-sour pot roast) in the Savoy on Kufurstendamn, you can drive to the Soviet Victory Monument and see Russian uniformed guards, go to the Brandenburger Tor and the 28-mile-long concrete Wall of Shame that separates East from West, or to the inspiring Platz der Luftbrucke to see the three-pronged monument in tribute to those who ran the amazing airlift in the late 1940s when Berlin was shut off from the rest of the world.

Back in West Germany, the signs of war are hard to find now. The rubble is cleared away, the trees that once grew in the doorway of St. Michael's church in Hamburg have been transplanted, and what has not been restored has been replaced. Cologne's great cathedral still stands, magnificent as ever, and from the top, a climb of 500 steps, you see a panorama of the city that is still the pride of the Rhineland. Heidelberg, once overrun with American servicemen, is now less crowded and the thick beef soup in the Student Prince's inn, the Red Ox, is rich and pleasing as ever.

High in the Bavarian alps, at the Braustuberl in Garmisch-Partenkirchen, the bratwurst in beer tastes so good with a frothy stein of Lowenbrau that you are reluctant to ever leave.

And when I'm home, I can be in Bavaria or Berlin anytime I want, thanks to some imported Blue Nun Liebfraumilch, a dish of *Königsberger Klopse* (a veal-pork-dumpling goulash) from an authentic Old Country kitchen recipe, and my phonograph playing traditional German songs by Fritz Wunderlich and Elisabeth Schwarzkopf.

A Germanophile? Who isn't!

Appetizers

Zwiebelbissen
(onion puffs)

rye or white bread, sliced	medium size sweet onions
mayonnaise	grated Parmesan cheese

Cut bread into circles about 1½ inches in diameter. Spread some mayonnaise on each piece. Place a thin slice of onion on this, then spread more mayonnaise on the onion and top with Parmesan cheese. Place in preheated 400 degree oven until cheese is lightly toasted, about 10 minutes.

Asternöilchen
(oyster in the blanket)

bacon slices   large oysters

Lay one large oyster on a very thin slice of bacon. Wrap the bacon around the oyster and fasten with a toothpick. Fry and serve hot.

Käsestangen
(cheese sticks)

½ pound butter
1 pound cheddar cheese, grated
2 cups flour
1 teaspoon salt
¼ teaspoon cayenne pepper
2 teaspoons baking powder
1 teaspoon caraway seed

Cream the butter. Add cheese and cream well. Sift together flour, salt, cayenne pepper and baking powder and add to cheese mixture. Add caraway seeds. Roll out dough and cut into strips 1 inch wide with a pastry wheel. Cut each strip into pieces of equal length, about 4 inches. Bake on ungreased cookie sheet in 350 degree oven for 10 to 12 minutes. Serve with cocktails, soups, or salad. Yield: 2 dozen sticks.

Bierkäse
(beer cheese)

1 pound aged natural cheddar cheese
1 pound natural Swiss cheese
1 garlic clove, mashed
1 teaspoon dry mustard
2 teaspoons Worcestershire sauce
1 cup beer

Grate cheese finely. Mix with garlic, dry mustard, and Worcestershire sauce. Gradually beat in enough beer until mixture is well blended and of spreading consistency. Store in a covered container in refrigerator. Serve at room temperature with dry rye bread.

Soups

Rotweinsuppe
(red wine soup)

a little cinnamon or cinnamon
stick
2 cloves

¼ cup tapioca or rice
2 cups red wine
⅓ cup sugar

Add cinnamon and cloves to 2 cups water and bring to boil. Sprinkle in tapioca or rice, stir and simmer gently until done. Stir in the wine, season with sugar. Reheat without boiling. Serve hot or cold. Yield: 4 servings.

Weisse Kartoffelsuppe
(cream of potato soup)

6 potatoes, cubed
2 teaspoons onion, chopped
2 ribs celery, chopped
¼ cup flour
1 quart milk, heated

2 teaspoons salt
dash of cayenne pepper
⅛ teaspoon pepper
2 tablespoons butter
1 teaspoon parsley, chopped

Cook cubed potatoes, chopped onions, and celery in a pint of water until all are soft. Mash, add hot milk, salt and pepper. Melt butter and stir in flour. Add flour and butter mixture to soup. Stir until soup thickens. Sprinkle chopped parsley on top. Yield: 4 to 6 servings.

Apfelbrotsuppe
(apple-bread soup)

8 large cooking apples
6 slices pumpernickel bread
3 tablespoons sugar
¼ cup seedless raisins

⅛ teaspoon cinnamon
3 tablespoons lemon juice
1 tablespoon grated lemon rind

Peel and slice apples, combine with 2 quarts water in saucepan. Soak the bread in water, then squeeze dry. Add to apples. Cook over medium heat for 20 minutes or until apples are very soft. Force apple mixture through a sieve. Return the puree to saucepan and reheat. Add sugar, raisins, cinnamon. Cook over medium heat for 10 minutes. Add lemon juice and rind. Cook 5 more minutes and serve very hot. Yield: 4 to 6 servings.

Salads

Heisser Kartoffelsalat
(hot potato salad)

4 potatoes, cooked in jackets
4 strips bacon
4 green onions
4 tablespoons bacon drippings
4 tablespoons vinegar

1 teaspoon salt
½ teaspoon dry mustard
¼ teaspoon pepper
2 teaspoons sugar

Skin potatoes and slice into top of double boiler over hot water. Fry bacon until crisp and crumble over potatoes. Add diced onions, including green tops. Mix together bacon fat, vinegar, salt, mustard, pepper, and sugar. Heat to boiling point and pour over potatoes. Stir until all potatoes are coated and keep covered until serving. Yield: 4 to 6 servings.

Sauerkraut Salat
(sauerkraut salad)

1 No. 2½ can sauerkraut,
    drained and chopped
2 cups celery, chopped
1 cup green peppers, chopped

¼ cup pimentos
¾ cup sugar
¾ cup vinegar

Mix ingredients and refrigerate at least two hours, or make the day before serving. Leftovers can be refrigerated. Yield: 4 servings.

Roher Rübensalat
(raw turnip salad)

2 cups turnips, shredded
½ cup onions, chopped
½ cup carrots, shredded
½ cup celery, chopped
1 teaspoon salt

¼ cup vinegar and oil salad
  dressing
1 teaspoon sugar
1 teaspoon parsley, chopped

Mix and chill all ingredients. Yield: 4 servings.

Vegetables

Sauerkraut mit Äpfeln
(sauerkraut with apples)

4 tablespoons bacon drippings
1 onion, sliced
2 pounds sauerkraut
3 apples, peeled, cored, and
  quartered

salt
1 teaspoon caraway seeds
2 raw potatoes, grated fine
soup stock or boiling water
brown sugar

Heat bacon drippings, add onion and fry until brown. Add sauerkraut and cook for 5 minutes, then add apples, salt, caraway seeds, and grated potatoes. Cover with boiling water or soup stock and cook uncovered over low heat for 30 minutes. Cover tightly and continue cooking another 30 minutes. Sweeten to taste with brown sugar. Yield: 4 servings.

Deutscher Spinat
(German spinach)

2 pounds fresh spinach
1 cup water
1 tablespoon flour

1 tablespoon butter
dash of nutmeg
salt and pepper to taste

Cook spinach in water until tender, drain (save the liquid), chop spinach. In separate pan, brown flour and butter. Add spinach, heat again, and add 1 cup of the reserved liquid. Cook 5 minutes longer, add dash of nutmeg, and season to taste. Yield: 4 servings.

Kohlrabi

8 medium size kohlrabi
1 teaspoon salt
2 tablespoons butter

1½ tablespoons flour
1 cup beef bouillon
1 cup light cream

Pare and slice kohlrabi, cook in 2 quarts salted water until tender. Drain. Melt butter, add flour and blend, add bouillon and cream, cook over low heat stirring constantly until mixture boils and thickens. Add kohlrabi, cook 5 more minutes. Yield: 4 servings.

Gefüllte Zwiebeln
(stuffed onions)

6 medium onions
1½ cups soft bread crumbs
1 cup cooked, ground ham or
  beef
salt and pepper

melted butter
2 boiled carrots, chopped
  finely
1 egg

Parboil onions, remove part of center leaving root end intact. Fill hole with mixture of onion just removed, 1 cup bread crumbs, chopped meat, salt and pepper to season, moisten mixture with melted butter. Place stuffed onions close together in a buttered cooking dish and cover with ¼ cup white sauce (see index). Sprinkle with remaining bread crumbs, carrot, eggs, and parsley to garnish. Bake in moderate oven at 350 degrees until brown. Yield: 4 to 6 servings.

Potatoes and dumplings

Spätzle
(German noodles)

3¼ cups flour
1 teaspoon salt

3 eggs

Put flour in a bowl, make a well, put salt and slightly beaten eggs and 1 cup water into well and mix thoroughly. Put spoonfuls on spatula and snip off pieces with knife into boiling salted water. As spätzles rise to top, scoop out with slotted spoon and put in covered bowl to keep warm until all are made. Also can be fried: Put generous piece of butter in a heavy frying pan, add 1 tablespoon minced onion, brown slightly. Add spätzle, keep turning until slightly browned. Good served with sauerkraut.

Kartoffel Klösse
(potato balls)

9 medium sized potatoes	3 teaspoons salt
3 eggs	½ cup butter
1 cup flour	½ cup bread crumbs
⅔ cup bread crumbs	1 teaspoon minced onion
½ teaspoon nutmeg	

Boil potatoes in their jackets until tender. Chill at least 12 hours. Peel and force through a potato ricer. Add eggs, flour, ⅔ cup bread crumbs, nutmeg, and salt. Beat with fork until light and fluffy. Shape into small balls and drop them into boiling salted water. When potato balls come to surface, allow them to boil about 3 minutes. Remove from water and drain. When potato balls are cooked, centers should be dry. Arrange on large platter and cover with following sauce: Allow the butter to brown in a skillet. Add ½ cup bread crumbs and onions. Cook 1 minute. Yield: 1 dozen balls.

Fish

Gesprickter Fisch, Gebracken
(baked stuffed fish)

2¼ lbs. fish fillet	chopped parsley
salt	mustard
vinegar	2 slightly heaped teaspoons
4 slices fat bacon	cornstarch
1 onion, chopped	2 tablespoons tomato puree
small can evaporated milk	2 tablespoons bread crumbs

juice of 1 lemon
1 pickled gherkin, diced

¼ cup grated cheese
1 ounce butter

Cut fish fillet into two even pieces, wash, rub with salt and vinegar, and leave to stand about ½ hour. Fry diced bacon and just when it begins to brown, add chopped onion and fry until brown. Whisk the milk with lemon juice, stir in the cooled bacon and onion, diced gherkin, and parsley. Season with mustard and salt, then stir in cornstarch. Dry fish thoroughly and put half into greased pie dish or casserole. Cover with stuffing, brush remaining fish thinly with tomato puree and place on top of the stuffing, puree side up. Sprinkle with bread crumbs and cheese and dot with flakes of butter. Bake at 400 degrees for about ½ hour. Yield: 4 servings.

Poultry
Huhn in Burgunder Wein
(chicken cooked in Burgundy wine)

5 tablespoons butter
3 slices bacon
1 medium onion, thinly sliced
1 broiling or frying chicken,
    cut in pieces
1 tablespoon flour
2 tablespoons brandy
2 cups Burgundy or dry red
    wine

1 bay leaf
2 tablespoons chopped parsley
½ teaspoon crumbled dry
    thyme
1 teaspoon salt
½ teaspoon pepper
⅛ teaspoon nutmeg
1 cup chopped fresh mush-
    rooms, sauted in butter

Melt 4 tablespoons butter over medium heat, stirring occasionally. Cook bacon (cut in matchstick pieces) with onion in butter until soft and transparent. Remove bacon and onion with slotted spoon and save. Brown chicken in remaining fat on all sides. Sprinkle with flour, add brandy, wine, bay leaf, parsley, thyme, salt, pepper, and nutmeg. Cook covered in preheated 375 degree oven for 30 minutes or until tender. Stir in reserved bacon and onion and mushrooms. Return to oven and cook, covered, another 5 to 10 minutes. Remove, stir remaining butter into sauce. Serve with noodles or mashed potatoes. Yield: 4 servings.

Apfelgefüllte Hühchen
(apple-stuffed chicken)

2 small chickens	2 tablespoons raisins
salt and pepper	1 cup cubed cooking apples
lemon juice	2 tablespoons Madeira wine
Stuffing;	2 tablespoons butter
½ lb. ground lean pork	2 strips bacon, diced
1 tablespoon butter	1 cup chicken bouillon

Rub chicken with salt, pepper, lemon juice. Brown pork in butter and toss with raisins, apples, and moisten with the wine. Stuff the birds. Saute diced bacon in the butter and brown birds slowly on all sides. Use Dutch oven. Arrange birds in pot, breast side up, and add 1 cup hot chicken broth. Cover and simmer slowly about an hour, until done, basting often. Add more wine to pan juices for gravy and season to taste. Serve sauce over chicken.

Meats

Sauerbraten
(sweet-sour pot roast)

3 pounds beef, larded	12 cloves
salt and pepper	¼ cup sugar
cider vinegar or white wine	3 tablespoons shortening
3 medium onions, sliced	6 gingersnaps
3 bay leaves	½ cup flour
1 teaspoon peppercorns	1 cup sour cream

Use top sirloin or bottom round of beef and have butcher lard it with salt pork. Wipe meat with damp cloth and rub well with salt and pepper. Place meat in large crock or bowl. Heat equal parts vinegar and water, or white wine and water to half cover the meat. Add sliced onions, bay leaves, peppercorns, cloves, and sugar. When mixture is hot, pour over meat. Cover crock with a tight-fitting lid and refrigerate 3 days in summer or 8 days in winter, turning meat once each day. Remove from the marinade and drain thoroughly, saving the marinade. Heat shortening in heavy iron skillet or Dutch oven, add meat and brown well. Add marinade and the gingersnaps. Cover pot tightly and simmer very slowly from 2 to 3 hours. When meat is tender, remove to hot platter. Mix the flour with the sour cream and add to the liquid in the pan, Stir until mixture thickens. Strain and serve with the meat. Yield: 4 to 6 servings.

Königsberger Klöpse
(pork-veal with dumplings)

3 slices white bread	1 pound ground veal
½ cup mik	2 tablespoons vinegar
1 egg	4 tablespoons butter
1¼ tablespoon salt	4 tablespoons flour
1 teaspoon pepper	1 tablespoon capers
1 pound ground pork	

Remove crusts from bread and soak in milk. Combine egg, salt and pepper, work into meats. Add bread and form into small balls. Heat 2 quarts of water to boiling, add vinegar, meat balls, salt and pepper. Reduce heat and cook for 15 minutes. Blend butter with flour, slowly add 4 cups meat stock. Cook for 10 minutes. Pour sauce over drained klopse. Add capers, simmer 10 minutes. Yield: 8 servings.

Hasenpfeffer
(ragout of rabbit)

1 rabbit or hare	½ teaspoon poultry seasoning
vinegar	½ teaspoon peppercorns
1 onion, sliced	3 whole cloves
1 teaspoon salt	4 tablespoons butter
¼ teaspoon red pepper	1 cup thick sour cream

Clean and disjoint rabbit. Place in large jar and cover with equal parts vinegar and water. Add onion and all of the spices. Allow meat to remain in this solution for 2 days. Melt butter and brown the meat in it, turning often. Add some of the marinade and cover pan with tight-fitting lid. Cook slowly until meat is tender, then add sour cream and cook a few minutes more. Serve with the sauce. Yield: 4 servings.

Schwalbennester
(swallows' nests)

4 strips bacon	½ cup butter
4 thin slices veal	2 teaspoons cornstarch with
½ cup chopped onions	1 teaspoon water
4 hard-boiled eggs	2 teaspoons sour cream

Place a strip of bacon on each slice of veal, top with 2 tablespoons chopped onion and 1 hard-boiled egg. Roll and tie each slice securely. Brown each roll in butter in skillet. Carefully add 1 cup water, cover and braise, gently, until done (about 1 hour). Thicken gravy with cornstarch and water, add sour cream. Correct seasoning. Cut each roll in half, pour gravy over and serve. Yield: 4 servings.

Bratwurst in Bier
(sausages in beer)

18 pork sausages	½ teaspoon salt
1 tablespoon butter	2 cups beer
4 onions, sliced	2 tablespoons water
1 bay leaf	3 tablespoons potato flour
6 peppercorns	

Pour 2 cups boiling water over sausages, drain and dry them. Melt butter in a skillet, add sausages, and brown on all sides. Remove sausages and pour off all but 2 tablespoons of the fat. Add onions and saute 10 minutes. Return sausages to pan and add the bay leaf, peppercorns, salt, and beer. Cook over low heat 20 minutes. Mix water and potato flour to smooth paste and add sausages, stirring constantly until mixture reaches the boiling point. Cook over low heat for 5 minutes. Serve with mashed potatoes. Yield: 6 servings.

Pastries, Desserts

Rhamkuchen
(cheese cake)

1½ cups rolled Zwieback
   crumbs
3 tablespoons butter
2 tablespoons sugar
1 pound cream cheese
2 eggs, separated

½ cup sugar
rind of 1 lemon
½ teaspoon vanilla
1 tablespoon lemon juice
1 tablespoon sugar
1 cup sour cream

Blend rolled crumbs with melted butter and 2 tablespoons sugar. Press into bottom of a 9-inch spring-bottom pan. Place in warm oven for 5 minutes to set the crust. Cool. Warm the cream cheese to room temperature and break up with a fork. Blend in egg yolks, one at a time, and beat well after each one. Beat egg whites stiff and fold into mixture with a spatula. Slowly add ½ cup sugar and lemon juice. Pour over crumb base and bake 45 minutes at 300 degrees. Mix 1 tablespoon sugar and vanilla into the sour cream. Spread lightly over top of cake and return to oven to bake 10 minutes more. Let cake cool and remove rim of the spring pan to serve.

Pfoertchen
(raisin doughnuts)

2 packages dry yeast
1 cup milk
1 cup cream
½ teaspoon salt

½ cup sugar
6 eggs, beaten
1 cup raisins
4 cups flour

Dissolve yeast in 2 tablespoons warm water. Combine milk and cream (both at room temperature), salt and sugar. Add yeast and mix well. Blend in eggs, mixing thoroughly. Add raisins and flour to make a soft dough. Let rise 2–3 hours. Drop from tablespoon into hot lard. Fry until brown. Shake in mixture of sugar and cinnamon. Yield: 5–6 dozen.

Anise Drops

3 eggs	2 cups flour
1⅓ cup powdered sugar	1 teaspoon anise seed

Beat eggs and sugar for half an hour (a necessity). Add flour and anise seed and mix well. Drop batter from teaspoon onto greased baking sheet in drops the size of a walnut. Decorate with colored sugar. Cover with a sheet of waxed paper and let stand at room temperature 8 hours or overnight. Bake in 300 degree oven about 15 minutes. (These should be made to store for 2 or 3 weeks before serving.) Keep in tightly covered tin box with an apple. Ideally, the cookies will have a hollow bubble in the top.

Spritzgebäck
(spritz cookies)

1 cup butter	2½ cups flour
¾ cup sugar	1 teaspoon salt
3 egg yolks	½ teaspoon baking powder
1 teaspoon almond extract	

Cream sugar, butter, and egg yolks. Add flavoring and then flour, salt, and baking powder sifted. Mix well. Roll dough to ¼ inch thickness, cut with cookie cutter, and place on well-greased cookie sheet. Bake at 400 degrees until light brown.

Kastanienauflauf
(chestnut soufflé)

½ pound chestnuts, blanched	3 egg yolks, beaten
½ cup milk	1 tablespoon brandy
¼ cup butter	3 egg whites, beaten stiff
4 tablespoons sugar	

Cook chestnuts in milk until tender, then force through a ricer. Cream the butter well, slowly adding the sugar. When thoroughly blended, add the chestnuts and egg yolks and beat well. Add the brandy. Fold in the stiffly beaten egg whites. Pour soufflé into a well-buttered baking dish and bake at 350 degrees for about 40 minutes. Yield: 4 servings.

Blitz Torte
(almond cream cake)

½ cup butter
½ cup sugar
4 egg yolks, well beaten
1 teaspoon vanilla
1 cup flour
1 teaspoon baking powder

3 tablespoons milk
5 egg whites
¾ cup sugar
½ cup chopped almonds
1 tablespoon sugar
½ teaspoon cinnamon

Cream the butter and slowly add ½ cup sugar; beat well. Add egg yolks and vanilla. Sift the flour and baking powder and add alternately with the milk. Pour batter into two well-greased cake pans and cover with the following meringue: Beat egg whites until very light, gradually add the ¾ cup sugar and continue beating until whites are stiff. Spread on the batter and sprinkle top with the chopped almonds and sugar and cinnamon which have been mixed together. Bake in 350 degree oven about 30 minutes. Cool and spread with custard filling (see below).

Custard filling

1 tablespoon cornstarch
¼ cup sugar
1 cup milk, scalded ·

2 egg yolks, beaten
3 tablespoons butter
½ teaspoon vanilla

Mix cornstarch and sugar together; add the hot milk. Gradually pour some of the hot liquid over the slightly beaten egg yolks. Put in a double boiler and cook, stirring constantly, until mixture becomes thick. Add butter and stir until it melts. Cool and flavor with vanilla.

Lebkuchen
(gingersnaps)

1 pound butter
1 pound brown sugar
3 eggs
1 pound corn syrup
1 teaspoon cinnamon
3 teaspoons baking soda
    dissolved in ¼ cup milk

½ teaspoon each of nutmeg,
    cloves, allspice
1 cup candied fruit
1 cup chopped nuts
1 cup milk
4 cups flour

Cream butter, sugar, and eggs. Add remaining ingredients and mix well. Roll dough to ½ inch thickness and cut out cookies with cutter. Place on greased cookie sheet and bake at 350 degrees until light brown. Cool and either ice or sprinkle with powdered sugar. Yield: 1 dozen.

Walnussfinger
(Christmas black walnut sticks)

2⅔ cups brown sugar
½ cup butter
3 eggs
5 cups flour

½ teaspoon nutmeg
½ teaspoon baking powder
¾ cup black walnuts
egg yolks

Cream together butter, sugar, and eggs. Add 2½ cups flour, nutmeg, baking powder, and walnuts, and mix again. Add remaining 2½ cups flour and beat thoroughly. Roll in long strips like a pencil. Cut off pieces about 2 inches long and paint top with lightly beaten egg yolks. Bake in 350 degree oven until brown.

Chapter 3

Czechoslovakia

European composers loved to write music about their rivers. Johann Strauss's immortal "The Beautiful Blue Danube" captured the grace and romance of nineteenth century Vienna. Bedřich Smetana wrote about his river, the Moldau, which runs through Prague, major city of Czechoslovakia.

Today walking the streets of this ancient, majestic capital called the "Golden City of a Hundred Spires," hearing Smetana's haunting music, you sense the reasons for his patriotism, his pride of country. Like the river, the city and the country abide, despite domination from foreign powers which dates back to the tenth century.

Hungarians, Poles, Turks, Austrians, and Germans all controlled the land now called Czechoslovakia at one time or another. It did not even exist as a sovereign country until after World War I, when the Treaty of Versailles joined two peoples, the Czechs and the Slovaks, into one nation.

Two more dissimilar peoples rarely have been joined. The Czechs in the north are traditionally a sober, hard-working, industrialized people, and their homeland of Bohemia-Moravia strongly reflects these traits. Slovaks in the south are of peasant stock: agrarian, rural, and friendly. What has joined them harmoniously as a nation is their fierce independence. As a landlocked nation in central Europe, bounded by Germany, Austria, Hungary, Poland, and Russia, and since World War II

Russia's westernmost Socialist Republic, the Czechoslovaks have tried several times to regain their freedom from foreign domination. Each time they have failed, most recently in August 1968 when their uprising for independence was crushed by Soviet troops and tanks.

Today the Czechoslovaks work in their mills and mines and factories or farm the land and, like the Moldau, they endure. Another opportunity will come to make themselves free and, meantime, the food is good and plentiful, the local Pilsener beer perhaps the finest in the world, the spirited Slavic music is to dance to, and life, like the river, goes on.

If there is any doubt of this, you drown it in beer and wine and satiate yourself with peasant beer soup, potato dumplings, goose with apple stuffing, and poppy seed cake. Try these at the elaborate hotel restaurants in Prague or in one of the many Czech or Slovak inns along the countryside.

The Waldstein Tavern in Mala Strana, Prague's Old Town, is an old inn with wine cellar where the food justifies its reputation as the best in town. It's a perfect dining stop after touring the magnificent walled Hradcany castle, which once was the seat of Bohemian kings and today is a wonderland of many European architectural styles. When the Nazis occupied Prague in World War II, the jeweled crown of Bohemia was hidden in a bread oven in a twelfth century wing of the castle.

Waldstein Tavern lies just below the castle, past lovely terraced gardens and down narrow winding cobblestone streets with medieval and Baroque houses. After such a stroll, you are ready for the old inn and its fabulous menu. Westward from Prague through Bohemia's fertile rolling countryside with medieval castles and villages, south through thickly forested mountain country, north to the recreational and sports centers, and eastward to Slovakia's mountains, valleys, and farmland, you will also find inns with menus to tempt you. The food reminds you that Czechoslovakia indeed was a crossroads for the armies of central and eastern Europe, which left behind some of the world's most palate-pleasing recipes.

Czechoslovakia is a fertile country, rich in game, fish, grain, and fruit, all of which are reflected in their cooking. Added to the variety of schnitzels, steaks, borschts, and potato dishes that have crept in from neighboring countries, the favorite native foods are pork and goose, served with sauerkraut and dumplings, fresh-water fish, Prague-style ham which is canned and shipped all over the world, and of course sausages. No other country has such a variety of sausages, which along with Pilsener beer constitute a cult among the Czechs. Not much for vegetables, the Czechs do share with their Polish neighbors a great love for mushrooms, which are used in many ways. And Czechs make soup of practically anything. (I find the beer soup too bland, but it may taste good to a peasant after working all day in the Carpathian mountains.)

Caraway, like mushrooms, goes with everything. It is sprinkled on pork, goose, and duck before roasting. It goes into soups and stews, and into Czech cabbage and potato dishes. Sour cream, adopted from the Hungarians, is used widely.

Czech desserts are world-famous. *Kolacky,* fruit or jelly filled sweet buns, and short-dough coffeecakes are Czechoslovakia's contribution to the world of baking. There are also Austrian and Hungarian-inspired baked goods such as fancy tortes, pastries of paper-thin strudel dough, and crusty salt rolls sprinkled with caraway or poppy seeds.

My brother John married a Chicago girl whose parents came to this country from Czechoslovakia. If all the girls in her parents' homeland are as pleasant, lovely to look at, and cook as well as Mitzi, beer and dumplings no longer will be regarded as the Czechs' main tourist attractions.

Appetizers

Spinat Rohlicky
(spinach rolls)

½ pound spinach
1 cup white sauce
salt and pepper to taste
1 slice bread
2 tablespoons butter or

margarine
2 eggs
1 cup milk
2 ounces grated cheese

Wash the spinach and reserve 8 large leaves. Cook the rest, drain, and chop. Mix with white sauce (see index), season with salt and pepper. Cut bread into small cubes, fry in butter or margarine. Mix with spinach mixture on the blanched (par-boiled) spinach leaves, roll and place in a shallow baking dish. Beat eggs with milk, cook slowly until mixture thickens, stir in grated cheese. Pour over the spinach rolls. Bake at 350 degrees for 20 minutes. Yield: 4 to 6 servings.

Sandviče s Husi Jatra
(open sandwich with goose liver)

1 goose liver, broiled, per serving
hot goose fat
1 slice of bread per serving

1 slice tomato
salt, pepper
egg white, chopped

Brown goose liver in hot goose fat in skillet (enough fat to half cover liver); brown both sides. Toast bread slices. Cut in fancy shapes if desired. Place thin slice of tomato on each slice of toast. Season with salt and pepper. Slice liver and place a slice on top each tomato slice. Garnish with chopped white of a hard-cooked egg. Yield: 1 serving.

Soups

Pivní Polévka
(beer soup)

1 quart beer
2 tablespoons sugar
1 tablespoon butter

3 egg yolks
1 cup heavy cream

Combine beer and 1 quart water in saucepan. Bring to boil and add sugar and butter. Cook over low heat for 30 minutes. Beat egg yolks in a bowl. Add cream and beat again well. Gradually add beer mixture to egg and cream mixture, beating constantly. Pour mixture back into saucepan and heat again but do not boil. Yield: 6 servings.

Česnečka
(garlic soup)

4 or 6 potatoes
dash of powdered caraway
   seeds
¼ cup shortening

4 cloves garlic
salt
4 to 6 slices toasted rye bread

Dice potatoes. Boil in 6 cups salted water with caraway seeds until tender, 20 to 30 minutes. Add shortening. Mash garlic with a pinch of salt and add to soup. Serve with toasted rye bread. Yield: 4 to 6 servings.

Polévka z Oháňky
(oxtail soup)

1 pound oxtails
2 carrots, diced
1 parsnip, diced
½ medium celery root, diced
1 tablespoon shortening
3 peppercorns

1 medium onion, diced
1 small cauliflower or 1 cup
   green peas
¼ pound mushrooms
1 tablespoon minced parsley

Cut oxtail into pieces and cook in 6 cups water until tender, about 2 hours. Fry carrots, parsnip, and celery root in shortening with peppercorns. Strain soup. Remove meat from bones and cut into small pieces. Return meat to soup, add fried vegetables, add cauliflower or peas and mushrooms; cook until tender, 10 to 15 minutes. Add parsley. Yield: 4 servings.

Salads

Pražský Salát
(Prague salad)

1½ cups thin strips roast veal
1½ cups thin strips roast pork
1½ cups thin strips of pickles
1 cup thin strips of onion
1 cup thin strips of sour apples

1 tablespoon lemon juice
salt to taste
pepper to taste
mayonnaise

Mix together cut up ingredients. Sprinkle with lemon juice, salt, and pepper. Bind with mayonnaise. Chill for several hours before serving. Yield: 8 servings.

Salát z Květáku
(cauliflower salad)

Salad:
3 cups cauliflower, broken into
    flowerets
salt to taste
1 bay leaf
3–4 peppercorns

Dressing:
½ cup water
3 tablespoons vinegar
salt to taste
½ teaspoon sugar
1 small onion, grated
3 tablespoons oil

Boil cauliflower in 4 cups salted water with bay leaf and peppercorns about 10 minutes. Drain. Mix dressing, pour over flowerets, and chill. Yield: 4 servings.

Vegetables

Pečené Houby
(baked mushrooms)

¼ cup finely chopped onion
4 tablespoons butter
2 tablespoons minced fresh
    parsley
1 pound mushrooms, washed
    but not peeled
½ teaspoon caraway seeds

½ teaspoon salt
dash white pepper
1 tablespoon flour
¾ cup sour cream
1½ teaspoons vinegar
buttered bread crumbs

Saute onion in 2 tablespoons butter until golden. Add parsley and 2 more tablespoons butter. Slice and add mushrooms; saute lightly. Add caraway seeds, salt, pepper. Cover skillet and cook on low heat 10 minutes or until mushrooms are tender. Sprinkle 1 tablespoon flour over contents. Blend in. Combine sour cream and vinegar. Add, and cook gently on medium heat about 5 minutes. Turn contents of skillet into a small buttered casserole, sprinkle thickly with buttered bread crumbs and bake at 350 degrees for 15 to 20 minutes or until topping is browned. Yield: 6 servings.

Rotkohl
(red cabbage)

1 red cabbage
2 tablespoons suet
2 tablespoons butter
1 onion, chopped fine
1 green apple, diced
1 cup water

2 tablespoons light brown
   sugar
2 tablespoons vinegar
2 teaspoons caraway seed
salt and pepper

Shred cabbage fine and saute in the hot suet and butter. Add onion and apple. Cover pan and simmer slowly for 30 minutes. Add remaining ingredients and continue cooking slowly for 1 hour. Stir occasionally. Yield: 4 servings.

Dumplings and Potatoes

Knedliky
(potato dumplings)

1 pound potatoes, boiled in
   their skins
2 cups flour

pinch of salt
1 egg

Skin and mash potatoes. Add flour, salt, and egg. Knead into a firm dough. Shape into balls or rolls and cook in boiling water for 20 minutes. (Chopped meat added to the dough makes these dumplings a meal in themselves). Also can be served as a dessert by adding fruit or jam to the dough. Yield: 6 dumplings.

Topfenknödel
(cheese dumplings)

1 pound pot cheese
2 egg yolks
1 tablespoon flour
½ teaspoon salt

1 roll, soaked in water and
   well-drained
2 tablespoons bread crumbs

Mix all ingredients together and place in refrigerator for 1 hour. Shape into dumplings and dust with flour. Drop into boiling salted water and boil on low heat for 5 minutes. Remove carefully from water with perforated spoon. Serve sprinkled with sugar and cinnamon and pour hot melted butter over all. Yield: 6 dumplings.

Fish

Kapr na Modro
(blue carp)

3 pounds carp	4 whole allspice
salt to taste	dash of thyme
2 medium onions, sliced	½ cup boiling vinegar
1 cup sliced vegetables (celery root, parsnip, carrot)	parsley
10 peppercorns	¾ cup butter, melted
½ bay leaf	lemon wedges

Clean carp, cut lengthwise. Cook vegetables and spices in 3 cups salted water for 20 minutes. Put carp in deep skillet, skin side up, and slowly pour vinegar over it. (The skin will turn blue.) Pour in vegetables with water, but not directly over the fish. Cover and simmer 15 to 20 minutes. Remove carp to a warm plate. Garnish with lemon wedges and parsley and serve with butter. Yield: 4 to 6 servings.

Ryba na Víně
(stewed fish in wine)

1 onion, chopped	3 pounds fish (carp or pike)
6 tablespoons butter	1 cup red wine
1 bay leaf	¼ cup flour
5 peppercorns	½ to 1 cup fish stock or water
2 whole cloves	lemon juice to taste
salt to taste	

Saute onion in half the butter. Add bay leaf, peppercorns, cloves, and fish sprinkled with salt. Add wine. Simmer about 15 minutes. Remove fish to a heated platter. Melt remaining butter; blend in flour. Blend in wine sauce and fish or water stock. Simmer for 5 minutes. Strain sauce over fish and sprinkle with lemon juice. Yield: 6 to 8 servings.

Poultry

Husa s Jablkovou Nadivkou
(goose with apple stuffing)

10 to 12 pound goose	3 cups sliced apples
3 teaspoons salt	1 cup bread crumbs
1 teaspoon pepper	1 small onion, chopped
2 teaspoons caraway seeds	⅛ teaspoon cayenne pepper

Wash goose and remove any remaining feathers. Dry thoroughly. Combine salt, pepper, and caraway seeds and rub into the skin and inside of the goose. (This should be done about 8 hours before using, to allow seasoning to be absorbed.) Place sliced apples in saucepan with ½ cup water. Cook over low heat until soft, about 20 minutes. Mash apples with a fork and add the bread crumbs, minced onion, and cayenne pepper. Mix well. Stuff goose with apple mixture and fasten the opening with skewers or thread. Roast in shallow pan at 350 degrees for 3 hours. Pour off fat as it accumulates. At end of 2 hours, carefully pour over the skin 1 cup of ice water. Baste several times during final hour of roasting for a crisp and brown skin. Yield: 4 to 6 servings.

Meat

Székely Goulyas
(veal and pork goulash)

1 pound veal shoulder	1 1-pound, 11-ounce can and 1
1 pound pork shoulder	14-ounce can sauerkraut
2 tablespoons salad oil	1½ cups sour cream
2 tablespoons caraway seeds	paprika
1 teaspoon salt	

About 1 hour, 45 minutes before serving, saute veal and pork (cut in 1½-inch cubes) in salad oil until brown on all sides. Stir in caraway seeds, sauerkraut, salt. Cover and simmer over low heat 1½ hours or until tender. Blend in 1 cup sour cream and bring to boil. Heap on serving platter. Spoon on rest of sour cream over sauerkraut and sprinkle with paprika. Serve with boiled potatoes. Yield: 6 servings.

Hovězí Dušené Přírodní
(braised beef)

2 pounds brisket or round beef	salt and pepper to taste
2 medium onions, chopped	1 tablespoon flour
¼ cup bacon fat	

Pound meat. Brown onion in fat. Add meat, salt, pepper. Brown meat well on both sides. Pour ¾ cup of water over meat, cover, and simmer until tender, 2 to 2½ hours. When tender, remove meat. Dust drippings with the flour, stir until browned, and add 1¼ cups water. Simmer 5 minutes. Slice meat and return to the gravy. Serve with noodles, potatoes, dumplings, or rice. Yield: 4 to 6 servings.

Cikánský Guláš
(Gypsy goulash)

1 medium onion, chopped	½ teaspoon caraway seeds
¼ cup shortening	salt to taste
¼ teaspoon paprika	2 tablespoons flour
1½ pounds fresh pork shoulder, cubed	2 peeled, chopped tomatoes
	1 large sliced onion

Fry 1 medium chopped onion in shortening. Add paprika, meat, caraway seeds, salt. Brown well. Add ½ cup water. Simmer in covered pan until meat is tender (about 1 hour). Dust drippings with flour. Stir until brown. Add 1½ cups water and simmer for 10 to 20 minutes. During last 5 to 10 minutes, add 2 peeled, chopped tomatoes and simmer. Fry 1 large sliced onion in 1 tablespoon shortening. Serve sprinkled on top of meat. Yield: 4 servings.

Pastries and Desserts

Kolacky
(yeast pastries)

Dough:	*Fruit filling:*
½ cup sugar	½ pound prunes
1 teaspoon salt	4-ounces dried apricots
4 cups flour, sifted	¼ teaspoon allspice
½ cup softened butter	½ cup sugar
2 eggs	1 tablespoon lemon juice
2 packages dry yeast	1 tablespoon grated lemon rind

Simmer prunes and apricots in water to cover for 30 minutes. Drain and finely chop. Add sugar, spice, lemon juice and rind. For dough: Cream sugar, butter, salt and eggs thoroughly. Dissolve yeast in ¾ cup warm water. Add to creamed mixture with 1½ cups flour. Beat on low speed with electric mixer for 10 minutes. Stir in remaining flour. Let rise in large buttered bowl in warm place for 1½ hours. Stir down. Turn out onto a well-floured board. Divide dough into 24 equal pieces. Shape into smooth round balls. Let rest 15 minutes. Make a depression in each ball. Fill with fruit filling as prepared above. Place on ungreased baking sheet. Let rise 30 minutes. Bake at 350 degrees until brown. Brush with melted butter. Yield: 24 pastries.

Jablkovy Dort
(apple tart)

butter	½ cup sugar
breadcrumbs	½ cup flour
6 cooking apples, sliced in rings	2 tablespoons milk
	1 egg

Butter a pie dish and sprinkle thickly with breadcrumbs. Place sliced apples over bread crumbs. Make some pastry by blending the sugar, flour, milk, and egg, mixing to a thick batter, and pour over apples in the dish. Bake for 20 minutes at 425 degrees. Serve hot. (If using fresh apples, stew them a little before putting them into the pie dish.)

Makovec Bramborový
(poppy seed cake)

1 egg yolk
¾ cup sugar
4 tablespoons milk
2 cold boiled potatoes, grated
¼ cup farina
¾ cup ground poppy seed
3 teaspoons baking powder

¼ teaspoon cinnamon
pinch of ground cloves
½ teaspoon ground lemon peel
½ teaspoon vanilla
2 egg whites, stiffly beaten
fine breadcrumbs
jam

Beat egg yolk, sugar, and milk together until creamy. Add potatoes, farina, and poppy seeds mixed with baking powder, cinnamon, and cloves. Blend in lemon peel and vanilla. Fold in egg whites. Grease a spring form and sprinkle with bread crumbs. Pour in batter. Bake in preheated 350 degree oven for 40 to 50 minutes. When cake is cool, spread jam on top and decorate with cocoa or rum icing.

Cocoa icing:

6 tablespoons butter
⅔ cup powdered sugar
1 tablespoon milk

2 tablespoons cocoa
2 tablespoons potato starch

Melt butter. Stir in sugar. Mix until smooth. Heat over low flame. Add cocoa and milk and bring just to boiling but do not let icing boil. Add potato starch and blend well. Remove from heat and serve.

Rum icing:

2 cups powdered sugar   3 tablespoons rum

Sift sugar into a bowl, add rum and 2 to 3 tablespoons boiling water. Stir with wooden spoon until white and thick.

Chapter 4

HUNGARY

Of all the peoples behind the Iron Curtain, the Hungarians seem to be the most prosperous and happy. Not that they always have been so. For ten centuries Hungary has been dominated by foreign powers.

Indelible in my memory is the autumn of 1956 when I heard on the radio in Germany, where I was living, that the Hungarians were staging a counterrevolution against the Soviets. Budapest became an armed camp. On television I saw a young secretary standing on the high ledge of an office building waving the Hungarian flag over her comrades below. Machine guns were spouting bullets, tanks were set ablaze, and many were killed. When the uprising was suppressed after less than two weeks, 200,000 Hungarians went into exile.

The revolt was not all defeat, however, because since then Hungary's Communist government has become more liberal, giving in to some of the people's demands. Private enterprise has been introduced into industry and commerce; Hungarians once again may travel outside their borders; writers and artists can express themselves more freely; and the secret police's powers have been reduced. And while Hungary still has the closest economic and political ties with Russia, life is not so dreary and drab as in some other Communist satellites.

Hungarians have survived the Mongols, Tartars, Turks, their own despotic kings, the Austrian Hapsburgs, and even an admiral who ruled them after World War I despite the fact that Hungary has no outlet to the sea. Descendants of oriental invaders, brave, fun-loving, quick to become fired up to defend a cause and just as quick to let the fire die and get back to enjoying life, the Hungarians have no little gypsy blood in them. Perhaps that is what keeps them going.

In Budapest today you see the gayest, most prosperous capital of all the Communist countries. The gardens on Margaret Island in the middle of the Danube, which cuts through the city, are lovely and peaceful. Old and young sit at sidewalk cafes sipping local Tokay wine (Hungarians are primarily wine drinkers) and exchange jokes, which they love with a passion. Store windows are well stocked with consumer items, and the girls, among Europe's loveliest, are dressed more smartly than in any other Communist country.

Hungarian food is synonymous with paprika, but the spice is only common to them because Turkish invaders in 1526 brought it with them from India. Hungarians add sour cream to make their paprika dishes more distinctive. *Gulyas* (goulash), the famous stew, is one of Hungary's oldest dishes, and was named after the cooking pot of the nomadic shepherds and gypsies who roamed its hills. *Gulyas* is served almost as thin as a soup, while *porkolt,* another type of stew, is much thicker.

Soups are varied and usually a meal in themselves, served with dumplings, noodles, or potatoes. Veal and pork are the favorite meats, and chicken and goose are popular. Hungary's lakes and rivers provide fish and shellfish.

Hungarians love pastries and so their variety is great, usually served at home with tea because coffee is more expensive. Budapest coffeehouses and pastry shops are close rivals to those of Vienna in popularity, serving delicacies such as strudles and tortes.

Many fine restaurants and inns throughout Hungary serve gourmet food or the delicious, substantial food of the people.

In Budapest, you'll run out of time before you run out of good and charming places to dine, from elegant hotel restaurants to historic, Magyar, and foreign eating places. At many of them a gypsy band will serenade you, for a few *fillérs* extra, of course.

At the Royal, along the Grand Boulevard, you can enjoy the

delicious Tokay goulash, red cabbage salad, and nut torte while the gypsies play, then stop in the beer garden just outside. Or go to the Pilvax, a cafe-restaurant in the heart of the old inner city of Pest where young patriots gathered in 1848 and later dethroned the Hapsburg dynasty. Again to gypsy music, you might try the veal rolls and *Ujhazi* chicken soup, rounded off with a dessert called apple pie which you may think you've never tasted before. In Matyas Pince, a beer cellar in the morning and also a restaurant from noon on, the atmosphere with medieval carved wooden tables and benches is strictly Magyar, honoring their storied King Matthias.

Among the many pastry shops, all roads lead to Hungaria on the Grand Boulevard, which the old-timers still call the Cafe New York. Nearly a hundred years old, it has been called the most beautiful cafe in the world, with its Venetian chandeliers, twisted marble columns, gilt balconies, bronze statues, and murals depicting Hungarian history and countryside. On the luxurious lower level, world-famous artists, writers, film stars, and composers gathered. The pastries at Hungaria are rich but light, filled or topped with walnut, poppy seed, hazelnut, chocolate, or fruits and jellies.

Two hours from Budapest is the resort area of Balaton with the largest inland lake of Europe. Szeged, second largest city in Hungary, is a handsome Baroque town. Pecs, in the southwestern mountains, has many Turkish relics. North of Budapest is the Danube Bend, a romantic and scenic stretch of river. Gourmet dishes or the daily fare of the people is served in atmospheric inns and hotel restaurants throughout Hungary which may not be as famous as those in Budapest, but the food is every bit as good.

Westward on the Austrian frontier is Sopron, a small but beautifully preserved Gothic and Baroque town popular for its holiday festivals. Esterhazy palaces, Gothic churches and monasteries, medieval and rococo houses, and gardens on the eastern outcrop of the Alps provide settings for dining at places like the Windmill, on Kuruc Hill, with glass walls, dance floor, and panorama of the city and lake country. A glass of Tokay, an Esterhazy beef stew, a cherry torte, a little gypsy music, and you know why you have come to Hungary.

Soups
Cseresnyeleves
(spiced cherry soup)

1 pound sweet red cherries
rind of ½ lemon
6 whole cloves
1 3-inch stick cinnamon
⅓ cup granulated sugar
½ teaspoon salt

3 tablespoons tapioca
 (quick-cooking)
1 cup red wine
4–6 thin lemon slices
sour cream

Pit cherries, wash, and remove stems. Peel rind from lemon in strips, then stick cloves into rind. In saucepan, combine cherries, lemon rind with cloves, cinnamon, sugar, salt and 3 cups water. Simmer uncovered for 15 minutes. Gradually stir in tapioca. Bring to boil, then remove from heat. Stir in wine, allow to cool. Remove and discard lemon rind and spices. Refrigerate. Serve by ladling ice-cold soup into bowls. Top with a lemon slice and spoonful of sour cream. Yield: 4 servings.

Ujhazi
(chicken soup)

1 boiling chicken
1 carrot
1 parsnip
1 onion

1 tomato
salt and pepper
vermicelli, cooked

Clean and joint the chicken and stew together with vegetables in seasoned water, enough to cover, about an hour. When tender, add cooked vermicelli and serve meat, vegetables, and liquid together in a deep dish. Yield: 2 servings.

Salads
Voros Kaposzta Salata
(red cabbage salad)

½ head medium-sized red
 cabbage, finely shredded
1 tablespoon salt

¼ cup granulated sugar
½ cup vinegar
¼ teaspoon pepper

In large bowl, sprinkle cabbage with salt. Let stand ½ hour. In saucepan, combine sugar, vinegar, ½ cup water, pepper. Bring to boil and pour over cabbage. Refrigerate until serving time. Drain. Serve with pot roast or pork. Yield: 2 to 3 servings.

Paprikasalata
(paprika salad)

5 green peppers	2 teaspoons sugar
3 tablespoons white wine vinegar	salt and pepper
	1 cup mayonnaise

Roast peppers on a rack in hot oven until outer skin starts to blister and turn black. Remove and peel off black skin. Discard the seeds and cut peppers into thin, long strips. Put in bowl. Combine 1 cup water with 2 teaspoons sugar and 3 tablespoons of white wine vinegar and pour over peppers. Salt and pepper and let stand covered overnight in the liquid. Drain thoroughly and mix with mayonnaise. Let chill in refrigerator before serving. Yield: 4 to 6 servings.

Vegetables

Paprikas Gomba
(mushrooms paprika)

1 pound mushrooms	1 tablespoon paprika
1 onion, sliced	1 tablespoon minced parsley
3 tablespoons butter	2 tablespoons flour
½ teaspoon salt	1½ cups sour cream

Wash well, trim, and slice the mushrooms. Brown onion in butter and add mushrooms, seasonings, and parsley. Cook about 10 minutes. Take mushrooms out of onion mixture, dredge with flour, and return to onion mixture. Add sour cream, and bring to a boil. Serve with fried eggs or croutons.

Dumplings

Caraway Dumplings

¾ cup flour
1½ tablespoons baking powder
½ teaspoon salt

pepper
1 teaspoon caraway seeds
1½ ounces fat

Mix dry ingredients and rub in the fat with the fingertips. Mix to a firm, light dough with cold water. Divide into 10 or 12 equal-sized portions, roll into balls, and cook in salted boiling water, covered, about 25 minutes. Yield: 4 dumplings.

Csipetke
(boiled dough with cheese)

6 eggs
4 cups flour
½ teaspoon salt

1 cup sour cream
¼ pound dry cottage cheese
4 slices bacon

Beat eggs and add flour and salt which have been sifted together. Add only sufficient water to make a stiff dough. Chill dough for 20 minutes, then roll out quite thin. Break into small pieces about the size of a thumbnail; spread out on a board to prevent them from adhering to each other. Drop into rapidly boiling salted water and cover. When they rise to the surface, they are cooked. Remove and rinse in cold water, drain and brown in shortening. Before serving, crumble the cottage cheese over the pastry; pour the sour cream over the top and sprinkle with cubes of bacon fried to a crisp brown. Yield: 6 to 8 servings.

Fish

Sult Hal Feherborban
(baked sole)

½ pound mushrooms
4 cold cooked medium
   potatoes, sliced thinly

1 teaspoon paprika
⅔ cup white wine
1 cup sour cream

2 tablespoons butter
1½ teaspoons salt
½ teaspoon pepper

2 pounds fresh fillets of sole
parsley or chives

Heat oven to 375 degrees. Wash, trim, and slice mushrooms. Arrange potatoes in buttered 12-inch by 8-inch by 2-inch baking dish. Top with mushrooms. Dot with butter, sprinkle with half of salt and pepper and ½ teaspoon paprika. Pour wine over all. Spread with half of sour cream. Arrange pieces of fish over all, sprinkle with rest of salt and pepper and ½ teaspoon paprika. Top with rest of sour cream. Bake 30–40 minutes or until fish is done. Sprinkle with paprika and parsley. Yield: 6 to 8 servings.

Poultry

Csirkepaprikás
(chicken paprika)

1 4-pound chicken
2 tablespoons butter
2 onions, chopped
1 teaspoon paprika
2 tablespoons flour

1 can tomato sauce
4 tablespoons sour cream
1 teaspoon salt
¼ teaspoon pepper

Cut chicken into small portions. (Lamb or veal, cut into small portions, may be used instead). Heat butter and brown chicken or meat. Add chopped onions. When golden brown, stir in paprika and flour; mix well. Slowly add 4 cups water and stir until well blended. Add tomato sauce, sour cream, salt and pepper. Cook slowly until tender. Yield: 4 to 6 servings.

Kaposztas Facan
(pheasant with sauerkraut)

1 pheasant
8–10 slices bacon
½ cup white wine
salt
8–10 peppercorns

1 bay leaf
1½ pounds fresh or canned
    sauerkraut
½ cup beer

Clean pheasant, wrap in bacon slices, and truss. Place in deep saucepan. Fry first, turning all over until bacon is rendered. Drain fat after browning. Pour white wine over pheasant, add salt, peppercorns, bay leaf. Cover and gently stew for one hour, until almost tender. Add sauerkraut, beer. Cover and stew 25 minutes more. Yield: 6 to 8 servings.

Meat

Gulyas
(goulash)

1 pound brisket of beef
2 teaspoons sweet paprika
2 large onions, chopped
½ teaspoon salt
4 or 5 potatoes, diced

1 tomato, sliced
1 egg, well-beaten
1 cup flour
½ teaspoon salt

Cut brisket of beef into cubes and wash in cold water. Put meat in saucepan with tight-fitting lid, and add chopped paprika, onions, salt, and ½ cup water. Onions may be browned in butter if desired. Allow mixture to simmer 1½ hours, adding more water if necessary to prevent meat from burning. Add diced potatoes and 1 cup water. Let simmer until meat and potatoes are tender, then add the tomato. Just before serving make dumplings of the flour mixed with egg and ½ teaspoon salt. Roll out very thin, cut into small squares, and boil in goulash for 1 or 2 minutes. Yield: 3 to 4 servings.

Marjoram Tokany
(beef stew)

5 onions, chopped
6 tablespoons butter
2 pounds stew beef
½ teaspoon salt
dash of marjoram

¼ teaspoon pepper
1 clove garlic
¾ cup white wine
½ pound bacon
2 cups sour cream

Brown onions in butter, then add meat which has been cut into long strips. Season with salt, marjoram, pepper, and garlic. Add wine and stew until meat is nearly tender. Add bacon which has been browned. Stir in sour cream and cook over low heat until meat is tender, 30 to 45 minutes.

Esterhazy Beef Stew

4 ounces bacon fat
3 carrots, chopped
2 onions, chopped
2 stalks celery, chopped
½ green pepper, chopped
salt and pepper
2 teaspoons paprika

2 teaspoons capers
1 cup beef stock
⅛ cup flour
3 tablespoons sour cream
2 pounds stew beef
3 tablespoons Madeira wine

Melt half the bacon fat in an ovenproof dish. Add vegetables and seasoning. Cover and saute gently for 10 minutes. Do not stir. Remove cover and raise heat. Without stirring, shake the pan and brown the vegetables, adding a little stock (beef boullion and water). Sprinkle in flour. Stir gently, blending, and adding remaining stock and sour cream. In another pan, heat remaining drippings. Sear beef (rump or chuck steak cut into small steaks and flattened out) quickly on both sides. Add meat to vegetables and gravy. Cover and cook in 350 degree oven for about 30 to 45 minutes. Add wine 5 minutes before serving. Yield: 4 servings.

Borju Rolada
(veal rolls)

1¼ pound veal, cut ¼-inch
  thick
1 tablespoon prepared
  mustard
¼ cup grated Parmesan cheese
1 teaspoon salt

1 tablespoon flour
1 teaspoon paprika
¼ cup butter
2 tablespoons chopped
  parsley

Cut veal into 4 pieces. Spread each with mustard, then sprinkle with cheese, parsley, salt. Roll each up and tie with string. Combine flour and paprika and use to coat rolls on all sides, reserving any leftover flour. In hot butter in pan, brown rolls well on all sides. Add ½ cup water; simmer, covered, for 30 minutes until tender. Remove rolls to heated platter. Thicken liquid in pan with remaining flour. Heat, stirring, until smooth. Pour over rolls. Sprinkle with parsley. Yield: 4 servings.

Porkoltborju
(veal porkolt)

6 onions, sliced
2 tablespoons shortening
1 tablespoon paprika
3 pounds veal, cubed

salt
3 tomatoes
3 green peppers, sliced

(This dish also may be prepared with pork, mutton, fowl, hare.) Brown onions in shortening. Add paprika and meat. Season to taste. Stew slowly, adding water if necessary. When meat is half cooked, add tomatoes and sliced peppers. Cover and cook until tender. Yield: 4 to 5 servings.

Pastries, Desserts

Apple Fool

4 or 5 cooking apples
2 egg whites

½ cup sugar
4 fresh plums

Peel and core apples. Cook with very little water until tender. Rub through a sieve. Beat egg whites until very stiff. Fold in sugar; gradually add the apple puree. Decorate with fresh plums, stoned and cut in half, or with any fresh fruit. Serve cold.

Apple Pie

3 apples
¾ cup flour
¼ pound butter or margarine
1 egg yolk

¼ cup sugar
strawberry jam
1 egg white
egg white and sugar to glaze

1–2 tablespoons sour cream or milk

⅔ cup ground almonds

whipped cream and glacé cherries

Stew apples about 20 minutes. Sift the flour and rub in the butter, mix to a dough with egg yolk and sour cream or milk, knead, and put aside in cool place for 30 minutes. Line a 7-inch pie tin with half the pastry and party bake about 10 minutes in 400 degree oven. Mix ground almonds with the sugar. Spread pastry with strawberry jam and sprinkle half of the sugar and almond mixture on top. Fold the stiffly whisked egg white into the stewed apples and put into the pie; sprinkle the rest of the almond and sugar mixture on top. Cover with the rest of the pastry, glaze the top with egg white, sprinkle with sugar, and bake in 400 degree oven about a half hour. Decorate with whipped cream and glacé cherries.

Nut Torte

7 eggs

¼ cup sugar

¼ cup fine dry white bread crumbs

few drops vanilla

blanched nuts to decorate

½ cup chopped walnuts and toasted almonds

¾ cup powdered sugar

2 ounces chocolate

Separate 4 eggs and whisk yolks with ¼ cup sugar until thick and creamy. Whisk egg whites until stiff. Mix together breadcrumbs and nuts. Add egg yolk mixture, fold in egg whites. Put mixture into three 8-inch greased layer cake tins and bake in 350 degree oven about 25 minutes or until firm and lightly browned. Allow cakes to cool in the tins before carefully turning them out. When cold, fill and top with the following soft chocolate icing:

Put 3 eggs and ¾ cups of powdered sugar into a double saucepan. Stir until mixture thickens, being careful it does not overheat and curdle. Remove from heat and stir in two ounces melted chocolate and a little vanilla extract. Beat until filling is thick enough, then spread it between the cakes and over the top. Decorate with a few nuts.

Chapter 5

SWITZERLAND

The Swiss must have everything they want right between their borders, because you rarely hear of a Swiss immigrant. I know I've never met one. And it would seem they choose to stay in their homeland for good reason.

Following the path of neutrality, the Swiss have not been in a war for over a hundred years, preferring to be active in humanitarian causes. Their economy and the value of their currency are among the best in the world. A highly electrified country, air and water pollution are practically unknown. The mountain and lake scenery is nothing short of spectacular. And the sports-and-outdoors-minded people appear to be happy and content, possessed of a serious respect for quality craftsmanship in everything they produce that is almost unique among other peoples. You've heard the expression, "It works like a Swiss watch." The Swiss reputation for craftsmanship certainly is deserved.

Some people can't forgive the Swiss for not taking up arms in World Wars I and II. Perhaps the Swiss take their stand of neutrality because they alone among nations have come to realize the futility of war. Their own history of domination by foreign powers dates back to the Roman Empire. Afterward they were ruled at various times by the French, Germans, and Austrians. By the late thirteenth century, three communities of Uri, Schwyz, and Unterwalden formed a Confederation to free themselves from the Hapsburgs. More communities joined in, and by the fifteenth century Switzerland emerged as a nation. The process was not dissimilar from the thirteen original colonies that joined together to form the United States of America.

Nearly two centuries of troubles plagued the fledgling Swiss nation. First, defeat in 1515 by the French in another war, then the Reformation, the Protestant revolution that divided the country on religious issues, followed by more internal disputes. Then came Napoleon's armies in 1798, but Switzerland emerged from that war still an independent nation. Civil war in 1847 failed to destroy the nation and since then the Swiss have regarded war in general as an inadequate way of solving problems.

Twenty million tourists flock each year to Switzerland, which in area is not quite twice the size of Massachusetts. When I was there, the bulk of tourists must have been out climbing the Jungfrau, because I never had trouble getting a table in a restaurant, tours were limited to reasonable numbers, hotel rooms were readily available, and not once did I bump into anyone I knew from Chicago. Perhaps it's because Switzerland is so well prepared for its tourist invasion each year and there are so many out-of-the-way places to see, tourists can be gobbled up in the mountains and towns, not concentrated in large cities.

My Switzerland is snowcapped mountains, meadows multicolored with wildflowers, gardens which must rival those in paradise, cobblestone streets and gingerbread houses and shops, murals depicting folklore painted on outer walls of homes, concerts in the park and, of course, cafes and restaurants.

Swiss food is a happy blend of the culinary arts of their neighbors, especially France, Germany, and Italy. The only major contribution the Swiss make to the world's cuisine is *fondue,* a melted dish made with Swiss cheese, white wine, and *kirsch,* a clear cherry brandy. A favorite *apres ski* appetizer or meal, the dish has been altered by Europeans and Americans to produce various meat variations. In Bern province, the local speciality is the *Berner platte,* a tray of assorted meats and sausages. St. Gall province is the home of *St. Galler bratwurst,* a veal sausage. Lucerne is noted for its *kuegeli-pastete,* a puff filled with sweetbreads, mushrooms, and other delicacies. The southern provinces serve Italian-style food.

Swiss cheese and chocolates are, of course, known throughout the world. And being wine drinkers like the French, the Swiss produce noteworthy wines such as Neuchatel and Riesling-Sylvaner. Where to dine in Switzerland is as much an adventure as where to ski next.

Zurich is cosmopolitan; to me a womanly city, like a small Paris. Smart little shops front on tree-shaded boulevards, flower gardens spread out around quaint villas where even the lower class live, historic churches and museums and art galleries are works of art in themselves, the blue of Lake Zurich and wooded green hills are within a few minutes walk, and charming dining places such as the Kronenhalle are plentiful. There, over a deep plate of *geschnetzeltes,* a beef and veal stew with dumplings, you can look up at original Matisses and Picassos on the walls, or sit at the table that was the favorite of the late author James Joyce.

Bern, the capital, is a storybook city unlike any other in Europe. Most of its shops are lined inside arcades, tucked under stone archways. From the balcony of the parliament buildings high above the river, one especially clear August afternoon allowed a spectacular view of the snow-covered Jungfrau range. Later, actually up in the mountains, on the terrace of the Berghaus, at 11,723 feet the highest hotel in Europe, the Swiss veal and cheese cake were as out of this world as the panoramic view of the three incredible glaciers.

Switzerland also is Interlaken, Lugano, Gstaad, Grindelwald, St. Moritz, Zermatt and the magnificent Matterhorn. It has always been my ambition, for some strange reason, to drink a glass of beer at the *bottom* of the Matterhorn. I'm sure when I do that, all my world's travel wishes will have been fulfilled, so I'm saving that adventure for last.

Lucerne remains my favorite Swiss city. It has perhaps the world's best blend of old and new atmosphere. Fifteenth century houses, medieval covered bridges, picturesque water towers, baroque chapels, old city walls, and truly beautiful parks and gardens all live harmoniously with modern architecture.

The Wilden Mann hotel restaurant with its medieval charm has been delighting tourist palates since it opened in 1517. My favorite is the less imposing Old Swiss House near the Lion of Lucerne grotto. In an old patrician home converted into a restaurant, the fondue was especially delicious and fun to eat. The *struzels*, horseshoe-shaped raisin pastries, were light and so tasty. And afterward an outdoor evening band concert in the park, looking out over Lake Lucerne to see the distant lights of chairlifts taking riders up to resorts high in the mountains. Ah, Switzerland, no wonder your people stay at home.

Appetizers

Swiss Fondue
(also a meal)

French bread	dash of pepper
3 tablespoons Kirsch or brandy	dash of nutmeg
2 tablespoons cornstarch	¾ pound natural Swiss cheese
1 clove garlic, crushed	(Emmenthal or Gruyere, or
2 cups dry white wine	half and half)

Half an hour before serving, cut French bread into small cubes; place in breadbasket or bowl. Stir together cornstarch and Kirsch until smooth; set aside. Rub inside of ovenproof casserole with garlic. Pour in wine, heat gradually until just below boiling. Add pepper and nutmeg. Gradually add cheese, stirring constantly with a fork. Add cornstarch mixture and stir until smooth and bubbly. Place over alcohol burner, warm enough to keep it bubbling slightly. To serve: each person heaps some bread cubes on his plate. Using fork, dip bread cubes one by one into fondue. (Fondue also may be prepared in a chafing dish or other fireproof vessel.)

Käsekugeln
(fried cheese balls)

2¾ cups grated Swiss cheese	¼ teaspoon pepper
½ cup flour	⅛ teaspoon nutmeg
2 eggs, beaten	fat for deep frying

1 egg yolk　　　　　　　　parsley
1 teaspoon salt

Combine grated cheese, flour, eggs, egg yolk, salt, pepper, and nutmeg. Work into a stiff paste (slowly add more flour if necessary). Shape into balls with teaspoon. Fry in deep fat at 380 degrees for 6 minutes or until golden brown. Drain on paper towels. Garnish with parsley. Yield: 4 to 6 servings.

Soups

Braune Mehlsuppe
(Swiss brown soup)

¼ cup butter or bacon　　　　salt and pepper
　　drippings　　　　　　　　grated cheese
¾ cup flour

Melt butter or bacon drippings in large kettle. Add flour and stir constantly until golden brown. Slowly add 5 cups cold water, again stirring constantly until all water has been added. Season to taste with salt and pepper. Cover and simmer 2 hours. Serve with grated cheese. Yield: 4 servings.

Kässuppe
(cheese soup)

1 pound stale brown bread　　⅓ pint dry white wine
1¼ pound cheese　　　　　　salt

Cut bread and cheese into small, thin slices, and arrange in layers in a tureen. Pour in 5 cups boiling water. Let set for about 3 hours. Pour into saucepan and cook, carefully crushing the bread and cheese with a wooden spoon. Add wine and seasoning before serving. Yield: 4 servings.

Salads

Zwiebeln Salat
(onion salad)

4 large onions
4 tablespoons margarine
1 tablespoon flour

1 teaspoon salt
2 tablespoons vinegar

Slice onions ½ inch thick. Melt butter or margarine in saucepan. Add onions and saute until light brown, stirring often. Sprinkle with flour and cook for 3 minutes. Remove from heat. Add salt and vinegar. Mix well. Serve hot or cold. Yield: 3 servings.

Grüner Bohnensalat
(green bean salad)

1½ pound green beans
½ cup olive oil
2–3 tablespoons vinegar
salt and pepper

1 teaspoon prepared mustard
1 medium onion, minced
2 tablespoons parsley
1 teaspoon dried tarragon

Cook beans in boiling salted water until tender but still crisp. Make dressing with the oil, vinegar, salt, pepper, mustard, onion, and parsley. Drain cooked beans and put in a bowl. While they are still hot, toss with the dressing. Add tarragon. Let stand at room temperature for 2 hours. Do not chill (salad will lose some of its flavor if cooled). Yield: 3 servings.

Vegetables

Tomatoes Stuffed with Apple and Celery

6 large tomatoes
1 teaspoon salt
¼ teaspoon pepper
2 cups celery, finely chopped

¼ cup sour cream
3 tablespoons salad oil
1 tablespoon horseradish
½ teaspoon salt

2 cups unpeeled apples,
  coarsely grated
¼ cup lemon juice
½ teaspoon salt
1 teaspoon sugar

½ teaspoon pepper
chopped chives
watercress
radishes

Cut a ¼-inch slice from the stem end of each of 6 large tomatoes. Using a spoon, scoop out and keep and pulp. Sprinkle tomato cups with 1 teaspoon salt and ¼ teaspoon pepper. Invert on a plate. Put 2 cups finely sliced celery in a bowl with 2 cups coarsely grated unpeeled apples, ¼ cup lemon juice, ½ teaspoon salt, 1 teaspoon sugar. Combine ¼ cup sour cream, 3 tablespoons salad oil, 1 tablespoon horseradish, ½ teaspoon salt, and ¼ teaspoon pepper. Drain tomato pulp and coarsely chop enough of it to make 1 and ¼ cups. Chill all ingredients. Combine apple and sour cream mixtures, then add tomato pulp. Use to fill the tomato cups, arrange on a large dish and sprinkle with chopped chives. Garnish with watercress and radish roses. Yield: 6 servings.

Dumplings, potatoes

Swiss Rice

3 cups milk
1 teaspoon salt
1 cup rice

½ teaspoon vanilla
2 cups cream, whipped
raspberry juice

Scald the milk in top of a double boiler. Add salt. Stir in well-washed and drained rice. Cook over boiling water 45 minutes or until rice is tender and milk is absorbed. Remove from heat and add vanilla. Cool. Whip the cream and reserve ½ cup of it for garnish. Fold remaining cream into the cooled rice and mix well. Fill sherbet glasses and chill. To the ½ cup of whipped cream remaining, add enough raspberry juice to color. When serving rice, garnish top with the rose-colored whipped cream.

Eierduenkli
(egg dice)

½ loaf white bread
1 cup warm milk
2 tablespoons butter
3 eggs, well-beaten

salt and pepper
3 tablespoons Swiss cheese,
   grated

Cut bread into small cubes and cover with warm milk and allow to soak for 5 minutes Melt butter and add bread. Saute until brown. To well-beaten eggs add salt and pepper and grated cheese. Pour mixture over the bread and continue cooking until eggs are set. Serve at once. Yield: 3 servings.

Funggi
(potato apples)

2 apples
6 potatoes
1 onion, sliced
3 tablespoons sugar

3 tablespoons butter
1½ teaspoons salt
2 tablespoons cider

Pare and quarter apples. Peel and cube potatoes. Slice onion. Combine apples, sugar, and 3 cups water in saucepan. Bring to a boil and cook 3 minutes. Melt butter in a large saucepan. Add onion and saute for 10 minutes, stirring frequently. Add potatoes, salt, cider, and apple mixture, including any liquid. Cover and cook 30 minutes or until very soft. Mix well. Serve hot in individual small dishes. Good with roasts, other meats. Yield: 4 to 6 servings.

Fish

Lachs, Baseler
(Basel style salmon)

6 slices fresh salmon
2 teaspoons salt
1 teaspoon pepper
4 tablespoons flour

¼ pound butter
2 onions, chopped
3 tablespoons stock or water
paprika

Sponge but do not wash salmon slices. Combine salt, pepper, flour and pat into the fish on all sides. Melt half the butter in a skillet. Fry salmon slices 5 to 8 minutes on each side or until golden brown. Place on heated platter and keep warm. Melt remaining butter in same skillet. Saute onions over low heat for 15 minutes, stirring frequently, until soft and yellow. Pour onions over salmon. Place stock or water in same skillet, bring to boil and pour over fish. Sprinkle a little paprika on the fish. Serve with very thin slices of lemon.

Lucerne Fish Fillets

2 lbs. fish	butter or margarine
beef bouillon	flour
2 or 3 potatoes	salt, pepper, mustard
dry white wine	grated cheese

Cook fish in beef bouillon until tender. Peel and cook potatoes at same time. Place fillets side by side in a buttered ovenproof dish and surround by slices of potato. Make a piquant sauce with dry white wine, butter, flour, salt, pepper, and mustard, and pour over the fish. Top with plenty of grated cheese and bake about 20 minutes in 350 degree oven.

Fillets de Perches Gourmet
(gourmet's fried perch)

1½ perch fillets	flour
salt	2–3 ounces butter
juice of 1 lemon	1–2 tomatoes
1 egg	⅔ cup béarnaise sauce
1 teaspoon olive oil	boiled potatoes

Salt perch fillets and sprinkle with lemon juice. Dip in beaten egg mixed with a little olive oil, flour them, then cook in butter in skillet until golden brown. Skin, seed, and dice tomatoes. Put béarnaise sauce (see index) in a hot dish and scatter the diced tomatoes over it. Arrange fillets on the dish and garnish with boiled potatoes.

Poultry

Poulet im Topf
(chicken in a pot)

2 3-pound chickens	2 pounds peas
¼ cup butter	6 medium carrots
salt and pepper	1 small head cauliflower
paprika	6 small potatoes
1 tablespoon cornstarch	

Cut chickens into quarters. Brown in butter in large Dutch oven. Sprinkle with salt, pepper, paprika. Cover tightly and cook slowly until tender. Add a little water as needed. Remove chickens from pot. Stir in cornstarch dissolved in ¼ cup water. Cook, stirring constantly, until smooth and thickened. Pile chicken into center of pot. Surround with peas that have been shelled and cooked (or equivalent frozen peas that have been cooked), carrots that have been sliced and cooked, cauliflower that has been broken into flowerets and cooked (or frozen and cooked), and potatoes that have been cooked. Cover and reheat for 10 minutes. Yield: 6 servings.

Meat

Geschnetzeltes
(pan stewed meat with dumplings)

4 tablespoons butter	salt
3 medium onions, chopped fine	pepper
	½ pound round steak, diced
1 tablespoon minced parsley	½ pound veal, diced
1 tablespoon flour	lemon juice or wine

Melt butter in skillet and add onions and parsley. Cook for several minutes. Sprinkle all with flour and add some salt and pepper. When flour is blended, add meat and fry over high heat about 2 minutes, stirring constantly. Cover the skillet, reduce heat and simmer meat slowly about 45 minutes or until tender. When ready to serve, add a little lemon juice or wine and serve with small dumplings. Yield: 2 servings.

Veau á la Suisse
(Swiss veal)

6 thin veal cutlets (about 1½ pounds)	⅓ cup butter
6 thin slices Swiss cheese	1 cup sauterne or Rhine wine
6 very thin slices cooked ham	1 cup beef gravy
2 tablespoons flour	½ cup light cream
paprika	salt
	6 drops lemon juice

Pound each cutlet flat by using edge of a heavy saucer, then cut each slice in half. On each half, place ½ thin slice cheese, 1 paper-thin slice ham, ½ thin slice cheese. Top each with second cutlet half and fasten with toothpicks. Mix flour with paprika and use to coat cutlets. In skillet place butter and when quite hot, saute cutlets until well browned on each side. Add ½ cup wine and cook slowly, uncovered, until liquid is almost evaporated. Slowly add ½ cup wine, beef gravy, and cream, stirring with wooden spoon. Cover skillet and simmer cutlets 10 minutes or until tender. Before serving, stir in salt and lemon juice, then remove toothpicks. Serve with rice. Yield: 4 servings.

Hackbraten
(meat loaf)

½ pound ground beef	½ cup rolled oats soaked in milk
½ pound ground pork	6 green olives, stoned
½ pound veal	2 eggs
1 large cooking apple, peeled and chopped	salt and pepper
4 ounces mushrooms, sliced	

Mix all ingredients well. Bind with beaten eggs. Season lightly with salt and pepper. Bake in 350 degree oven in a greased bread tin for an hour and a half. Yield: 3 servings.

Äpfelschnitte
(bacon and apple)

¾ pound dried apples
1½ ounces butter
1 tablespoon sugar

1¼ slices lean bacon
1½ diced potatoes
½ pound smoked sausages

Soak apples in cold water 6–8 hours beforehand to let them swell. Melt butter and sugar in saucepan. Add soaked apples and bacon. Moisten with a little water and cook about 1 hour. Mix in diced potatoes and sausages. Cook another 25 minutes. Add salt if desired. Cut up bacon and dish it up on top the apples. Yield: 3 servings.

Pastries

Chäs-Tange
(cheese sticks)

2 cups sifted flour
¼ teaspoon salt
1 cup butter
1 egg

2½ tablespoons milk
1 egg, beaten
1½ cups grated Swiss cheese
caraway seeds

Sift flour with salt in large bowl. With pastry blender, cut in butter or margarine until mixture is coarse. Blend in one egg, beaten with milk. Wrap the dough in wax paper and refrigerate for 1 hour. Heat oven to 375 degrees. Grease two cookie sheets. Roll out half the dough on a lightly floured surface. When ⅛ inch thick, cut into strips 5 inches by ½ inch with pastry wheel. Twist two strips together. Place on cookie sheet, pinch ends together. Repeat with rest of strips. Brush twists with some of beaten egg, sprinkle with ¾ cup grated cheese, 1 tablespoon caraway seeds, and 1 teaspoon salt. Bake 15 minutes or until golden, then remove. Serve warm or cool by themselves or with soup or salad. Yield: about 36 sticks.

Strüzels
(horsehoofs)

2 cups sifted flour
3 tablespoons sugar
2 tablespoons butter
1 egg, beaten

½ cup milk
2 tablespoons seedless raisins
1½ teaspoons baking powder
fat for deep frying

Sift flour and sugar together into a bowl. Cut in butter with pastry blender or two knives. Add egg and milk, mixing well. Add raisins and baking powder and mix well again. Shape a tablespoon of the dough into a horseshoe shape. Heat fat in deep saucepan to 360 degrees. Drop horseshoes into fat and fry until golden brown. Drain and dust with powdered sugar. Serve either hot or cold.

Käse Kuchen
(cheese cake)

1 cup flour
6 tablespoons butter
3 egg yolks
rind and juice of 1 lemon
¼ cup sugar

¼ cup currants
¼ cup candied peel
½ pound cream cheese
2 egg whites, beaten

Make a dough with the flour, butter, and one egg yolk and roll it out. Line a 10 inch tart tin. Blend cream cheese with 2 egg yolks, grated lemon peel, lemon juice, sugar, currants, and candied peel. Fold in the beaten egg whites. Fill tart tin with mixture. Bake in 350 degree oven about a half hour.

2

The Baltic

Poland, Estonia, Latvia, Lithuania

The cultural and culinary history of the Baltic countries is tied to Poland, a mixture of Slavonic races, and to Russia.

The food comes basically from peasant appetites. The people, for the most part, being rugged and robust and hardworking, are possessed of a great sense of camaraderie. A newcomer in the community, whether back in the Old Country or in America, is greeted with open arms and made the occasion of a celebration that includes a staggering quantity of palate-pleasing food, polkas and waltzes you can't stop dancing to, and vodka, beer, and wine.

Polish weddings, even in this country, last usually a weekend. My parents' wedding in Chicago forty years ago lasted a week. Dozens of relatives in half a dozen cars followed them one hundred miles on their honeymoon before they returned to the party. The wedding party, without the bride and groom, lasted until the food and drink was gone, and that took a week of evenings and the entire next weekend.

Cooking, under the influence of peasant Russia, is simple but more than ample. Beef, ham, cabbage, rice, a multitude of soups and stews, and a constant supply of fresh fish from the sea, lakes, and streams provide Polish, Estonian, Latvian, and Lithuanian cooks with staples to which they add local herbs, spices, and greens to flavor the dishes in their own unique style.

Spices from the Far East once were used abundantly by the upper classes with the idea that the more used, the better the result, especially in showing generosity to a guest.

Peasants could rarely afford the spices, but they used mushrooms, which the upper class seldom ate because they thought that forest pickings were beneath them.

In the sixteenth century the cuisine of the French court, which became the standard of gourmet excellence throughout Europe, found its way up to the Baltic countries, and cooks there adapted some of the French refinements.

Dairy products are plentiful in the primarily agricultural Baltic countries, and eggs, milk, cheese, and butter are used extensively in many recipes.

The Baltic states, being bordered on the west by the Baltic Sea and on the east by Russia, were and still are bound by their geographic location to be dominated by the vastly greater political and economic influences of their neighbor, the Soviet Union.

But though the countries exist today as Russian satellites, Poland and its northern neighbors continue to assert their national identities. Politically, when they can. Gastronomically, every day.

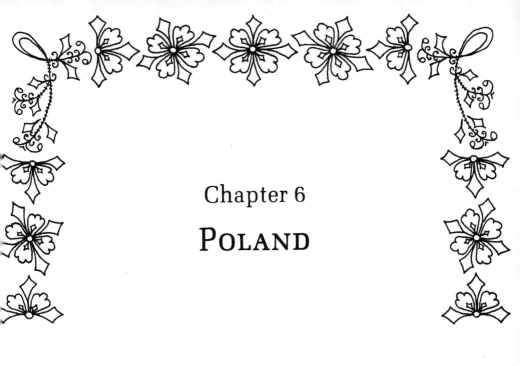

Chapter 6

POLAND

Once off limits to Westerners, Poland now welcomes visitors. Most of the cities of Poland were completely destroyed during World War II, when more than six million Poles lost their lives. Today, Warsaw and the other ancient cities of this ancient country are almost completely restored, in a blending of old and new.

Poles have been living in or on the brink of disaster for so many hundreds of years, they have learned how to get a lot of enjoyment out of very little. For this reason, you will find on a visit to Warsaw that you may have to wait in line to get into a night club or a very good restaurant. The wait is worth it.

Poles are considered to be the most friendly and courteous of all peoples of countries under the Russian yoke. Perhaps it is because they are also considered to be the most Western minded of the people's democracies. Americans are fussed over and asked to sit down and take a vodka while being questioned about everything from jazz to an uncle someone may have in Detroit.

You have only to see the contented faces of the native Poles, young and old, dining on baked pike with anchovies or breast of lamb stewed in wine at the Krokodyl on the marketplace in the old quarter of Warsaw to know that some things never change. A good meal and some vodka can make you forget just about anything.

Poland originally was inhabited by a Slavonic tribe called

the Polans. In the year 962, these people united under a king, and there followed about 300 years of wars with Germany. In the thirteenth century, the Mongols swarmed out of the East and conquered the Poles. As a result, the Slavic races divided into independent municipalities which included many Germans and Jews.

Late in the seventeenth century, the peasants found themselves no longer under the domination of the Mongols but under the thumb of a hierarchy of noblemen. Under the leadership of the Cossacks, the peasants created an uprising that freed them from the rule of the nobles but put them under the protection of Russia. The decline of Poland's political autonomy dates from this time, and its borders continuously shrank from partitions by Russia, Prussia, and Austria.

Today Poland is a republic of about 33 million people living in 121,000 square miles, wedged between Eastern Germany and the U.S.S.R. But though a republic, Poland is dominated by Russia.

In its food Poland also is tied to Russia, but adds dishes from its Slavic beginnings that give Polish food its own zesty distinction.

Kwas, a sour beverage or liquor made from fermented cereals, gives many Polish dishes a distinctive flavor.

A national Polish dish is *Zupa Flaczkowa*, a soup made with tripe, filled with vegetables and barley.

Barszcz (borst) is a beet soup popular in Poland as it is in Russia.

Bigos is a hunter's stew, of cabbage, sausage, sauerkraut, pork, and beef, eaten after a day of outdoor sport on a cold winter's evening.

Another favorite meal is cabbage leaves stuffed with ground beef and rice, seasoned with onion, and cooked in tomato sauce flavored with bacon.

Hussar's Roast is a glorified pot roast, scalded with hot vinegar, sliced and heated in gravy, and served with stewed cabbage and potatoes.

A holiday meal such as on Easter Sunday might consist of ham, sausage, meat pie, roast suckling pig, roast of jellied turkey, cooked eggs, *Babkas* (yeast cakes), *Kielbaza* (sausage with horseradish), and a fantasmagoria of pastries.

When most people think of Polish food, they think of the pastries. Some dough creations begin as though they were intended as desserts, but end up as meat or fish meals.

Pierozhki are noodle dough pockets or turnovers, stuffed with sauerkraut, cheese, meat, or buckwheat groats. Sweet ones are filled with berries or jam.

Cukiernia are pastry and coffee shops in Polish cities which serve rich chocolate desserts with even richer fillings. You might try *Pierogi,* dough filled with prunes or plums; *Kolacki,* pastries filled with apricot, strawberry, prunes, cheese, or nuts; or *Chrusciki,* bow ties made from a rich sour cream dough and deep-fat fried, then sprinkled with confectioner's sugar. They are crispy, flaky, and delectible.

When I was a boy, one Christmas dinner my mother served *Czarnina* at our feast table in Chicago. I took one look at the murky brown soup and pushed the bowl away. I had heard what it was made of: goose blood, vinegar, prunes, raisins, and sour cream. Any one of those ingredients by itself would have turned me off; mixed together, I was overwhelmed.

Blood soup aside, I have always considered the Polish dishes my mother brought to our table to be among the most delicious of all.

Appetizers

Polish Stuffed Eggs

4 hard-boiled eggs
salt and pepper
chopped chive or sauted onion

2 tablespoons butter
2 tablespoons sour cream
bread crumbs

Cut cold hard-boiled eggs lengthwise. Take out the egg yolks without breaking the whites. Chop the egg yolks. Add a dash of salt and pepper, chopped chive, or onion sauted in butter, and two tablespoons sour cream. Refill the egg halves, sprinkle tops with bread crumbs and brown face down in frying pan in 2 tablespoons of butter, or sprinkle with buttered bread crumbs and brown under broiler. Yield: 8 halves.

Pierozki

1 4-ounce package cream cheese	¼ pound butter
	1 cup flour

Mix cream cheese with soft butter in a mixing bowl. Add flour and mix with a fork. When smooth, place dough in refrigerator at least 1 hour. Now prepare filling:

1 cup mushrooms	salt
butter	pepper
1 onion, chopped	

Fry onions with mushrooms in butter. Add seasoning. Roll out small squares of dough and fill with mushroom-onion filling. Seal edges, making walnut-sized balls. Place on baking sheet and bake at 350 degrees for half an hour until lightly colored. (You also may fill with cheese, melted, or cut up cocktail frankfurters.) Yield: 4 to 6 servings.

Nadziewane Grzyby
(stuffed mushrooms)

1 pound mushrooms	2 tablespoons dry bread crumbs
1–2 tablespoons butter	
1 small onion, chopped	salt and pepper
1 tablespoon chopped parsley	

Remove stems from mushrooms. Put caps in pan of salted boiling water. Cook gently 5 minutes. Chop stems and brown in butter with onion. Stir in parsley. Add bread crumbs to thicken. Season to taste. Fill mushroom caps with mixture and place under broiler to brown. Yield: 4 to 6 servings.

Soups

Zupa Kartofli
(potato soup)

1 medium onion, chopped	dash of pepper
3 tablespoons fat	3 cups scalded milk

3 medium potatoes, diced   butter
1½ teaspoons salt

Saute onions in fat until lightly browned. Add 3 cups boiling water, potatoes, seasoning. Cook until potatoes are tender. Mash potatoes to desired consistency. Add scalded milk. Heat to boiling point. Top with a few pats of butter.

Czarnina
(blood soup)

wings, neck, liver, and gizzard   2 cups prune juice
    of 1 domestic duck, goose,   1 cup raisins
    or turkey   1 pint blood of any of above
3 pounds pork neck bones   birds
salt and pepper to taste   vinegar
2 carrots, cut in large pieces   3 tablespoons flour
1 onion, cut in half   2 tablespoons sugar
1 pint whole prunes

Put duck, goose, or turkey wings, neck, liver, gizzard and pork neck bones in large kettle. Add 6 quarts water, salt and pepper, carrots and onion. Cook soup slowly until meat is tender, about 1½ hours. Strain and return broth to pot. Add 1 pint jar of whole prunes and 2 cups prune juice and 1 cup raisins.

    Some butchers will drain your duck, goose, or turkey and give you a jar of the blood. Dilute with a little plain vinegar, strain into a bowl. Blend in 3 tablespoons flour and 2 tablespoons sugar. Mix to a smooth liquid. Add blood contents to steaming broth and keep cooking slowly, stirring occasionally. Let simmer about half an hour. Taste. Broth should be sweet-sour. If too sweet, add vinegar. If too sour, add sugar. Serve with noodles. Yield: 8 servings.

Kapuśniak
(sauerkraut soup)

3 pounds pork neck bones   4 whole cloves
1 medium onion, sliced   salt and pepper

1 quart jar or can of sauerkraut   ½ cup barley
1 16-ounce can tomatoes   ½ cup rice
4 peppercorns or allspice

Cover neck bones with water in deep pot and let come to boil. Skim off surface. Lower flame and add sliced onion, sauerkraut, tomatoes, spices, and salt and pepper to taste. A teaspoon of salt is usually sufficient. Also add barley and rice. Let soup come to a boil again, then simmer about 1½ hours, covered. (Spare ribs may be substituted for pork neck bones, but fat should be removed from ribs.) Yield: 8 servings.

Salads

Sałatka z Buraczków
(beet salad)

1 pound cooked beets   1 or 2 tablespoons horseradish
1 teaspoon sugar   1 teaspoon salt
½ teaspoon caraway seeds   juice of 3 lemons

Peel and slice beets. Mix other ingredients together (1 or 2 tablespoons horseradish, to taste). Pour over beets and serve.

Sałatka z Czerwonej Kapusty
(red cabbage salad)

1 head red cabbage   juice of 1 lemon
2 tablespoons sugar   salt and pepper
4 tablespoons olive oil

Scald grated cabbage in a collander with boiling water. Drain. Toss with other ingredients and serve. Yield: 4 servings.

Sałatka Ziemniaczana z Selerem
(potato salad with celery)

4 or 6 potatoes   dill
4 stalks celery   3 tablespoons olive oil

salt and pepper   2 tablespoons vinegar
1 onion, chopped

Peel and cook potatoes until tender in salted water. Cook celery
separately. Dice both potatoes and celery and mix together,
adding seasoning. Add chopped onion and dill. Mix olive oil
with vinegar and pour over potato and celery. (Raw celery may
be used instead of cooked celery, and chive may be substituted
for onion.) Yield: 4 to 6 servings.

Vegetables

Ziemniaki Nadziewane Grzybami
(potatoes stuffed with mushrooms)

4 potatoes   2 hard-boiled eggs, chopped
butter   1 tablespoon parsley, chopped
2 tablespoons mushrooms,   salt and pepper
   chopped   bread crumbs
1 onion, chopped

Coat potatoes with butter or oil and bake. When tender, cut in
half, lengthwise. Scoop out insides. Mash together with sauted
mushrooms and sauted onion, chopped eggs, and parsley.
Season. Refill potato shells. Sprinkle with bread crumbs. Cover
with melted butter and bake 15 minutes at 450 degrees. Yield: 4
servings.

Nadziewane Ogórki
(stuffed cucumbers)

5 cucumbers   butter
1 onion, chopped   1 egg
½ cup mushrooms   bread crumbs
½ pound chopped meat   salt and pepper

Cut cucumbers lengthwise. Scoop out seeds. Saute onion with
mushrooms and meat. Add 1 egg and mix. Fill cucumber halves
and place in greased baking dish. Cover with crumbs, season,
and bake at 350 degrees for ½ hour. Yield: 5 servings.

Noodles

Kluski do Zupy
(soup noodles)

1 egg
⅛ cup flour

chopped parsley
salt

Beat egg. Mix with flour and parsley. Season with salt. Add mixture slowly into boiling soup. It will cook quickly and take on shape of ribbon noodles.

Fish

Karp w Czerwonej Kapustsche
(carp in red cabbage)

1 head red cabbage
1 large onion
1 tablespoon butter
1 tablespoon flour
1 cup red wine

salt
juice of 1 lemon
1 tablespoon sugar
1 carp

Pour boiling water over shredded red cabbage in a colander. Chop onion and saute in butter. Sprinkle flour over onion and stir in cup of red wine. Salt cabbage and add lemon juice. Mix cabbage with wine sauce and add sugar. Cover and cook over a low flame. When almost tender, add cleaned carp cut in small diamond-shaped pieces. Mix with cabbage and stew for 30 minutes. Bone and skin fish and serve covered with the cabbage. Yield: 2 servings.

Swfle z Ryby
(fish soufflé)

2 pounds perch or flounder
1 tablespoon butter
salt and white pepper

nutmeg
6 egg whites
grated Parmesan cheese

Chop raw fish meat fine and mix 1 tablespoon soft butter or margarine into it. Add salt and pepper and dash of nutmeg. Fold in egg whites beaten until stiff. Mix thoroughly. Put in greased pan and sprinkle with grated cheese. Bake in 350 degree oven for 25 minutes. Test with a straw before removing from oven. When straw comes out clean, serve. Yield: 4 servings.

Poultry

Pieczona Kaczka Lub Geś
(roast duck or goose)

1 duck or goose
salt and pepper
3 garlic cloves
6 oranges, peeled

your favorite stuffing,
chestnut, or sauerkraut
stuffing (see below)

Rub duck or goose with salt, pepper, and squeeze garlic inside and out. Stuff with as many peeled oranges as will fit, in addition to chestnut stuffing (see below) or sauerkraut stuffing (also below) or your favorite. Cover bird with sliced oranges. Roast in 325 degree oven for 30 minutes to a pound. Baste occasionally. Pour off excessive fat. (Unpeeled apples may be substituted for oranges as a stuffing). Yield: 3 servings.

Chestnut Stuffing

goose or duck liver, chopped
butter
1 large onion, chopped
2 pounds chestnuts

¾ cup black raisins
3 apples, peeled
salt and pepper

Fry liver in butter with onion. Boil chestnuts about 45 minutes. Shell, take off skins, and grate. Combine all ingredients and stuff bird. Bake as above recipe.

Sauerkraut Stuffing

1 cup sauerkraut
butter

1 onion, chopped

Saute sauerkraut in butter with chopped onion. Stuff and roast duck or goose as above.

Meat

Golabki
(stuffed cabbage leaves)

1 large head cabbage	1 small onion, minced
1 cup rice	1 egg
1½ pounds ground beef	salt and pepper

Remove core from cabbage. Scald in boiling salted water. Remove one leaf at a time. Set leaves aside. Cook rice in boiling water about 10 minutes. Drain. Mix together beef, onion, rice, egg, and salt and pepper. Place large spoonful of meat mixture on each cabbage leaf. Fold and roll. Chop leftover cabbage and put in roasting pan. Place cabbage rolls on top. Roast, covered, about 1 hour in 350 degree oven with following tomato sauce poured over the top:

4 slices bacon, diced	1 can (small) tomato sauce
1 small onion, chopped	1 bay leaf

Brown bacon. Add onion and saute several minutes. Add tomato sauce and bay leaf. Simmer about 1 minute. Yield: 4 servings.

Bigos
(cabbage stew)

1½ pounds sauerkraut	1 pound leftover meat
1 pint beef stock	1 glass white wine
1 onion, sliced	salt
1 tablespoon butter	paprika
⅛ cup flour	

Simmer sauerkraut in beef stock for 1½ hours. Saute onion in butter. Add flour and cook 1 minute. Chop sauerkraut and add onion mixture. Cut meat into small pieces. Put meat and sauerkraut mixture into a casserole. Add wine, season with salt and paprika. Mix well. Cook in slow oven with lid on for 1 hour. Yield: 4 servings.

Pieczeń Husarska
(hussars roast)

2 pounds sirloin steak	1 onion, chopped
salt	1 tablespoon bread crumbs
4 tablespoons flour	salt and pepper
¼ pound butter	1 egg yolk
juice of half a lemon	

Beat the sirloin, sprinkle with salt, and dredge with flour. Melt butter, brown meat on both sides. Add lemon juice and a little water. Simmer. Saute half the chopped onion in the rest of the butter until lightly sauted. Add bread crumbs, season with salt and pepper. Mix with the egg yolk. Cut pockets into the meat and fill with the stuffing. Fry the rest of the onion in a casserole. Add meat and about half pint of water. Cook covered at 325 degrees for 1 hour, until meat is tender. Serve with following sauce:

1 ounce butter	½ pint vegetable stock
2 onions	2 glasses red wine
1 clove garlic	juice of half a lemon
1 slice carrot	½ cup ham
parsley	1 tomato
½ bay leaf	2 tablespoons horseradish
basil	1 teaspoon sugar
2 tablespoons flour	

Melt butter. Chop onions, garlic, carrot, and parsley. Saute in butter with bay leaf and pinch of basil until browned. Stir in flour, add vegetable stock. Simmer 40 minutes and strain. Return to pan, add wine and lemon juice. Cut ham into strips. Peel tomato, remove seeds, cut into slices. Add ham, tomato, horseradish, sugar. Serve hot, poured over roast.

Ogonki Wołowe z Soczewica
(oxtails with lentils)

1 large oxtail, disjointed	salt
3 large carrots, sliced thickly	½ pound lentils

Place oxtail in a pan with enough water to cover. Salt to taste. Add carrots and lentils. Cook until done.

Zeberka z Kapusta Kminkiem
(spareribs with caraway kraut)

3 pounds spareribs
2 teaspoons salt
¼ teaspoon pepper
1 No. 2½ can sauerkraut
2 medium carrots, shredded

1½ cups tomato juice
3 teaspoons caraway seeds
1 unpared tart apple, chopped
2 tablespoons brown sugar

Season ribs with salt and pepper. Cut in serving pieces and put in Dutch oven. Combine kraut, including liquid, with remaining ingredients and spoon over ribs. Bake, covered, in oven at 350 degrees for 2½ hours until ribs are done. Baste kraut with juices seven times during the last hour. Serve with some of the juice. Yield: 4 to 6 servings.

Kiski
(sausages)

1 whole pork liver
4 pounds pork kidneys
butter
6 or 7 pounds pork snouts
2 pounds fat back with skin

5 pounds pork butt, cut in
   large pieces
2 pounds very fine barley
salt and pepper to taste
sausage casings

Cook liver and kidneys in butter in Dutch oven until tender. Cool. Set aside. In another pot, cook pork snouts, fat back, and pork butt in water until tender. Remove snouts, fat back, and pork butt and boil barley in same water about 1 hour until soft. Cut pork butt, fat back, snouts and kidneys into small pieces. Grate liver. Mix barley, cut meat, and liver. Add salt and pepper to taste, adding water if mixture is too thick. Put in big sausage casings. When done, boil 3 kiski at a time gently, about 10 to 15 minutes, careful not to burst casings. Remove and drain. Serve with ketchup.

Pierogi
(sauerkraut dumplings)

1 No. 2 can sauerkraut
2 medium onions, sliced
¼ cup pork drippings
2 teaspoons salt

pepper
4 eggs
½ cup milk
4 cups flour

Boil sauerkraut 20 minutes, then drain. Saute onions in pork fat. Mix in sauerkraut and season with salt and pepper. To make dough: place eggs in bowl, add salt and milk and mix well. Add flour and mix until dough is heavy.

Flour a breadboard and rolling pin and roll out dough as thin as a pie crust. Cut dough into 4-inch squares and place a portion of sauerkraut into the center of the square. Fold over and pinch ends together. When all pierogi aremade, put 6 at a time into pan of boiling water and boil about 3 minutes. Pierogi will rise to the top when done. Remove from water and let dry in a collander. After cooling, fry in butter until golden brown. Yield: 3 dozen. Good with soup, stews, meat dishes.

Kielbasa z Kapusta
(Polish sausage with sauerkraut)

1 pound smoked Polish
  sausage
1 pound can of sauerkraut
salt and pepper

1 teaspoon caraway seeds
2 slices bacon, diced
1 teaspoon onion, chopped
2 tablespoons flour

Place Polish sausage in Dutch oven. Add small amount of water and cook in 350 degree oven about 1 hour. If water remains, place pan on top stove and saute until sausage is lightly browned and water evaporates. Rinse sauerkraut with water. Drain. Cover sauerkraut with water. Add salt, pepper, and caraway seeds. Simmer about 30 minutes. Saute together bacon and onion, until bacon is almost crisp and onion is soft. Stir in flour. If necessary, drain some water from sauerkraut. Stir in bacon mixture. Cut browned sausages into 1-inch pieces. Combine with sauerkraut. Serve hot.

Pastries, Desserts

Chrusciki
(twist pastries)

6 egg yolks
1 cup sour cream
jigger of dark rum
3 cups flour

pinch of salt
shortening
powdered sugar

Beat egg yolks. Add sour cream and rum. Combine flour and salt. Form flour into a round, make a well in the center, and pour in egg mixture. Knead dough and form into a solid ball. Roll out dough to ⅛-inch thickness. Cut strips of dough 6 inches long by 1 ½ inches wide. Cut a slit two inches long in the center of the strip. Pull end of strip through center, forming a type of twist. Deep fry strips in shortening until golden brown. Drain finished strips on paper towels. Sprinkle strips with powdered sugar.

Placek z Jabłkami
(apple coffee cake)

¼ pound butter
1 cup sugar
2 eggs
1 teaspoon vanilla
2 cups flour, sifted
1 teaspoon baking soda
1 teaspoon baking powder
½ teaspoon salt
1 cup sour cream

2 apples, finely chopped
1 pear, finely chopped
   (optional)

Topping:
½ cup chopped nuts
1 cup brown sugar
1 teaspoon cinnamon
2 tablespoons soft butter

Cream together butter and sugar. Add eggs and vanilla. Beat well. Sift flour, baking soda, baking powder, and salt together. Add to batter, alternating with sour cream. Fold in apples. Spread batter in greased 13×9×2-inch pan. Combine topping mixture in a bowl and spread over batter. Bake in 350-degree oven for 35 to 45 minutes. (Cake will be lighter and more flavorful if a peeled, finely chopped pear is added when apples are folded into the batter.)

Ponczki

2 cups milk
1 cake yeast
7 cups flour
1 whole egg
4 egg yolks
1 cup sugar

½ cup butter
½ teaspoon vanilla
grated rind of ½ orange
1 teaspoon salt
fat for frying

Scald milk, then cool to lukewarm. Dissolve yeast in lukewarm milk. Add 2 cups flour. Mix. Let stand in warm place for ½ hour. Beat 1 whole egg, sugar, butter, 4 egg yolks, vanilla, rind, and salt until light. Add this mixture to flour and yeast mixture. Add 5 cups flour, mix with your hands. Cover and allow to rise about 1 hour until dough is double its bulk. When dough feels light, turn onto floured board and pat with hands until dough is ½ inch thick. Cut with top of rounded glass or doughnut cutter. Put on floured board and cover. Let rise once more until at least twice its size.

Use a deep fryer or deep frying pan large enough for the dough to float. Heat shortening until a piece of white bread, dropped into fat, browns quickly. Fry dough until done, drain on paper towels, and cool. Sprinkle with powdered sugar. Fill with custard or preserves, by punching a hole in the side with a pastry tube and filling.

Baba

8 egg yolks
¾ cup powdered sugar
1 ounce yeast
½ cup milk

vanilla
½ teaspoon salt
saffron
¼ pound melted butter

Beat egg yolks and sugar over hot water until white and thick. Dissolve yeast in a little warm milk. Add yeast and all other ingredients except butter to the eggs. Beat until blended. Pour in butter and beat again. Fill a greased tin with mixture to ⅓ its depth. Cover and leave to rise in warm place. Bake in 425 degree oven for 1 hour.

Smazone Jablka w Cieście
(deep-fried apple rings)

5 sour apples
3 eggs, separated
1 cup warm milk
½ cup sugar
flour

fat
vanilla
cinnamon
powdered sugar

Peel apples. Scoop out core and slice apples in rings. Prepare batter: Mix 3 egg yolks well, warm milk, and sugar. Beat with enough flour to make thick batter. Beat and fold in egg whites. Dip apple rings into batter and fry in very hot fat. When brown and crisp, sprinkle with vanilla, cinnamon, and powdered sugar. Serve hot.

Bułeczka Maślana
(butter horns)

1 cup butter
½ cup sugar, granulated
¾ cup almonds, blanched

1 teaspoon vanilla
1½ cups flour
powdered sugar

Beat softened butter with sugar. Grind almonds. Add almonds with vanilla to butter-sugar mixture. Blend in flour. Roll out on floured board. Cut into cookie shapes. Bake on cookie sheet in 325 degree oven until lightly browned. While warm, sprinkle with powdered sugar.

Korzenny Placek
(spice cake)

1 cup shortening
2 cups brown sugar
2 whole eggs
2 egg yolks
2⅔ cups flour
1 teaspoon baking powder
1 teaspoon cinnamon
1 teaspoon baking soda

1 teaspoon cloves
½ teaspoon salt
1 cup sour cream or milk

Topping:
2 egg whites, stiffly beaten
1 cup brown sugar
½ cup nuts, chopped

Cream shortening and brown sugar together until light and fluffy. Add well-beaten eggs and egg yolks. Sift and combine dry ingredients and add to creamed mixture, alternately with sour cream or milk. Pour into an 8½ by 12½ inch greased pan. While beating egg whites, add sugar gradually and spread topping over batter. Sprinkle with nuts and bake 45 minutes in 350 degree oven.

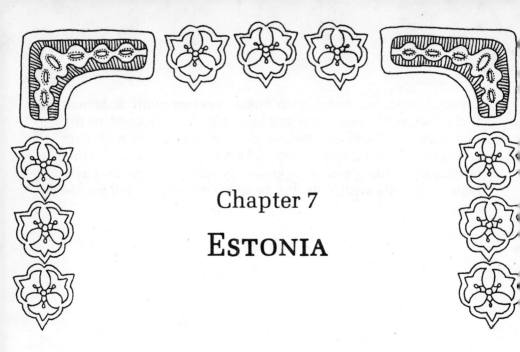

Chapter 7

ESTONIA

Northernmost of the Baltic states, Estonia has both Russia and Finland as neighbors. Helsinki is just north, across the Gulf of Finland, and Leningrad lies just to the east.

Tallinn, capital of Estonia and once a Hanseatic city, has the most contact with the West, from among its Baltic neighbors of Latvia, Lithuania, and Poland. This is largely due to shiploads of Finns who depart Helsinki daily on brief excursions almost directly south across the Gulf to Tallinn.

The city is also the most picturesque of the Baltic capitals, with a whole section left over from medieval times. Tallinn's 350,000 people are drawn compactly around the base of a hill upon which sits the remains of an old castle and its town. Its cathedral, a mixture of thirteenth century Gothic and seventeenth century Baroque, is one of northern Europe's most beautiful.

Historically, Estonians are more Scandinavian than they are European. They are a branch of the Finno-Ugrian family of nations and linguistically closely akin to the Finns. Their first invaders were the Norman vikings who passed through Estonia and Latvia in the mid-ninth century on their way to the Slavonic hinterland. In reprisal, the Russians crossed the Estonian border and in 1030 a Russian prince, Yaroslav, built a fortress at Tartu which he called Yuryev, and shortly after he found resistance from the Germans. It all involved making Christians out of the then pagan people living in the north Baltic area. The Germans finally won, the Estonians were finally Christian, but they had lost their land and freedom and had become serfs of their conquerors.

Later Estonia was partitioned between Poland and Sweden, then won in war by Russia under Czar Peter I who instituted some land reforms including abolition of serfdom.

Estonia gained its independence during the Russian Revolution of 1917, only to be invaded by Germany the next year as World War I increased momentum.

Between the two great wars, Estonia was independent but suffered as most of the rest of the world from the great depression. In June, 1941, Germany invaded the Soviet Union, and for three years Estonia was under German occupation. Late in 1944, Soviet troops took Tallinn, and over the next five years, 60,000 Estonians were deported.

Today Estonia suffers the same fate as its neighbors, Latvia and Lithuania, as subject countries of the U.S.S.R., with even tighter restrictions than Poland.

Kadriorg Palace, built by Peter the Great in Tallinn in 1718–23, now houses the Estonian art museum. Paintings reveal the beauty and courage of the Estonian land and people. Nearby is the Pegasus coffee house, where students gather to drink and talk, and the Gloria Restaurant, where the menu reflects the Baltic taste for beef, fish, cheese, and filling pastries. And beet soup, of course. With Leningrad only five hours away by rail, why not?

Soup

Potato Barley Soup

½ cup cracked barley or pearl barley	4 cups milk salt
1½ cups water	1 tablespoon butter
2 medium potatoes, cubed	

Bring salted water to a boil, add washed barley. Boil about half an hour until barley is half-done. Add cubed potatoes, boil 20 minutes to half an hour until done. Add milk and bring to a boil. Before serving, add butter. Yield: 4 servings.

Salad

Mushroom Salad with Potatoes

1 cup potatoes, cubed
1 cup mushrooms, slivered
2 tablespoons butter
½ cup dill pickles, cubed
½ cup sour cream

1 small onion, finely chopped
salt to taste
vinegar to taste
celery leaves or dill

Cook potatoes, cool, then cube them. Saute mushrooms in butter. Mix all ingredients with sour cream, decorate with chopped celery leaves or dill. Yield: 4 servings.

Vegetable

Mulgikapsad
(sauerkraut, country style)

1 pound pork tenderloin
salt
1 can sauerkraut (1 lb., 11 ounces)

1 small onion (optional)
¼ cup barley
sugar

Rub meat with salt. Wash sauerkraut and squeeze dry. Place pork in a pot between layers of sauerkraut and slices of onion. Place washed barley on top. Add enough boiling water to cover. Cover pot and cook over low heat about an hour until everything is done. Lift out the pork and cube it. Stir sauerkraut, add salt and sugar to taste. Mix cubed meat in with the sauerkraut. Serve with hot boiled potatoes. Yield: 3 servings.

Dumplings

Blood Dumplings

½ pound back fat of pork (or bacon)
1 medium onion
1 cup blood from poultry
½ teaspoon salt

¼ teaspoon pepper
2 tablespoons barley or rye flour
¼ cup water

Cube the fat and brown lightly, add finely chopped onion and heat together, then cool. Strain the blood, add salt and pepper, flour and cooled fat (or bacon), and onions, mix into a sticky dough. With wet hands, form dumplings about the size of a potato and boil in salted water 15-20 minutes. Lift out of water and cool. Cut into slices, less than half an inch. Brown in fat on both sides. Serve with sour cream, melted butter, fried pork.

Meat

Mutton Stew with Rutabaga

2 pounds mutton (shoulder or breast)
2 tablespoons fat
1 medium onion
2 stalks celery
salt
1 can tomato puree or sauce

1 medium rutabaga
1 tablespoon flour
2 tablespoons sour cream
dill weed
caraway seeds
parsley leaves

Cut mutton into large cubes. Brown in fat. Place in stewing pan, add cut onion and celery stalks, salt, and tomato paste, and a little boiling water. When meat is half done, add cubed rutabaga, a little water, if needed, and continue cooking. Add flour, heated in fat and mixed with water. Cook until thickened, add sour cream. Before serving, sprinkle with dill weed, caraway seeds, and parsley leaves. Serve with boiled potatoes and beet or pickle salad. Yield: 4 servings.

Pastries
Mulgi-Korbid
(curd tarts)

4 cups flour	2 ounces yeast
¾ cup milk	½ cup butter
½ teaspoon salt	2 tablespoons sugar

Put two cups of flour in a bowl, add warmed milk, salt and yeast. Mix a thin dough. Cover with a clean cloth, let stand in a warm place for 1 to 1½ hours. When doubled in bulk, add the rest of the flour and ½ cup butter which has been creamed with 2 tablespoons sugar. Knead to an even, resilient dough. When dough separates cleanly from bowl and hands, smooth out top, sprinkle with flour, cover with cloth, let rise 1½ to 2 hours in a warm spot. Form small oblong-shaped buns. Place on a greased baking sheet, let rise. Bake in 350 degree oven until light brown. When cool, cut in half. Cover both halves with sweet cottage cheese or cream of wheat topping (see below).

Cottage Cheese Topping

2 pounds dry cottage cheese	¾ cup sour cream
5 eggs	⅓ cup butter, melted
¾ cup sugar	salt

Put cheese through a sieve. Cream 4 eggs and sugar, add sour cream, butter, and salt, mix into cheese. Spread on bun halves, brush with 1 beaten egg and bake until light brown.

Cream of Wheat Topping

3¾ cups milk	4 eggs
½ teaspoon salt	5 tablespoons sugar
⅔ cup cream of wheat	1 tablespoon butter

Bring milk and salt to a rapid boil. Slowly sprinkle cream of wheat on top of milk, stirring constantly. Bring to a boil again, lower heat, and cook for 10 minutes or until thickened, stirring frequently. Cream eggs with sugar, add to cooled cream of wheat. Add butter. Cover both halves of bun with mixture, brush with beaten egg and bake in oven until light brown.

Chapter 8
LATVIA

Latvia shares her history and culture with neighboring Lithuania. Together with Prussia in ancient times, they constituted a Baltic group of peoples akin to the Slavs. In the course of history, especially after the German conquest of Latvia and Estonia, the north Baltic tribes fused together into one racial and linguistic group.

Until 1561 Latvia was an integral part of Livonia, the domain of the Teutonic Order. Then it was partitioned, became part of Poland, then was conquered by the Swedes, and since 1721 has been handed between Poland and Russia. In 1939 Latvia fell victim as a pawn in a German-Soviet nonaggression treaty and a year later was invaded by Soviet troops. During the first year of Soviet occupation, 35,000 members of Latvian intelligentsia were deported to Siberia.

Latvia was a battleground throughout World War II between the Nazis and the Soviet Union. Finally the Soviet Union won control of Latvia after the war and established the nation as a Soviet Republic.

Slightly larger than West Virginia, Latvia is a low-lying country with one-fifth of it being less than 130 feet above sea level. The land is heavily forested, with nearly 3,000 lakes, and the climate is damp.

Its major port city, Riga, was opened to tourists a few years ago. Westerners are especially welcomed, yet they will see that behind the cheerful faces, this is a conquered country and its people wish it were otherwise.

In early August, Riga's citizens forget their cares in the annual "Ligo," a holiday of song festivities, with singing and dancing, fireworks, bonfires, and beer. Food adds to the holiday atmosphere, including a tempting appetizer called *piradzini*, bacon rolls made from a yeast dough and shaped as half moons, filled with luscious mixtures of diced bacon, onion, and smoked pork shoulder roll seasoned with a dash of nutmeg. *Cukas cepetis*, roast fresh ham, and a custard fluff are a main course favorite and a popular dessert.

Riga's old section shows the scars of wars, but its medieval churches along narrow winding streets and fourteenth century Riga Castle and Domsk Monastery are important tourist attractions, even though the castle is now the Palace of Pioneers and the monastery is the Riga Museum. On Lake Yuma is a museum that contains a reproduction of a whole ancient rural community to show how Latvian peasants once lived. Barns, cottages, and furnishings were collected from throughout Latvia to reconstruct life in earlier times.

The easiest way to do that, of course, is to go to the kitchen and whip up some *piradzini*, those half-moon shaped bacon rolls. Which is what Latvians abroad and in America do when they want to sojourn back to the Old Country and remember the good old days.

When I was at Michigan State University, working on the soup line in the dormitory to help make ends meet, a handsome dark-haired tall woman stood next to me many a day, serving up mashed potatoes with an ice cream scoop. While talking, she told me she was from Latvia. Her parents had been concert musicians before the war. She herself was just starting her career as a concert pianist.

When the Nazis invaded, she was separated from her parents and the rest of her family and never learned what happened to them. Friends helped her to escape and eventually she came to America. I didn't have to ask what became of her career as a concert pianist. Her hands were swollen, testimony of the hard years that followed.

Appetizer

Piradzini
(bacon rolls)

¾ cup milk
¼ cup butter
2 teaspoons salt
3 tablespoons sugar
1 package active dry yeast

¼ cup warm water
1 whole egg
3½ cups flour
1 egg yolk, lightly beaten
bacon filling (see below)

Scald milk. Remove from heat and add butter, salt, and sugar. Set aside to cool to lukewarm. Dissolve yeast in warm water. Beat 1 egg. Add to lukewarm milk mixture. Stir in yeast. Add flour, ½ cup at a time. Cover bowl and let dough rest for 10 minutes.

Remove dough to a floured board or pastry cloth. Knead for 5 to 6 minutes. Place in a clean, lightly greased bowl and cover with a damp cloth. Let rise until dough doubles in bulk, about 2 hours. Remove half of the dough from bowl. Using a rolling pin, roll out dough on a floured pastry cloth or bread board to ⅛-inch thickness.

Starting at one corner, put ½ teaspoon filling on dough; fold over and cut a half-moon-shaped roll, using a floured tumbler or cooky cutter (2 to 2¼ inches in diameter) to cut. Continue until all dough is used. Place rolls on a greased cookie sheet. Brush with lightly beaten egg yolk. Let stand in warm place, free from draft, until rolls double in size. Bake in preheated 400 degree oven for 10 to 12 minutes until golden brown. Yield: 6 to 8 servings.

Bacon Filling

¼ pound lean thick-sliced
   bacon
1 onion
¼ pound smoked butt,

precooked
pinch of nutmeg
salt
pepper

Dice bacon and onion; saute in skillet until bacon is crisp and onion is soft but not brown. Carefully remove bacon and onion from skillet. Add diced smoked butt and brown quickly on high heat for from 1 to 2 minutes. Remove pork from skillet and mix with bacon and onion. Add nutmeg and season to taste with salt and pepper. Refrigerate until time to use.

Salad

Tomato-Cucumber Salad

Peel a large cucumber and cut into thin slices. Cut two tomatoes into wedges. Toss together lightly. Season dairy sour cream with dill weed, salt, and pepper to taste. Pour over cucumbers and tomatoes, toss lightly, and serve. Yield: 2 servings.

Vegetables

Latvian Sauerkraut

6 tablespoons bacon fat
1 can sauerkraut (No. 2½ size)
3 large cooking apples

4 tablespoons dark brown
  sugar

Place fat in Dutch oven. Heat until lightly browned. Add sauerkraut, including juice. Do not stir. Add water to cover. Peel and slice apples and place on top of kraut. Cover and bring to a boil. Reduce heat to simmer and cook 2 to 3 hours, until liquid evaporates and kraut has thickened. Add brown sugar; stir and continue to cook for 15 to 30 minutes. Serve hot. Yield: 6 servings.

Meat

Cukas Cepetis
(roast fresh ham)

1 medium size fresh ham (8 to
  10 pounds)

salt
paprika

Wipe ham with damp cloth. Rub with salt and sprinkle with paprika. Place ham in roasting pan and roast in 450 degree oven for 15 minutes. Reduce heat to 350 degrees and continue roasting for 30 minutes. Remove from oven and score top. Add ½ to 1½ cups hot water. Baste roast with pan juices every 20 to 30 minutes, until done. If necessary add more water. Allow 35 to 45 minutes per pound. Remove roast from oven and let stand for 15 minutes. Slice and serve.

Pastries

Custard Fluff

⅔ cup sugar
6 egg yolks
2 cups milk

2 teaspoons vanilla
6 egg whites, stiffly beaten

Beat sugar and egg yolks until smooth and creamy. Scald milk and add to egg yolk mixture gradually. Return to saucepan in which milk was scalded and cook slowly, stirring constantly until mixture comes almost to a boil. Do not allow to boil. Remove from heat and add vanilla. Cook, stirring vigorously at first while it is still hot and then occasionally to prevent skin from forming on top. Before mixture becomes stiff, fold in stiffly beaten egg whites. Pour into individual serving dishes and refrigerate for several hours. Serve with well-chilled red currant sauce (see below). Yield: 6 servings.

Red Currant Sauce

2 cups frozen red currants,
    defrosted
1 cup sugar

1 cinnamon stick
2 tablespoons cornstarch

Combine currants, 2½ cups water, sugar, and cinnamon stick. Bring to boil. Reduce heat and simmer for 15 minutes. Remove from heat. Discard cinnamon stick. Put mixture in a blender on low speed. Return to heat and bring to a boil. Dissolve cornstarch in 2 teaspoons water. Add to sauce and bring to a boil, stirring continuously. Remove from heat and let stand at room temperature for 30 minutes. Stir occasionally to prevent skin from forming. Refrigerate. Serve very cold over custard fluff.

Chapter 9

LITHUANIA

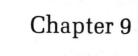

The Republic of Lithuania and its sister countries Estonia and Latvia, situated on the eastern shore of the Baltic Sea between Russia and Germany, are all-but-forgotten nations which became absorbed by Russia during World War II. Despite resistance from both within and without the country, all three nations remain locked firmly under Soviet domination.

The Lithuanian nation has been in existence since 3000 B.C., when a great migration of people started from what is now India and progressed through Greece and Hungary to finally settle on the Baltic. The climate appealed to them. Like that of northern Maine, it is ideal for growing wheat, potatoes, sugar beets, and for timbering. The Baltic Sea, lakes, and streams provide abundant fish, so many coastal Lithuanians are fishermen.

There isn't much in Lithuania to interest a conquering country. The land, heavily forested, is flat, low lying, and overlaid with glacial deposits, in some places 400 feet thick. Yet it has been a bone of contention for centuries, falling under the Prussians, Tartars, Poles, Nazis, and now the Soviets.

Lithuania flourished briefly between 1918 and 1940, but in June of that year 300,000 Soviet soldiers occupied the country and, despite resistance efforts, Lithuania became a component Republic of the U.S.S.R.

Travel out of the country is not allowed, and both religion and education that would help perpetuate Lithuanian history and culture are suppressed. Yet Lithuanians both in their native country and living abroad have not given up working toward the day when they again will be free.

About 2.7 million people live in Lithuania today, including about a quarter of a million Soviet colonists. Many thousands of Lithuanians emigrated to America early in World War II. Chicago has more than 100,000 Lithuanians, and other thousands are spread out throughout the country. While many Lithuanians in America keep their culture and history alive with festivals, they also work to keep news of their homeland and its struggle before the eyes of the free world, to remind them not to abandon Lithuania.

And some Lithuanians say their major enemy is not so much Russia or Germany or other conquerors as it is geography. Lithuanians have seen enemies come and go, but they are forever stationed on the dividing line between East and West. And since 1722 East and West have acted to maintain Lithuania, Estonia, and Latvia as a group of small nations to be either bufferzones or battlefields.

Lithuania's position straddling East and West is evident in its national food. Dishes reflect the influences of the Germanic, Slavic, and Eastern countries. Lithuanian cuisine bespeaks a good, solid, thrifty folk with a long background of farming. The food is substantial, nourishing, not highly seasoned.

In its more frugal aspects, the food of Lithuania is indicative of the arduous times endured by the people during invasions, wars, and several occupations by neighbors. The more lavish foods became favorites during periods of national affluence, particularly during its independence between the two great wars.

Beet soup, potatoes, cabbage, sauerkraut, pork and beef dishes, buckwheat bread, cheeses, herring and crabs, cucumbers, potato salads and puddings, and apple desserts are all popular Lithuanian favorites.

Perhaps an excursion into the food of Lithuania, such as you might find in emigrant homes throughout the United States any week night or especially on holidays will help keep alive the memory of yet another Old Country culture threatened with extinction.

As one Lithuanian puts it, "Mother Lithuania is sleeping, waiting until she is again free. But meanwhile the trees will be green again in summer, and if the sea wind is right, the orchards will bloom. The wheat still grows, and the children sing. Lithuanian children like to sing."

Soups

Alaus su Agunom Sriuba
(beer and poppy seed soup)

½ cup poppy seeds   2 tablespoons honey
1 quart beer

Pour 2 cups cups boiling water on poppy seeds. Let stand about 15 minutes. Pour off water. Pulverize seeds in a bowl. Add about 1 cup cold water, gradually. Pour into beer which has been heated (not boiled) with honey. Garnish with lemon slices and croutons of rye bread sprinkled with salt and caraway seeds. Yield: 4 to 6 servings.

Miezines Kruopos su Grybais
(barley and mushroom soup)

⅛ pound dried mushrooms   salt
¼ pound coarse barley   1 cup sour cream

Wash mushrooms thoroughly. Let soak one hour in cold water to cover. Add rinsed barley. Pour on 1½ quarts water. Salt to taste. Bring to boil, then simmer briskly until barley is soft. Remove mushrooms, cut into fine pieces, replace in soup. Remove soup from heat, and stir in sour cream gradually. Yield: 4 to 6 servings.

Salad

Ziemos Misraine
(winter salad)

1 cup each of boiled carrots, cauliflower, peas, dried white beans	1 chopped dill pickle
	1 cup sour cream
	salt
½ cup each of boiled, peeled, diced potatoes and beets	pepper
	1 chopped herring

Cook each vegetable separately. Cool. Cut carrots and cauliflower into small dice. Combine carrots, cauliflower, peas, and beans. Chill. Just before serving, mix in potatoes, beets, chopped pickle, sour cream, herring (optional), and salt and pepper. Serve on bed of lettuce.

Vegetables

Senoviskas Siupinys
(Lithuanian hash)

Boil as many dried peas and fava beans as you need. Strain. Mash. Add salt, pepper, and finely chopped onion. Stir in some bacon fat, and, if you wish, some very small pieces of leftover meat. Set in moderate oven until piping hot.

Kopustu Kotlietai
(cabbage croquettes)

2 small heads cabbage	½ teaspoon dill
1 small onion	3 eggs
1 tablespoon butter	salt to taste
½ teaspoon chopped parsley	bread crumbs

Boil cabbage in water until almost soft. Drain. Put through grinder. Add onion which has been chopped and sauted in butter, parsley, dill, and eggs. Season with salt. Add enough bread crumbs to hold form. Shape into croquettes. Roll in fine bread crumbs. Fry in butter. Yield: 6 servings.

Agurkai su Medum
(cucumbers and honey)

Scrub fresh green cucumbers. Refrigerate until cold and crisp. Slice cross-wise in generous slices. Arrange on serving dish, with small bowl of honey in the middle. Spread honey on cucumber slices as they are served.

Grybu Apkepas
(mushroom bake)

1 pound medium size fresh mushrooms	1 tablespoon flour
	½ teaspoon salt
2 tablespoons butter	⅛ teaspoon pepper
⅓ cup minced onion	½ cup bread crumbs
1 cup sour cream	butter

Wipe mushrooms with damp cloth. Leave them whole or if very large, slice in half lengthwise, through head and stem. Melt butter in skillet. Add onions and mushrooms. Simmer, covered, until onions are transparent, about 10 minutes. Blend sour cream with flour and seasonings. Pour over vegetables in shallow oven-proof dish. Sprinkle with bread crumbs, dot with butter. Bake in preheated 375 degree oven 10 to 15 minutes, until top is brown. Serve hot. Yield: 4 servings.

Potatoes, Dumplings

Suvalkieciu Bandukes
(potato buns)

Peel 4 to 6 potatoes. Grate fine. Remove excess water, straining grated potatoes in a thin towel. Salt to taste. Place wilted cabbage leaves on a cookie tin. Spoon potatoes on leaves, forming buns. Bake at 400 degrees until lightly brown. Remove from tin, pile buns one on top of another. Mince a small onion, fry with several strips of chopped bacon until bacon is crisp. Separate and discard cabbage leaves from buns. Pour the fried onion and bacon over buns. Yield: 4 to 6 servings.

Bandukes
(baked potato dumplings)

5 medium potatoes	1 small onion
1½ cups flour	2 tablespoons butter
2 teaspoons salt	½ pint sweet cream

Boil unpeeled potatoes until done. Cool and peel. Mash. Add sifted flour and salt. Roll into thick ropelike strips on floured board and cut diagonally into diamond shapes. Bake in 375 degree oven 20 minutes. While they are baking, prepare sauce:

Dice and saute onion in butter. When onion is tender, add cream. Pour over baked dumplings and serve. Yield: 6 servings.

Fish

Kimsta Zuvis
(gefillte fish)

2 pounds fish (pike, carp, whitefish)	1 teaspoon salt
	⅛ teaspoon pepper
2 large onions, sliced	1 stalk celery, diced
2 eggs	1 large carrot, sliced
¼ cup matzo meal or cracker crumbs	chopped parsley

Cut fish into 2-inch slices. Remove flesh and bones without breaking skin. Salt skin and bones and place in refrigerator while preparing filling. Put flesh and one onion through food chopper, then place in wooden chopping bowl and chop until smooth. Add 2 eggs, matzo meal or cracker crumbs, and salt and pepper to taste, and enough cold water to make a light soft mixture. Blend well.

Wet hands with cold water and form oval cakes of the mixture, then fit them into the skins. Place head bones and other bones in bottom of a deep heavy kettle. Add remaining onion, celery, carrot, and cold water to cover the fishcakes. Cover kettle and bring to a quick boil, then remove cover and reduce heat. Cook at very slow boil, 1½ hours to 2 hours, at which time liquid should be reduced by half. Serve warm or thoroughly chilled, garnish with sliced, cooked carrot and chopped parsley. If served cold, use jellied sauce to further garnish the fish. Yield: 6 servings.

If desired, in first step, instead of slicing the fish, skin it whole, then stuff and shape to resemble a whole fish. Tie in cloth before cooking.

Note: this famous Jewish dish originated in Lithuania.

Virti Veziai
(boiled crabs)

Plunge crabs into boiling water containing salt and some dill. When water starts boiling again, pour in 2 to 3 cups of beer. Continue boiling 10 to 15 minutes.

Zuvies Sriuba
(fish chowder)

2 pounds fish (bass, perch, whitefish, etc.)	2 onions
	1 carrot
1 teaspoon salt	2 potatoes
2 bay leaves	2 tablespoons butter
3 to 4 peppercorns	1 cup sour cream

Scale and clean whole fish. Place in 2 quarts water with salt, bay leaves, peppercorns, and one sliced onion. Boil until flesh separates from bones. Strain. To liquid add diced potatoes, carrot, and onion which has been lightly sauted in butter. Boil until vegetables are done. Add cooked fish (separated from bones). Before serving, blend in the sour cream. Yield: 4 to 6 servings.

Poultry

Kepta Antis ar Zasis
(duck or goose)

Stuff bird with 2 peeled, cored, and quartered cooking apples which have been sweetened very slightly with sugar. Or, stuff with sauerkraut which has been rinsed in hot water and thoroughly drained. For variety, add to sauerkraut chopped onion sauted in butter, or caraway seeds, or chopped tart apple.

Cut duck in pieces, salt. Prepare sauerkraut as above, add some caraway seeds. Place kraut with dabs of butter in baking dish. Set pieces of duck atop kraut. Bake until tender. Yield: 4 servings.

Meats

Versienos Vyniotinis
(veal roulade)

1 leg of veal	¼ pound bacon
4 hard-boiled eggs	4 slices white bread
2 onions	3 carrots
2 teaspoons salt	2 pork sausages or frankfurters
½ teaspoon pepper	(optional)
½ teaspoon nutmeg	1 bay leaf

Remove bone from veal leg, cut out meat from inside, leaving a smooth, flat outer piece. Chop fine or grind the cut-out pieces of meat with 2 hard-boiled eggs, 1 onion, salt, pepper, nutmeg, uncooked bacon, and bread which has been soaked in water and squeezed dry. Place the flat piece of meat on a board, skin side down. Spread with prepared mixture, top with 2 additional hard-boiled eggs, boiled whole carrots or sausages. Roll tightly, sew up, place in cheesecloth, tie or sew up cloth. Boil in water to cover, to which an onion, bay leaf, pepper, and 1 or 2 carrots have been added. Simmer from 2 to 3 hours, depending on size of meat. Remove from heat. Let cool in liquid. Remove from liquid, place the roll of meat under a weight for several hours. Remove cloth. Slice. Serve cold. Yield: 4 to 6 servings.

Krazai
(beef birds)

3 pounds sirloin
2 slices rye bread
2 onions
sliced bacon
mushrooms (optional)

salt and pepper
fat
beef bouillon
½ cup sour cream

Have sirloin sliced about ½ inch thick. Pound thin with edge of plate or rolling pin. Cut into uniform pieces. On each piece place in layers, a small piece of bread, thin slice of onion, piece of bacon, few slices of mushroom. Sprinkle with salt and dash of pepper. Roll up, tie with thread or fasten with toothpicks. Brown on all sides quickly in hot fat. Place in heavy cooking pot, pour on enough bouillon to barely cover. Cover pot tightly. Simmer 1 to 1½ hours. When tender, add cream. Remove birds, thicken liquid with flour for gravy. Yield: 4 servings.

Duonoj Keptas Kumpis
(dough-baked ham)

Mix a good rye bread dough, roll it out thick on well-floured bread board. Place on it a whole or half a ham which has been washed and soaked in cold water. Cover ham with another section of rolled dough. Press edges together tightly. Place in a well-floured roasting pan. Bake at 375 degrees for from 2 to 3 hours, depending on size of ham. When done, remove baked dough covering, skin ham, garnish, and serve.

Pastries, Desserts

Ausukes
(little ears)

5 egg yolks
½ cup sugar
5 tablespoons sweet cream

1 jigger rum or brandy
flour

Cream yolks and sugar. Add cream and rum. Add enough flour to make stiff dough. Roll thin on floured board. Cut in diamond shapes. Slit middle and pull one end of diamond through hole. Fry in deep hot fat till light brown. Drain on paper. Sprinkle with powdered sugar.

Meduolis
(honey cake)

1 cup honey	1 tablespoon mixed spices
1 cup sugar	(cinnamon, cloves, pepper,
1 cup sour cream	ginger, cardamon, grated
4 eggs	lemon and orange rind)
3 cups flour	2 tablespoons melted butter
2 teaspoons baking soda	½ cup almonds

Beat honey, gradually adding sugar and sour cream. Beat in eggs one at a time. Sift flour and soda. Add flour, spices, and butter gradually to honey mixture, beating constantly. (For a richer color, add 3 tablespoons carmelized sugar.) Pour batter (about one-inch thick) into a baking pan. Bake 30 minutes in 350 degree oven. For a more moist cake—when done, sprinkle top with sweetened water to which rum or flavoring has been added. Spread top of cake with fruit puree or with prune filling. Sprinkle with chopped almonds. Cut into triangular pieces.

Sviesto Sausainiai
(butter cookies)

½ pound butter	2 cups flour
½ pound cream cheese	

Cream butter and cheese, sift in flour. Mix and chill overnight. Roll thin, cut into squares. Fill 2 layers of squares with pureed stewed apricots, prunes, or jam. Bake in 450 degree oven until lightly browned. Remove from pan, sprinkle with powdered sugar.

Obuoliai Kepti su Slyvom
(baked apples with prunes and honey)

6 firm, tart apples, cored   6 tablespoons honey
12 presoaked or ready-to-eat   ½ teaspoon cinnamon
    prunes, pitted

Place apples in oven-proof shallow dish. Into the cavity of each apple put two moist prunes and one tablespoon honey. Sprinkle with cinnamon. Add water to cover bottom of dish, about ½ inch deep. Bake in preheated oven at 375 degrees for one hour or until apples are tender. Good served hot or cold. Yield: 6 servings.

Obuoline Putele
(apple snow)

12 cooking apples   1 teaspoon cinnamon
½ cup fine sugar   2 egg whites

Bake whole unpeeled apples. Cool. Force through sieve. Add sugar and cinnamon. Place dish on crushed ice, gradually add egg whites, beat until very fluffy. Spoon into dessert dishes, sprinkle with fine sugar. Serve at once.

3

The North Sea

Belgium, Luxembourg, Holland

To many, even some Frenchmen who prize their country's reputation for fine cuisine above all else, the best food in Europe is served in Belgium. Whether that is going too far or not won't be taken up here. The fact is, few will dispute that Belgian dishes and cooking can stand up against the best anywhere in the world.

Belgians cook even more lavishly with butter and cream than the French; beef is braised Flemish-fashion and cooked with onions in dark beer; steaks come sauted and garnished with braised endive; fish soups and stews are uniquely herbed;

rabbit is deliciously cooked with prunes; Brussels sprouts are better than you've ever tasted them; and Belgian pastries are rich with chocolate and cream.

There are even those who insist that there is a similarity between Flemish painting and cookery. And that isn't a bad description for the incredible pot herb soup of green peas, leek, chicken broth, shallot, chives, parsley, sorrel, chervil, Béchamel sauce, eggs, and heavy cream I experienced in Brussels one cold winter day at one of the small cafes along the Rue des Bouchers, "the street of restaurants." It would take a chef of the stature of a Van Dyck or Rubens to produce such a soup. And if that sounds extravagant, remember you can't eat a painting.

The food of Luxembourg, the tiny duchy to the south of Belgium, is influenced by Belgium and its other neighbors, Germany and France. Smoked pork with beans or sauerkraut dates back to Teutonic times, and jellied suckling pig is a favorite local dish. The duchy is perhaps best known gastronomically for its Ardennes ham, but its roast thrush or hare served in thick wine sauce should not be lightly dismissed.

Their northern neighbors, the Dutch, are heavily influenced in their cooking by the North Sea. The food in Holland is hearty and rather simple, but substantial enough to satisfy men who for centuries have earned their living by fishing the nearby waters. Exotic herbs and spices, influences from the earlier Dutch colonies in the East Indies, are still used profusely in Dutch dishes. Nutmeg is a particular favorite. Another Eastern influence, rice, remains almost a staple of Dutch diet. And Dutch vegetables deserve their reputation for freshness and flavor.

Fish, of course, are among the most popular and delicious of foods in the North Sea countries. A visit to any local fish market reveals a tempting variety of herrings, shrimp, oysters, mussels, and fresh fish of all sorts that have a deep-sea flavor seldom enjoyed by visitors accustomed only to eating fish that has been frozen.

Chapter 10

BELGIUM

The world knows Belgium perhaps best not through its exquisite cooking but through its famous painters. Rubens, Van Dyck, Breughel, Bosch and other Flemish artists have depicted outdoor peasant life, the landscapes of Flanders, and the lifelike indoor scenes of its ordinary citizens of two and three hundred years ago. A legacy of art and history perhaps more accurate than any written accounts.

Caeser, 58 years before the birth of Christ, called the hard-working, determined "Belgae" the bravest of the Gallic peoples. It has been their concentration on hard work and determination that have seen the Belgians through centuries of foreign domination that only as late as 1830 resulted in their independence.

Today Belgium is international headquarters of the European Common Market, NATO, and other organizations. Diplomatically, Belgium regards itself as "the capital of Europe."

Belgium's cities and towns contain some of Europe's most elaborate architecture. Flemish love of decoration is evident on great houses, guild halls, and churches throughout the land.

One cold, snowy Christmas Eve I found myself in Brussels, looking for a hotel. Not familiar with the city, I asked a citizen to direct me to one, and he pointed in a direction that I followed. It took me down winding narrow cobblestone streets past shops and houses until I wasn't sure where I was anymore. Then I turned a sharp corner and beheld a most magnificent spectacle. The gilt facades of the seventeenth century guild houses lining the Grand Place were illuminated by the golden glow of floodlights, the largest Christmas tree I had ever seen stood decorated and colorfully lighted in the center of the square where black-shawled old women were selling ornaments, crowds were milling about buying last-minute gifts and decorations from vendors at outdoor booths, and loudspeakers were playing carols sung by Flemish boys and girls.

It was my introduction to a northlands fairy tale city I never knew existed. My next discovery was its food. The grand Epaule de Mouton, a hotel restaurant famous for 300 years, serves a Flemish beefsteak and chocolate mousse that alone would explain why it is regarded as one of the great dining places in the world. But don't let that intimidate you from trying the chervil soup and brown fish at the Ravenstein, rich in Burgundian atmosphere.

Antwerp, over 50 miles from the sea but one of the great ports of Europe (ships come up the Scheldt river), holds the Rubens mansion, shops for the world's biggest diamond-cutting market, great commercial trading centers, and the new John F. Kennedy tunnel, a $62 million road and rail underground that is a major part of a project to link Stockholm with Lisbon. It is a typically active port city and restaurants such as the Criterium offer a memorable orange duckling.

The art towns of Flanders are among Belgium's greatest treasures. Bruges is a medieval city that is a work of art in itself. So are the pastries which lace-shawled ladies make in the local tea shops. Ghent, "the Florence of the North," also has its share of fifteenth century castles and cathedrals.

Belgium comes by its culinary treasures influenced by both Germany and France, with certain subtle refinements. Fish and shellfish are plentiful along the coastline of the North Sea. Vegetables are flavorful and tender. Belgian endive, a pale, bitter leaf, is especially delicious in salads.

Soups are popular and come in great varieties. The national favorite is *waterzooï*, made with either chicken or fish.

Only a confirmed vegetarian would fail to appreciate *boeuf à la flamande*, a beef, onion, and beer sensation.

Cheeses, souffles, Flemish waffles, and rich pastries such as honey cakes, Belgian tarts, and "little cakes" of cinnamon and raisins are notable desserts.

The thickly forested Ardennes country, a charming link between Belgium and Luxembourg, supplies both countries with the famous smoked Ardennes ham, trout, and fresh-water fish.

If your strongest impression of Belgium is the memory of a Breughel painting of dozens of peasants feasting at a banquet table in some courtyard, try some of the dishes of this culinary mecca, and you will know why so many of the peasants in the paintings have a contented look on their faces.

Appetizers

Oeufs Meulenmeester
(baked eggs)

6 hard-boiled eggs
2 tablespoons butter, melted
1 teaspoon minced chervil
¼ teaspoon dry mustard
1 teaspoon minced parsley
salt and pepper

½ cup shrimp, precooked, shelled, and chopped
1 cup sour cream
grated cheese
butter

Chop the eggs fine, add 2 tablespoons butter, seasoning, shrimp, and cream. Mix well. Pour into well-buttered baking dish, sprinkle top with grated cheese and dot with bits of butter. Bake at 450 degrees until cheese melts and begins to brown. Yield: 4 servings.

Canapés de Harengs Fumés
(smoked herring)

1 medium-sized roe
¼ teaspoon paprika

1 tablespoon prepared mustard

Save roe from herring. Poach roe for 5 minutes in boiling water. Drain on paper towels. Add prepared mustard and paprika. Spread on melba toast and serve hot.

Fritots à la Liégeoise
(cheese appetizers)

¼ cup bread crumbs (soft)
1 cup grated Parmesan cheese
1 egg yolk
¼ teaspoon prepared mustard

salt and cayenne pepper to taste
1 egg white, stiffly beaten
½ cup dry bread crumbs

Mix soft bread crumbs, cheese, egg yolk, and seasonings. Fold in egg white. Shape into balls the size of a walnut. Roll in dry bread crumbs. Fry in deep fat until golden brown. Drain on paper towels. Serve hot. Yield: 10 to 12 balls.

Soups

Le Waterzooï
(chicken soup)

1 stewing chicken
½ lemon
2 onions
4 cloves
½ cup diced celery
½ cup diced carrots

1 sprig thyme
3 leeks, minced
1 bay leaf
salt and pepper
2 cups dry white wine
1 tablespoon minced parsley

Leave chicken whole. Rub with lemon and place in large kettle. Add water to half cover chicken and bring to boil. Skim. Peel onions, leaving them whole and insert two cloves in each onion. Add to chicken with remaining ingredients except parsley. Cover kettle and simmer slowly until tender. When ready to serve, remove chicken from the broth and carve it, placing carved pieces in a soup tureen. Cover with the broth and garnish with sprigs of parsley. Yield: 4 servings.

Chervil Soup

2 leeks, sliced
1 medium onion, sliced small
2 large potatoes, sliced small
margarine

salt and pepper
1 bunch of chervil
1 tablespoon butter

Clean and wash leeks, peel onion and potatoes. Slice all into small pieces. Melt a little fat in a saucepan and gently fry the vegetables, stirring until they change color. Add 1 quart of boiling water, seasoning to taste. Bring back to a boil and simmer slowly at least half an hour. Meanwhile wash, clean and chop the chervil, and keep covered until required. Force vegetables through a sieve, then return them to the pan and boil for 5 minutes, then add the chervil and a tablespoon butter or margarine. Yield: 4 servings.

Soupe Verte
(pot herb soup)

1 leek, sliced
1 cup green peas
1 shallot, sliced
handful each of parsley, sorrel, chervil
few sprigs chives

2 cans chicken broth
2 egg yolks beaten with
¼ cup heavy cream
½ cup thick Béchamel sauce
salt and pepper

Wash leek under cold water to clean. Cook peas and leek in broth until tender. Meanwhile place all vegetables in wooden bowl and chop very fine. Blend broth and egg yolk-cream mixture with Béchamel (see below). Thicken by bringing to the boiling point. Remove from heat. Season to taste. Yield: 6 cups.

Sauce Béchamel
(Béchamel sauce)

2 tablespoons butter
2 tablespoons flour
1½ cups hot milk

salt and pepper to taste
½ cup heavy cream

Melt butter in saucepan. Add flour. Whisk to mix rapidly, adding milk slowly while sauce thickens and bubbles. When all milk has been added, boil 8 minutes, stirring slowly until thick and about half the liquid has evaporated. Season to taste. Stir in cream. Taste, correct seasoning. Do not boil again. Keep warm until using. Yield: 1 cup. (For white meats, use chicken broth instead of milk. For fish, use fish stock instead of milk.)

Ghentsche Waterzooie
(Flemish fish soup)

1 quart dry white wine	4 cloves
2 carrots, diced	salt and pepper to taste
1 onion, chopped	2 pounds fish (carp, brill, or
5 sprigs parsley	perch *and* eel)
1 bay leaf	6 small lake fish, or 12 smelts
¼ teaspoon mace	½ cup heavy cream

Simmer wine, 2 quarts water, carrots, onion, herbs and seasonings for 20 minutes. Add carp or other fish. Simmer until fish is cooked. Rub through food mill into a kettle. Place the small fish in a sieve. Lower sieve into soup and cook until done. Remove fish and reserve. Add cream to soup. Do not boil again. Serve with pumpernickel bread slices, well buttered, and place a small whole fish or 2 smelts in each plate before adding soup. Yield: 6 servings.

Vegetables

Purée des Choux de Bruxelles
(puree of Brussels sprouts)

2 pounds Brussels sprouts	2 egg yolks, beaten
4 tablespoons margarine	¼ cup sour cream
1 tablespoon flour	salt and pepper
1 tablespoon meat extract	

Boil the sprouts in 1 cup salted water for 10 minutes. Drain well. Melt margarine, add sprouts, and toss gently for 2 minutes. Sprinkle the flour on them, add meat extract, and 1 cup of water, mixing well. Cover and cook over low heat for 15 minutes. Force sprouts through a sieve. Beat egg yolks and sour cream together in a bowl. Gradually stir in the puréed sprouts. Season to taste with salt and pepper. Heat slowly but do not allow to boil. Yield: 6 servings.

Carottes à la Flamande
(Flemish carrots)

3 tablespoons butter
12 small carrots, scraped
1 teaspoon salt

¼ teaspoon pepper
1 teaspoon sugar
¼ cup sour cream

Melt butter in a heavy saucepan. Add carrots, salt, pepper, and sugar. Cover and cook over low heat for 20 minutes or until tender. Add sour cream, stir, and cook 2 more minutes. Yield: 4 to 6 servings.

Chicons Braisés
(braised endive)

1½ pounds Belgian endive
Juice of ½ lemon

3 tablespoons butter
salt and pepper

Boil endive in salted water for 18 minutes, adding lemon juice. Place endive and butter in heavy skillet. Simmer uncovered over medium heat until liquid has evaporated and edges of vegetables are golden. Season to taste. Yield: 4 servings.

Dumplings, Potatoes

Salade de Pommes de Terre
(potato salad Ardenaise)

4 cups potatoes, boiled,
    peeled, and sliced thinly
juice of 1 lemon
1 cup French dressing

½ cup diced smoked ham
1 teaspoon chervil
1 teaspoon parsley
1 teaspoon chives

Sprinkle potatoes with lemon juice. Mix potatoes, dressing, and ham thoroughly. Place in refrigerator and allow dressing to soak into potatoes for 1 hour. Add more dressing if needed. Season to taste. Before serving sprinkle top of salad with herbs (freshly chopped or powdered). Yield: 4 servings.

Salad

Salade de Blé
(field salad with endive)

4 stalks Belgian endive
1 head lettuce
¼ head red cabbage

1 cup mayonnaise
salt and pepper

Wash and drain vegetables. Cut endive into one-inch chunks and divide. Place endive in bottom of salad bowl. Make a ring around edge of bowl with lettuce leaves. Toward center make a ring of red cabbage and drop mayonnaise into center. Salt and pepper to taste. Yield: 4 to 6 servings.

Fish

Poisson Brun
(brown fish)

6 mackerel fillets
   (reserve head, skin, bones)
1 onion
2 teaspoons salt
1 teaspoon pepper
¼ pound butter

2 tablespoons flour
2 tablespoons chopped parsley
1 clove garlic, minced
⅛ teaspoon chervil
⅛ teaspoon sage
1 tablespoon grated lemon rind
½ cup red wine

Combine the head, skin, and bones of mackerels with the onion, salt, pepper, and 3 cups water in a saucepan. Bring to boil and cook over medium heat for 45 minutes. Strain reserving fish stock. Melt butter in skillet. Add flour and stir until smooth. Add the fish stock, stirring until boiling point is reached. Place mackerel fillets in the sauce and add parsley, garlic, chervil, sage, lemon rind, and wine. Cook over low heat for 20 minutes. Season to taste. Place under the broiler for 1 minute to brown the top. Yield: 4 to 6 servings.

Filets de Sole Vert-Pré
(fillets of sole with spinach)

1½ pounds fillet of sole	and drained
court bouillon for fish	4 cups Sauce Mornay
(see below)	(see below)
3 cups leaf spinach, cooked	

Roll fillets and fasten with toothpicks. Poach 4 minutes in court-bouillon. Remove and drain on paper towels. Spread out spinach in buttered ovenproof dish. Place fillets on top after removing toothpicks. Cover with the sauce. Brown lightly under broiler. Yield: 4 servings.

Court Bouillon

2 quarts white wine	2 quarts water
1 onion, sliced	1 clove garlic
2 carrots	1 small stalk celery
⅛ teaspoon powdered thyme	2 sprigs parsley
1 bay leaf	1 clove
14 whole peppercorns	salt to taste

Simmer all ingredients for 1 hour before adding fish. May be kept a week in refrigerator by adding 1 tablespoon vinegar per quart. Use as a fish stock base.

Sauce Mornay

2 cups Béchamel Sauce	2 tablespoons grated
(see under Belgium soups)	Parmesan cheese
3 egg yolks slightly beaten	2 tablespoons butter
with	3 tablespoons dry white
1 tablespoon cream	wine or sherry

Use Court bouillon instead of hot milk in the Béchamel sauce. Bring Béchamel sauce to boiling point. Remove from heat and stir in egg yolk and cheese mixture first adding some of the sauce to the mixture so the eggs won't cook. Yield: 2 cups.

Meat

Boeuf à la Flamande
(Flemish beefsteak)

4 tablespoons butter
6 onions, sliced
4 pounds sirloin
2 tablespoons flour
2 cups beer
2 tablespoons vinegar

2 teaspoons salt
½ teaspoon pepper
1 teaspoon sugar
3 tablespoons chopped parsley
2 bay leaves
½ teaspoon thyme

Melt butter in saucepan or casserole. Add onions and saute until brown, stirring frequently. Remove onions and set aside. Brown beef (cut into 12 pieces about 1 inch thick) on both sides and remove. Sprinkle flour on the pan juices and mix until smooth. Add 1 cup water, stirring constantly. Return onions and beef to the saucepan. Add beer, vinegar, salt, pepper, sugar, parsley, bay leaves, and thyme. Cover and cook over low heat for 2 hours. Yield: 4 to 6 servings.

Civet
(rabbit)

1 rabbit, jointed
½ bottle red wine
2 tablespoons vinegar
4 peppercorns
2 bay leaves
1 teaspoon thyme

4 tablespoons butter
¼ cup flour
salt and pepper
1 pound prunes
1 tablespoon red currant jelly

Marinate rabbit in wine and vinegar with peppercorns and herbs for 24 hours. Drain, pat dry with paper towels, and fry lightly on all sides in butter. Stir in flour. Add water to cover and season well. Add prunes (soaked if necessary). Cover pan and simmer for 1 hour or until tender. Stir in red currant jelly before serving. Yield: 2 servings.

Pastries

Mousse au Chocolat
(chocolate mousse)

8 ounces semisweet chocolate	1 teaspoon grated orange rind
3 tablespoons Grand Marnier	7 egg whites, beaten stiff
6 egg yolks	

Melt chocolate in Grand Marnier in top of double boiler. Add egg yolks and orange rind and stir until smooth. Fold chocolate into egg whites. Pour into small serving cups and set in refrigerator for 8 hours. Yield: 6 cups.

Petites Galettes Wallones
("little cakes")

1 cup melted butter	½ teaspoon salt
½ cup powdered sugar	2 teaspoons cinnamon
1 egg well beaten	½ cup milk
3 cups flour	½ cup raisins
1 teaspoon baking powder	

Mix butter and sugar. Add egg and beat. Sift flour, baking powder, salt, and cinnamon and add alternately with the milk. Add raisins. Form into small cakes and bake on well-greased cookie sheet in 350 degree oven until brown.

Gaufres à la Flamande
(Flemish waffles)

4 cups flour, sifted	8 eggs
½ ounce yeast	¼ cup brandy
pinch of salt	2 ounces butter
pinch of sugar	½ pint sweet cream

Mix 1 cup flour with yeast dissolved in warm water and set to rise. Work in rest of flour with salt and sugar, eggs slightly beaten, brandy, and cream which has been boiled and to which the butter is added. Knead well and let stand 2½ hours in a warm place. Heat and grease waffle iron. Batter should be sufficiently liquid to spread of itself over waffle iron. When evenly browned on both sides, sprinkle with sugar and serve hot.

Ghentsche Peperkoek
(honey cake)

2½ cups cake flour
1½ teaspoons double-acting
    baking powder

½ cup rye flour
¼ cup water
1½ cups lukewarm honey

Blend all ingredients together in a bowl until smooth, semistiff dough is formed. Place in well-buttered bread pan. Bake at 275 degrees for 2 hours without opening oven door. Test cake with toothpick (if it comes clean from center of cake, it is done). Allow cake to stand at least one day before serving. Serve sliced, buttered, and make into a sandwich with a thin slice of white bread.

Chapter 11

LUXEMBOURG

In Luxembourg it is easy to think you are in Camelot, a fairy tale land of knights and princesses, castles, turrets, moats, and medieval houses built like fortresses.

Luxembourg is all of that and a very progressive, industrial, economically sound grand duchy that is also the judiciary and banking center for the European Economic Community.

One of Europe's smallest countries, it is only fifty-one miles from north to south and thirty-five miles from east to west. Deep valleys dissect the picturesque country and some of the world's best wine comes from along the Moselle.

Its history dates to Roman times when what is now Luxembourg was inhabited by a Belgic tribe, the Treveri. There followed domination by Germany, France, Austria, and even Spain, until finally in 1815 after the Napoleonic wars, the Congress of Vienna gave Luxembourg as a grand duchy to William I, king of the Netherlands, and in 1867 Luxembourg attained its independence.

Luxembourg City is the capital, a fortress whose three rings of defense still include fifty-three forts linked by sixteen miles of tunnels and casements hewn into solid rock. No wonder it's called "the Gibraltar of the North."

All this physical appearance of defense does not apply today to Luxembourgers who are considered among the friendliest and happiest peoples of Europe. They seem to love a good time and are eager to share their music, dance, and food with others.

Food in Luxembourg is of the highest quality and reasonable in price, influenced strongly by the cooking of both Germany and France. Smoked pork is a favorite dish. Trout, pike, and crayfish from local streams are served with Franco-Belgian finesse.

After a visit to the National Museum in Luxembourg City, with works of art and a model of the citadel in ancient days, a stroll along the Promenade de la Corniche with its spectacular view of the deep valley below, the roast thrush in thick wine sauce at Au Gourmet makes you feel like a Burgundian prince, at least. The Cordial serves more simple fare such as beef carbonades and the popular dessert, rice tart.

After your fill of castles and palaces, a drive through the winding valleys of the Ardennes take you and your fishing pole to some of the world's best trout streams. Local inns serve fresh-caught trout cooked in wine sauce.

The Moselle Valley is a winelover's paradise, and a visit to the cellars of the Cooperative of Vinegrowers nets you several tall-stemmed glasses of champagne.

A small but beautiful country, rich in the lore of kings and palaces, Luxembourg has been called "The Land of Haunted Castles." You believe it when you see spotlights and floodlights illuminate Luxembourg City's medieval bridges, massive ramparts, and towering spires transporting you into your favorite fairy tale.

Soups

Bo'neschlupp
(peasant bean soup)

1 pound string beans	¼ cup fat
salt to taste	pepper to taste
2 pounds potatoes	1 tablespoon vinegar
2 tablespoons flour	1 cup sour cream (optional)

Cut string beans into half-inch pieces, pour boiling water over them, repeat two or three times and strain. Put them into 6 cups tepid water and bring to boil, adding salt to taste. Half an hour before serving, add 2 pounds raw potatoes, peeled and cubed. Cook until potatoes are done. Brown 2 tablespoons flour with 1¼ ounces fat in a saucepan and stir until blended. Add a little of the liquid from the soup and season to taste with pepper, salt, and 1 tablespoon vinegar. Add mixture to the soup a few minutes before serving and stir thoroughly. A cup of sour cream also may be added. Yield: 4 servings.

Porrettenzopp
(leek soup)

5 leeks	6 potatoes
4 tablespoons margarine	1 cup sour cream
salt	

Wash and chop leeks and brown lightly in margarine. Add 6 cups water and salt and boil 30 minutes. Add raw potatoes, peeled and cubed, and boil 20 to 30 minutes until cooked. Rub soup through a sieve, reheat, and just before serving add cup of sour cream. Yield: 4 to 6 servings.

Salad

Hierengszallot
(herring salad)

3 herrings	chopped parsley
1 teaspoon dry mustard	1 apple, minced
3 tablespoons salad oil	3 tablespoons sour cream
4 tablespoons wine vinegar	or sour milk
2 onions, finely chopped	

Wash herrings and soak at least 12 hours, then skin and bone them and cut the flesh into small cubes. If there are soft roes, mix them with the mustard, oil, and vinegar and pour this sauce over the herrings, then mix well with the onions, parsley, and apple. Add sour cream or sour milk, if desired. Yield: 3 servings.

Dumplings

Li'ewerkni'edelen
(liver dumplings)

1 pound liver

4 slices bacon

parsley

thyme

onions

shallots

chives

3 eggs

salt and pepper

bread crumbs

soaked bread

a little flour

Mince liver and 2 slices bacon and finely chop parsley, thyme, onions, shallots, and chives. Mix with eggs, salt, pepper, bread crumbs, soaked bread, and flour to a stiff dough. Form into small dumplings, using a teaspoon. Drop into boiling salted water and boil about 10 minutes, covered. Cut remaining 2 slices bacon in small cubes, fry gently so that it is almost melted. Pour over dumplings before serving. Yield: 4 servings.

Fish

Kribsen a la Lukembourgeoise
(crayfish)

1 large crayfish

milk or cream

small glass white wine

small glass cognac

2 tablespoons salt

2 tablespoons pounded
  peppercorns

thyme

parsley

tarragon

small piece butter

paprika

1 onion, quartered

Wash crayfish in cold water and drain. Remove the meat and soak in milk or cream. Meanwhile prepare a broth with a small glass each of water and white wine, a very small glass of cognac, 2 tablespoons salt, 2 tablespoons pounded peppercorns, a little thyme, a lot of parsley and tarragon, a small piece of butter, a little paprika, and 1 onion cut in quarters. Bring broth to a boil in a very large pan, put crayfish meat in it, cover and boil 5 or 6 minutes. Serve very hot, decorated with parsley.

Meat

Carbonaden vu Rendflesch
(beef carbonades)

1½ pounds sirloin	¼ cup vinegar
½ cup cooking fat	salt
3 carrots, diced	1 bay leaf
1 onion, sliced	parsley
2 tablespoons flour	¼ cup white wine

Cut meat in slices and fry lightly in cooking fat. Put alternate layers of meat, carrots, and onion in a pan, sprinkle with flour, and allow to brown slightly. Mix vinegar with ¼ cup water and bring to a boil. Add a very little boiling vinegar and water mixture, then the seasoning and herbs and stew for 2½ hours. Just before serving, add ¼ cup white wine and stir gently. Yield: 3 servings.

Vullen oni Kapp
(birds without a head)

3 thin slices sirloin	1 carrot, sliced
salt and pepper	finely chopped onion
chopped parsley	beef broth or water
3 slices bacon	¼ cup cooking fat
3 hard-boiled eggs	parsley
flour	

Roll slices of sirloin flat with a rolling pin. Place on each slice some salt, pepper, parsley, slice of bacon, and in center a hard-boiled egg. Roll up pieces of meat and tie with string. Roll in flour and fry slowly in an open pan, then add chopped onion and sliced carrot, sprinkle with a little salt, add a little hot beef broth or water, and stew gently about 2 hours, closely covered. Cut string and serve on top of mashed potatoes covered with chopped parsley. Serve gravy separately. Yield: 3 servings.

Pastries

Reiss Tart
(rice tart)

4 tablespoons butter
¼ cup cooking fat
2 cups flour
1 tablespoon rum, cognac, or
    cooking sherry
1 tablespoon cold water
1 tablespoon sour cream
6 tablespoons sugar
salt

Filling:
5 ounces rice
1½ pints milk
2 eggs, separated
a pinch of salt
1 ounce chopped almonds
2 ounces sugar
cinnamon

Rub the butter and cooking fat into the flour. Make a well and pour all the liquids into the center, with the sugar and salt, and knead into a dough. Leave in a cold place for an hour. Roll out dough, place in a greased baking tin and cover with the filling, made as follows: Wash the rice, put into boiling water and boil for 3 minutes. Drain and pour cold water over rice, then drain again. Meanwhile boil the milk, add the rice, and cook slowly until it is half done. Add egg yolks and remaining ingredients. Add the stiffly beaten egg whites last and spread the mixture over the pastry. Bake in 350 degree oven for 45 minutes.

Chapter 12

HOLLAND

Dikes and bikes, tulips and Rembrandt, windmills and canals, cheese and chocolates are all synonymous with Holland.

They call themselves Nederlanders; we call them Dutch. The people of Holland are an amazing lot. Who else in the world has reclaimed half of its land from the sea!

Half of Holland is below high-tide level, yet the people prosper. Floods threaten to wash away the dikes and levies, but with as much determination as the legendary boy who stuck his finger in a dike to save his town, the Dutch manage to keep things dry.

Holland dates to prehistoric times, when more than a dozen provinces united but remained under the influence of German rulers. In the sixteenth century the country came under the rule of Spain, and in 1648 achieved its independence. Despite domination by the Spanish, during the seventeenth century Holland was the most prosperous country in Europe, largely due to Dutch colonies in the East and West Indies from which were brought galleys laden with spices and other treasures for trade.

Today Holland is a blend of old and new, small farms and large commercial cities. The Dutch are a crowded people, over thirteen million in a country half the size of North Carolina. Yet their numbers are concentrated in their major cities, and the green countryside laced with blue canals and tree-bordered roads remains uncrowded.

Holland is perhaps best known for its tulips. From April to June the villages of Boskoop and Aalsmeer and the famous Keukenhof gardens, all near Amsterdam, put on the world's most beautiful display of colorful tulips.

For art lovers, Amsterdam's Rijksmuseum, Otterlo's Kroller-Muller museum, and The Hague's Mauritschuis exhibit the works of Rembrandt, Vermeer, Hals, Van Gogh, and other masters.

Hollanders in their native costumes including wooden shoes can be seen in Spakenburg, Volendam, and Marken on most Sundays. In the town of Staphorst are faces and settings Rembrandt would love to have painted.

I visited Amsterdam one early Spring. Tiny petals from the flowering trees drifted gently down into the canals as I rode a glass-roofed boat under bridges and along banks where narrow houses crowded next to each other. One house was little larger than one room wide, though three stories tall. At Prisengracht 263, Anne Frank and her family hid from the Nazis during World War II. And along the canals were flowerboats moored near bridges where local citizens stopped to buy a fresh bouquet for their tables.

Afterward I set out on foot to explore the Royal Palace, the Tower of Tears from which Hendrik Hudson set sail in 1609 and discovered New York, Rembrandt's house, and the Tropical Museum with its East Indian art treasures.

People who labor to keep the sea away from their door deserve a little fun, and the Dutch enjoy night life. The variety of places to spend an evening on the town is great.

Another popular way the Dutch enjoy themselves is to dine out. Traditionally, they get this started by partaking in the national institution of the *borreltje*, a little nip of gin at about 5 o'clock.

The Dutch love French cooking, which is served in many of the best restaurants, but typical Dutch dishes are also on the menu. The pea soup with bits of sausage or pig's knuckles, called *Erwtensoep*, is a meal in itself. Favorite meat dishes are *Hutspot*, a meat, carrot, and potato stew; *Hachee*, a beef and onion stew; and *Rodekool met Rolpens*, red cabbage and rolled spiced meat with sliced apple.

Gouda and Edam are favorite mild cheeses, and seafood is abundant and tastily prepared.

Indonesian and Chinese dishes are also popular in Holland, especially among those who have spent some years in the Indies.

Appetizers

Bitterballen
(cocktail savories)

1½ teaspoons powdered gelatin
½ cup veal stock
2 tablespoons Dutch unsalted butter
⅛ cup flour

½ cup milk
⅛ cup grated Gouda cheese
1 teaspoon chopped parsley
salt and pepper
⅓ cup toasted bread crumbs
1 egg, beaten

Dissolve gelatin in 3 tablespoons boiling veal stock. Make a white sauce using the butter, flour, the remaining stock, and milk, then add the dissolved gelatin, meat, cheese, and parsley. Season well, turn onto a plate and allow to cool until firm. Roll into marble-sized balls, dip into bread crumbs, then into beaten egg, and finally into crumbs again. Fry in hot fat until golden brown and drain on paper towels. Serve hot with mustard.

Kassballetjes
(cheese puffs)

3 tablespoons butter
5 tablespoons flour
1½ cups grated cheddar cheese
3 egg yolks, beaten

3 egg whites, beaten stiff
¼ teaspoon pepper
fat for frying

Melt butter, stir in flour, add 1 cup water. Cook and stir with a wire whisk until smooth and boiling. Add cheese and stir until it is melted. Take mixture off the fire, add the beaten egg yolks, and fold in the egg whites. Add pepper. Take a small spoonful of mixture and drop into hot fat. Drain on paper towel. Served with tomato sauce and green salad. Yield: 30 cheese puffs.

Soups

Sajor Kool
(cabbage and shrimp soup)

1 small cabbage
2 large onions
1 clove garlic
2 red peppers
2 tablespoons fat
2 cups stock for soup (or

bouillon and water)
salt
2 teaspoons vinegar
⅛ cup ground peanuts or
   peanut butter
2 cups shelled shrimps

Shred cabbage and onions, crush garlic, and slice the red peppers. Fry onions in fat, add cabbage, garlic, and peppers. Stir well. Pour on the stock, add salt, vinegar, and peanuts, and cook until cabbage is tender. Finally add shrimps and cook until done. Yield: 3 servings.

Erwtensoep met Worst en Kluif
(pea soup)

2 cups split peas
salt
2 pig's feet

3 leeks, chopped
1 stalk celery, chopped
½ pound beef sausage

Wash and soak peas in cold water for 12 hours. Drain and cover with fresh cold water and bring to a boil. Add salt, pig's feet, leeks, and celery. Simmer 3 or 4 hours. Half an hour before serving add the sausage. Serve with strips of toast. Yield: 4 servings.

Vegetables

Gestaafde Sla
(smothered lettuce)

6 heads Boston lettuce
2 tablespoons butter

½ cup beef bouillon
cracker crumbs

Use only the hearts of the lettuce. Wash thoroughly in several waters. Cover with boiling salted water and cook about 1 hour. Remove from water and drain. Arrange in a buttered casserole and dot with the butter. Add beef bouillon and sprinkle with cracker crumbs. Bake in 400 degree oven for 15 minutes. Yield: 3 servings.

Bieten met Appelen
(beets with apple)

4 tablespoons butter
6 medium beets, cooked and
    sliced
1 onion, chopped

4 tart apples, chopped
salt
½ teaspoon nutmeg

Melt butter, add beets, onion, and apples. Cook slowly until ingredients are reduced to a pulp. Season with salt and nutmeg, using more nutmeg to taste. Yield: 4 servings.

Potatoes

Aardappel Croquetten
(potato rissolés)

6 boiled potatoes
2 tablespoons melted butter
½ teaspoon salt
⅛ teaspoon grated nutmeg

2 egg whites, whipped stiff
1 tablespoon bread crumbs
fat for frying
2 egg yolks

Rub potatoes through a sieve, blend in the melted butter, salt, nutmeg, and beaten yolk of 1 egg. Fold in the 2 egg whites. Shape purée into small balls of about 1 inch in diameter. Dilute yolk of second egg with 2 tablespoons water. Roll potato balls in egg-yolk mixture, then in bread crumbs. Fry in deep fat until brown. Drain on paper towel. Yield: 4 servings.

Salad

Huzarensla
(Hussars' salad)

½ pound cold meat
2 cooked beets
6 cold potatoes
1 apple
a few onions

a few gherkins
mayonnaise
dry mustard
salt and pepper
1–2 hard-boiled eggs

Dice the meat, chop the beets, potatoes, apple, onions, and gherkins. Mix together with mayonnaise and add dry mustard and salt and pepper. Place salad on a platter and garnish with mayonnaise, beet, egg, and gherkins. Yield: 4 servings.

Fish

Gestoofde Paling
(baked eel)

2 pounds eel
8 tablespoons butter
bread crumbs

nutmeg
salt and pepper
2 teaspoons vinegar

Clean fish and cut into 2-inch lengths. Melt butter in a casserole and put in the eel. Sprinkle with bread crumbs, nutmeg, seasoning and vinegar. Cover and bake in 300 degree oven for 2 hours.

Viskoekjes
(fish cakes)

8 slices white bread, trimmed
1½ cups milk
1 pound fish fillets
8 tablespoons butter
2 eggs, beaten

2 teaspoons salt
1 teaspoon pepper
¼ teaspoon nutmeg
3 tablespoons chopped parsley

Soak bread in milk for 10 minutes. Mash until smooth. Grind fish twice in a food chopper and place in a bowl. Cream half of the butter until soft, and add to the fish, together with the bread, eggs, salt, pepper, nutmeg, and parsley. Mix well. Shape into small croquettes. If mixture is too thin, add a little cracker meal. Melt remaining butter in frying pan. Fry fish cakes over low heat until browned on both sides. Serve with small boiled potatoes. Yield: 4 servings.

Poultry

Kip met Tomaten Saus
(chicken in tomato sauce)

2 2-pound chickens
½ cup butter
1¼ cups chicken bouillon
4 tablespoons tomato puree
1 teaspoon grated onion

1 teaspoon sugar
¼ teaspoon pepper
1 tablespoon celery stalks and
  leaves, chopped
½ teaspoon salt

Pour boiling water over chickens, outside and in. Saute in butter until golden brown on all sides. Cut each in four pieces. Put back in pan and add bouillon and other ingredients. Cover and bake in 325 degree oven about 1 hour. Place chicken pieces on a dish and strain the sauce. Serve with macaroni and grated cheese.

Meats

Hachee
(beef and onion stew)

2 large onions, sliced
⅛ cup flour
3 tablespoons margarine
2 cups beef bouillon stock
3 bay leaves

5 cloves
1 tablespoon vinegar
½ pound cold meat, diced
salt and pepper
piquant table sauce

Saute onions and flour in margarine in a saucepan, and add stock gradually, stirring. Add bay leaves and cloves and simmer for 5 minutes with lid on. Add vinegar and meat and simmer another hour. Thicken if needed, then season to taste with salt, pepper, and the piquant table sauce.

Jachtschotel
(hunter's dish)

3 onions	salt and pepper
⅛ cup fat for frying	1 sour apple
¾ pound cooked meat, minced	4 potatoes, mashed
1 cup beef bouillon stock	bread crumbs
pinch of ground cloves	1 tablespoon butter

Slice onions and saute in fat until light brown. Add minced meat, stock, seasonings, peeled and chopped apple, and potatoes. Simmer gently for 15 to 30 minutes. Pour mixture into a greased ovenproof dish. Smooth out the surface and sprinkle with bread crumbs, dot with butter, and brown in 450 degree oven for 10 minutes. Yield: 3 servings.

Uien met Aardappelen, Rijst en Versche Worst
(onions with potatoes, rice, and sausage)

4 potatoes	½ pound sausage
2 onions	vinegar
¾ cup rice	salt

Peel potatoes, cover with water and bring to a boil. Chop onions and add to potatoes. Wash rice thoroughly and add to potatoes and onions. Add more water if necessary. Bring to a boil, add sausage and simmer for 30 minutes or until rice is tender. Place sausages on a hot plate and arrange vegetables and rice around them. Sprinkle with vinegar and salt to taste.

Stoofsla Kool
(cabbage stuffed with meat)

1 cabbage	¼ teaspoon nutmeg
6 ounces ground pork	¼ cup bread crumbs
6 ounces ground veal	beef bouillon stock
salt and pepper	butter or margarine

Remove outer leaves from cabbage and blanch them in boiling

water for 10 minutes, then drain well. Mix together ground pork and veal, salt, pepper, and nutmeg, add bread crumbs and mix a little beef bouillon stock with the filling. Arrange some of cabbage leaves on a clean cloth, then cover with a layer of filling, put another layer of cabbage atop this, and repeat until all meat is used. Gather cloth together, tie up and boil in salted water for 1½ hours. Remove stuffed cabbage leaves from the cloth, put into an ovenproof dish, top generously with pats of butter, and brown in 450 degree oven. Yield: 4 servings.

Pastries

Krenten Bollen
(currant rolls)

5 cups flour
1 teaspoon salt
¾ ounce yeast
⅛ cup sugar
2 tablespoons warm milk
1 egg

1 cup milk
6 tablespoons butter
1 cup currants
1 2-ounce chopped candied
   lemon peel

Sift flour and salt into a bowl and keep warm. Cream yeast with sugar and add 2 tablespoons warm milk. Make a well in the flour and pour in the yeast. Beat the egg, add milk and butter and blend thoroughly. Add this to the flour, mix well, and knead for 10 minutes. Add fruits and knead again. Cover with a damp cloth and place in warm place for 1 hour to rise. Divide into 16 small balls, knead into rounds, and place on a greased baking sheet. Set in warm place for 15 minutes, then bake in 450 degree oven for 20 minutes. Serve cold with butter.

Ontbijkoek
(breakfast cake)

8 eggs, separated
2¾ cups brown sugar
3 cups flour
1 teaspoon baking soda

2 tablespoons candied lemon
   peel, minced
4 tablespoons candied citron,
   minced

1 teaspoon cinnamon
1½ teaspoons ground cloves
½ teaspoon nutmeg

½ cup almonds, coarsely ground

Beat egg yolks until thick and lemon colored. Slowly add sugar and beat for 5 minutes. Sift the flour, baking soda, cinnamon, cloves, and nutmeg together and add slowly to the egg mixture. Add lemon peel, citron, and almonds and mix well. Fold in the stiffly beaten egg whites. Pour mixture into a well-greased pan and bake at 350 degrees for about 40 minutes.

Oliebollen
(Dutch doughnuts)

1½ cakes yeast
1½ cups milk
3 cups all-purpose flour
2 eggs
2 tablespoons sugar
2 tablespoons raisins

1 tablespoon chopped candied orange peel
½ teaspoon grated lemon rind
1 teaspoon salt
oil for frying
confectioners' sugar

Dissolve yeast in deep bowl in 3 tablespoons lukewarm milk. Put flour in another bowl. With a wooden spoon stir in the eggs, one at a time. Slowly add remaining milk. Stir until smooth. Add sugar, raisins, orange peel, grated lemon rind. Add this mixture to the yeast. Cover with a cloth and set to rise for about 1½ hours. Add the salt. Fry in deep oil, dropping in a tablespoon of the dough at a time. Drain on paper towels. Sprinkle with confectioners' sugar.

4

Scandinavia

Sweden, Denmark, Norway, Finland

Think of Scandinavia and most people think of *smorgasbord,* a long banquet table groaning under the weight of salads, meats, fish, and appetizers of great variety. Next to Swedish meat balls, *smorgasbord* has reached the broadest popularity outside of the four lands of the Midnight Sun (so called because in winter, the sun does not rise above the horizon). The worldwide popularity of *smorgasbord* is justified, for the sandwich table reflects the hearty, rich food of the Scandinavians.

Though the four countries are closely tied to each other geographically, they are distinctly different in nuances of culture, personality, and food. You know when you have crossed a border from one Scandinavian country to another, by its people and their national dishes.

Many of the dishes are similar, yet each country has its own special way of preparing or flavoring them, and most all have different names. *Smorgasbord* to the Swedes is *smorrebrod* to the Danes, *kold bord* to the Norwegians, and *voileipapoyta* to the Finns.

While the Swedes, Danes, and Norwegians are more closely tied to each other historically and culturally, the Finns belong to a completely different family of languages. All share one thing in common: their love of good food. Basically it is the meat and potatoes variety which appeals to most Americans, yet there are strong influences from both the delicate art of French cookery and the more hearty German fare.

Scandinavian food is richer than American food because of the cold climate of the North which demands that more fats be eaten. There are opulent sauces both hot and cold, thickened with eggs and sweet or sour cream. Fish is usually bought alive and prepared with great care. Potatoes, liked best boiled and steamed dry, are eaten by many at every meal. Salads and vegetables are virtually ignored, except for pickled cucumbers and pickled beets, which the people love.

Scandinavian desserts are among the most elaborate anywhere, from fresh fruit jellies to soufflés, many-tiered cream cakes, chocolate rolls, coffee cakes, and meringue tortes filled with jam. Almonds are served up every imaginable way and mountains of whipped cream are added to many delicious desserts. The berries of the far north countries are legend, especially arctic strawberries and cloudberries, which look like big yellow blackberries. Served under a cloud of whipped cream, you may forget that the Scandinavians are known primarily for their *smorgasbord*.

The people of Scandinavia are known to be among the world's most friendly, courteous, and honest. They enjoy their food and drink and like nothing better than to get together to talk and eat, take a little aquavit and beer, coffee and wines, listen to some music, and dance the night through.

The night is long in Scandinavia. What better way to enjoy the winter evening and wait for the next sun than to gather around a table, lift a glass, toast each other with "Skål!" and feast. In the old countries of the midnight sun, this is the joy of living.

Chapter 13

SWEDEN

Sweden is the largest, richest, most industrialized, and most welfare-conscious of the Scandinavian countries, but what most people like most about it are its beautiful, tall, blonde-haired, blue-eyed women and handsome, tall, blond-haired, blue-eyed men.

The sun doesn't shine in winter, but in summer the land is green and warm and bikinis are plentiful as flowers in the brilliant pastures. Any people with a Viking heritage is bound to get through a cold winter.

The Swedes are descendants of the Vikings who roamed the world and conquered Russia in the ninth century, penetrated as far as Constantinople where they protected the Byzantine Empire, saved the Protestant Reformation by entering the Thirty Years' War, drove out their enemies the Danes by capturing Copenhagen after a dramatic march across the ice from Jutland to Zealand, and showed the western world their military might in battle with their European neighbors during the eighteenth century.

All that swordplay and intrigue seemed to be enough for the Swedes afterward because for the last century and a half, they have pursued a policy of neutrality, despite provocation during both world wars.

At the turn of the present century, with old-fashioned farm methods that resulted in crop failure and famine, Swedes at the rate of 1,000 a week left their homeland and emigrated, most of them to America. The children and grandchildren of the emigrees hold their loyalty to the Old Country dearly and carry on their culture and traditions in states such as Minnesota and Wisconsin, whose geography and weather are similar to that of Scandinavia.

About eight million Swedes live today in a country larger than California that stretches from the sunny, fertile plains of the south to the northern home of the Lapps, who still herd reindeer as they did thousands of years ago, and on to the frozen tundra of the Arctic Circle. The Swedes are a remarkably homogeneous people, nearly pure Nordic. They are friendly, well-dressed, attractive people but more serious than the Danes, a bit heavier and slower than the Norwegians. Politically neutral, they are outspoken on everything from politics, art, and religion to the shortcomings of their neighboring countries and the rest of the world. They feel strongly that they have it good and enjoy telling you so.

Swedes refer to their country as a progressive democracy, with compulsory health, accident, unemployment insurance and old age retirement benefits which have provided them with complete social security. But with "too much equality" in pay and privileges, a young people questioning the ultimate benefits of being "over-socialized," and rising affluence, Sweden is not the tranquil paradise it might appear to be. Like the rest of the world, it is facing change.

Swedish women are among the most emancipated in Europe, living up to the beauty and independence we have come to admire in Greta Garbo and Ingrid Bergman. While Sweden has not exported an actor of similar stripe or stature, the male Swede we see in America fully lives up to what we expect the modern son of a Viking to be.

Stockholm is to Sweden as Paris is to France. It is the focal place of a nation, cosmopolitan and beautiful, with little competition from its sister cities. There is great prosperity, modern architecture blending with a quaint medieval Old Town.

A five-block glass-and-concrete "New Manhattan" business complex has terraced gardens among the skyscrapers to soften the twentieth century as it blends in with shops, restaurants, and relics of its ancient past.

Swedes are hearty eaters but you'll seldom see a Swede who has drunk too much. Sober is the word for Sweden, though of course you'll see Swedes raise their glass. They like their food well-flavored. Anchovies are popular and dill is the national food plant. Cardamom and other spices are used abundantly in baking.

Swedes also like their foods sweetened, so you find sugar used in what many Americans would usually consider nonsweet dishes.

Smorgasbord, the table of sandwiches and appetizers, is not normally found in Swedish homes or restaurants, except at holiday times. But four or five appetizers are usually served, which is still far more than most Americans enjoy at a meal. Herring is another national dish and comes in various forms. Smoked salmon, homemade liver pâté, and cheese are other typical smorgasbord treats.

Nourishing soups including fruit soups both hot and cold are in great number. Fish and seafood, especially salmon, fresh-water pike, and lobster are plentiful. If you're very lucky, you'll be invited to a boiled crayfish party. Crayfish is a national passion.

Meat is eaten at more everyday meals in Sweden than elsewhere in Scandinavia. Pork, veal, and lamb, boiled, pot-roasted, and minced into meatballs are the favorites, served with rich cream gravies.

Pastries are elaborate and usually made with almonds and served with heaps of whipped cream.

At the Berns Salonger, a hundred-year-old Stockholm restaurant that retains its antique atmosphere, the Oxrulader, a Swedish braised beef roll with sour cream gravy, and crown cake made from powdered sugar, eggs, butter, grated potatoes, and ground almonds and generally served with lemon cream will make you think of perfection. Just as will the attractive blonde young couple at the next candlelit table. Ah, to be in Sweden in the springtime.

Appetizers

Smorgasbord
(sandwich-appetizer table)

Many of the following dishes served as Swedish *smorgasbord* are typical of the other Scandinavian countries as well. Some are suitable as main dishes for lunch or dinner.

Dishes on a Tray for a Party

Stuffed celery
Pickled or smoked salmon
Pickled or smoked herring
Scandinavian bread

Liverwurst
Stuffed eggs
Smoked eel

Tidbits made of anchovies, chicken livers, sardines, and other delicacies fried in deep, hot fat.

Dishes for the Buffet or Smorgasbord Table

Any of above appetizers
Herring roe
Shrimp
Shrimp salad
Stuffed cabbage
Mixed green salads
Stuffed vegetables
Pork sausages
Mushrooms

Cheese
Creamed oysters
Crawfish
Meat balls
Ham
Fruit salads
Beef and potato hash
Chicken livers
Potatoes au gratin

Inlagt Sill
(herrings in vinegar)

2 salt herrings
3 to 4 tablespoons vinegar
1½ tablespoons sugar

½ teaspoon white pepper
2 tablespoons chopped onions

Soak herrings in cold water for 12 hours, dry them, and remove skin and bones. Cut into narrow strips and arrange in a dish. Mix vinegar with sugar and pepper and pour over the fish. Garnish with chopped onion. Yield: 6 servings.

Soups

Blandad Fruktsoppa
(cold fruit soup)

1 pound assorted dried fruit	2 apples
(other than prunes)	1 cinnamon stick or 2
½ pound prunes	teaspoons cinnamon
¾ cups sugar	2 tablespoons cornstarch

Wash the dried fruit and prunes thoroughly. Place in a saucepan with 8 cups water and sugar. Soak overnight. Peel and core apples. Cut into eighths. Leaving dried fruit in same water in which it was soaked, place the saucepan over medium heat. Add apples and cinnamon. Cook over medium heat for 45 minutes or until fruit is very soft. Remove fruit and force through a sieve, discarding any pits and cinnamon stick, if used. Return fruit pulp to soup and continue over medium heat. Combine cornstarch with 2 tablespoons cold water in a cup and stir until smooth. Gradually add to soup, stirring constantly until boiling point is reached. Continue cooking for 5 minutes. Chill and serve ice cold. Yield: 4 servings.

Arter ock Flaok
(pea soup with boiled pickled pork)

Put 1 cup yellow peas, previously soaked for 12 hours, in 4 quarts of cold water, with a pinch of soda. Bring to a boil and add 1 pound of pickled pork. Simmer for 3 hours until thick. The meat is sliced and eaten with pea soup or puree. Yield: 6 to 8 servings.

Salads

Sillsalad
(herring salad)

1½ pounds salt herrings
2 cups cold roast meat
2⅓ cups cold boiled potatoes
2 cups cold boiled meat
2 cups cooked beets
1 pickled cucumber
2 raw apples

4–6 tablespoons vinegar
pinch of sugar
pinch of white pepper
cream
beet juice
2 hard-boiled eggs

Cut ingredients into small pieces and mix with vinegar and sugar. Presoak herrings for 12 hours and skin and bone them before chopping. Serve salad with cream, mixed with a little beet juice to color. Garnish with hard boiled eggs cut in wedges. Yield: 4 servings.

Sallad Jonas
(seafood salad)

2 boiled lobsters
1 pound boiled shrimp
12 mussels (optional)
2 green onions, chopped
3 tomatoes, cubed
1 tablespoon prepared mustard

¾ cup olive oil
¼ cup vinegar
1 teaspoon salt
⅛ teaspoon pepper
1 head lettuce, shredded

Remove lobster meat from shells and cut into large pieces. Peel shrimp and cut each into four pieces. Combine lobster meat, shrimp, mussels, onions, and tomatoes. Mix well. In a bowl mix mustard and olive oil until smooth. Add vinegar, 2 tablespoons water, salt, pepper, and beat until blended. Pour over seafood mixture and mix carefully. Chill for 30 minutes. Arrange mounds of seafood mixture on individual plates and cover with shredded lettuce. Yield: 4 to 6 servings.

Vegetables

Blomkal med Agg
(Swedish cauliflower with egg sauce)

1 large cauliflower
¼ cup butter
⅔ cup minced onion
2 tablespoons fine dried bread
  crumbs

2 hard-boiled eggs, chopped
¼ cup minced parsley or dill
1 teaspoon salt
¼ teaspoon pepper

Boil cauliflower whole or broken into flowerets in salted water until soft but not mushy. While it is cooking, make the sauce. Melt butter in skillet and cook onion in it until soft and golden. Stir in bread crumbs, eggs, parsley or dill, and salt and pepper. Toss lightly until blended. Place cauliflower in serving dish and pour sauce over it.

Ugnstekt Svamp
(baked mushrooms)

12 large mushrooms
¼ cup butter
1 tomato, skinned and
  chopped
½ cup chopped cooked
  chicken

2 hard-boiled eggs, chopped
½ teaspoon salt
½ teaspoon white pepper
2 to 3 tablespoons cream or
  chicken stock

Wash mushrooms, separate caps from stems, and chop the stems. Cook stems in a little butter until tender. Add tomato, chicken, chopped eggs, and seasonings. Moisten with stock or cream and cook 2 or 3 minutes. Melt the remainder of the butter, dip mushroom caps in it, and fill with the mixture. Place filled mushroom caps in a buttered baking dish. Bake in 425 degree oven about 10 minutes, longer if mushroom caps are thick. Yield: 4 or more servings as an entree, 12 on the *smorgasbord*.

Potatoes, Dumplings

Skansk Potatis
(Swedish creamed potatoes)

6 tablespoons butter
2 medium onions, sliced thin
6 cups peeled, diced raw
   potatoes
1½ teaspoon salt

¼ teaspoon white pepper
1 cup light cream
3 tablespoons minced parsley
   or fresh dill

Melt 2 tablespoons butter in skillet and cook onions until soft and golden. Transfer onions to casserole. Melt remaining butter and saute potatoes in it until golden brown and half cooked. Transfer potatoes to casserole. Season with salt and pepper and mix thoroughly with onions. Add cream. Simmer covered over low heat until potatoes are done, about 15 minutes. Cream should be absorbed, and the potatoes creamy. Stir occasionally and check for dryness; add more cream if necessary. Before serving, sprinkle with parsley or dill. Yield: 6 servings.

Potatisuffle
(potato soufflé)

4 cups mashed potatoes
¼ cup butter
2 egg yolks
1 tablespoon chopped parsley
½ to 1 teaspoon salt
¼ teaspoon white pepper

1 tablespoon chopped pimento
1 tablespoon chopped or sliced
   blanched almonds
2 tablespoons buttered bread
   crumbs

Mix 3 cups of potatoes with butter, beaten egg yolks, and all ingredients except the crumbs. Pour into a buttered baking dish. Decorate the top with remaining potatoes put on as a garnish, using a pastry tube. Sprinkle the top with buttered crumbs. Brown in a 450 degree oven. Serve with roast, fish, or fowl. Yield: 6 servings.

Fish

Fiskfars
(mousse of fish)

2½ pounds fresh haddock
1¼ cups butter
4 eggs, separated
½ cup cream
½ cup flour

1 tablespoon salt
½ teaspoon pepper
a little sugar
bread crumbs

Wash and dry fish and remove skin and bones. Put fish and butter through grinder three times, then pound in a mortar to a smooth, creamy paste. Mix yolks of egg in a bowl with half the cream, adding flour, salt, pepper, and sugar. Mix in alternately fish mixture and cream, and work for about 1 hour. Add the stiffly beaten whites of egg and pour mixture into buttered pie dish and sprinkle with bread crumbs. Pie dish should be placed over double boiler and mixture steamed for about 1 hour. Served with lobster or mushroom sauce (see below).

Hummer Sas
(lobster sauce)

1 tablespoon butter
2 tablespoons flour
fish stock or milk

salt and pepper
cooked lobster meat
yolk of 1 egg

Melt butter in small saucepan, stir in flour without browning, and add hot fish stock or milk gradually, stirring constantly. Season with salt and pepper, add chopped lobster and yolk of egg previously mixed with a few tablespoons of the warm sauce. Simmer a few minutes without boiling.

Svamp Sas
(mushroom sauce)

Follow the directions for lobster sauce, but use chopped cooked mushrooms instead of lobster and water in which mushrooms were boiled instead of fish stock.

Kräftor
(crayfish)

(Crayfish are not shrimp. They resemble lobsters, but are much smaller. They are a national food of Sweden and the star attraction at parties in August, crayfish season, downed with plenty of aquavit and beer. Like lobster, crayfish should be alive before boiling.)

40 to 50 crayfish
5 tablespoons salt

1 bunch fresh dill, tied
together

Wash crayfish in fresh water. Pull off tiny wing in center of the tail. Combine 4 quarts water, salt, and dill. Bring to a boil and boil 5 minutes. Place 10 crayfish into boiling water. Bring water again to a rapid boil and add next 10 crayfish. Repeat with remaining crayfish. Simmer, covered, about 5 minutes. Remove from heat. Cool in stock and leave standing for 1 to 2 hours. Drain, arrange on platter, and garnish with dill sprigs. Yield: 5 to 6 servings.

Meat

Köttbullar
(meat balls)

½ pound ground beef
¼ pound ground veal
½ cup minced pork
2 eggs
3 cups milk

½ cup bread crumbs
2 tablespoons finely chopped
onion
salt and pepper
4 tablespoons butter

Put meat three times through a grinder. Beat eggs with milk, add bread crumbs, and let them soak until they swell. Saute chopped onions to a golden brown in 2 tablespoons butter. Mix meat with bread crumbs, work well together, add onion, season with salt and pepper. Shape into small balls and fry in 2 tablespoons butter. When brown, add 1 cup of boiling water and simmer about 15 minutes. Yield: 6 servings.

Dillkött pa Lamm
(boiled lamb in dill sauce)

Boil 3 pounds neck of lamb in 2 quarts of salted water with a few dill stalks. Cover saucepan and simmer for 2 hours. When done, divide into large pieces and serve with dill sauce (see below).

Dill-Sas
(dill sauce)

Mix 1 tablespoon hot butter with 2 tablespoons flour, without browning, and add gradually 1 pint of hot stock, stirring until smooth. Season with 2 tablespoons of dill-salt or fresh dill, 1½ tablespoons vinegar, 2 teaspoons sugar, and a little salt. Stir all well and finally add 1 egg yolk, previously mixed with a little of the sauce.

Oxrulader
(Swedish braised beef roll)

2 pounds round steak, cut ¼ inch thick	8 slices bacon, ¼ inch thick
¼ teaspoon pepper	flour
2 teaspoons prepared mustard	3 tablespoons butter
½ cup minced parsley	½ cup hot beef bouillon
	¼ cup sour cream

Pound meat as thin as possible without breaking it. Cut into 8 strips about 4 inches long and 2 inches wide. Season on one side with pepper and spread thinly with mustard and parsley. Place one slice of bacon on the mustard side of each strip of meat. Roll up and secure rolls with toothpicks or small skewers. Coat rolls with flour. Heat butter in heavy skillet. Brown beef rolls on all sides. Add hot beef bouillon. Simmer, covered, over low heat 45 minutes to 1 hour, or until meat is tender. Place beef rolls in hot serving dish and keep hot. Add sour cream to pan juices, scraping bottom of pan and stirring constantly. Pour over beef rolls and serve with any kind of potatoes and a green vegetable. Yield: 4 servings.

Slottsstek
(Swedish royal pot roast)

4 pounds beef, chuck or round
2 teaspoons salt
1 teaspoon allspice
½ teaspoon pepper
3 tablespoons butter
3 tablespoons brandy or
   whiskey

3 minced anchovy fillets
2 tablespoons white vinegar
⅓ cup hot bouillon
2 medium onions, sliced
2 bay leaves
2 tablespoons molasses

Rub meat with salt, allspice, and pepper. Heat butter and brown meat in it on all sides. Pour brandy or whisky over hot meat and flame. Add all other ingredients and blend. Simmer covered over very low heat about 2 hours, or until meat is tender. Remove meat to hot serving platter and keep hot. Make gravy (see below). Slice meat and surround with little mounds of buttered peas, carrots, and cauliflower buds, and decorate with tomato and cucumber slices and parsley. Pour a little gravy over the meat and serve the rest of the gravy separately. Yield: 4 to 6 servings.

Gravy

Make gravy by adding water or red wine to pan drippings, season with salt and pepper. Flavor with ¼ teaspoon anchovy paste and fold in 1 cup heavy cream, whipped.

Biff à la Lindstrom
(beef hamburgers Lindstrom)

¾ pound ground beef
1 finely chopped onion
1 teaspoon finely chopped
   parsley
¼ cup sour cream
¾ cup mashed potatoes

½ cup diced pickled beets
2 tablespoons chopped capers
salt and pepper
2 egg yolks
fat for frying

Mix very finely ground meat with chopped onion, parsley, and sour cream. Add potato, beet, capers, salt, pepper, and then bind with beaten egg yolks. Form into flat cakes about ½ inch thick and fry in smoking-hot fat until both sides are brown and crisp. Serve with fried potatoes or salad or place on toast and top with a fried egg. Yield: 3 servings.

Pastries, Desserts

Plattar
(Swedish pancakes)

2½ cups flour
½ teaspoon salt
2 eggs

4 cups milk
2 tablespoons melted butter

To make a pancake batter, mix flour and salt in a bowl, add eggs, previously beaten with 2 cups milk. When mixture is smooth, add 2 tablespoons melted butter and remaining milk. Let mixture stand 1 hour. Beat again just before using. Heat pancake skillet, put a little butter on it, and make pancakes in the usual manner.

Limpa

1 package dry yeast
1 cup milk, scalded
2 tablespoons shortening
2 teaspoons caraway seed
1 tablespoon salt

¼ cup molasses
3 cups rye flour
1 tablespoon grated orange
    rind
3½ cups sifted flour

Dissolve yeast in 2 tablespoons lukewarm water. Combine milk, shortening, caraway seed, salt, molasses, and 1 cup water; cool to lukewarm. Add yeast mixture, rye flour, and orange rind; beat well. Gradually stir white flour to make stiff dough. Knead on floured board. Place in lightly greased bowl. Cover; let rise in warm place for 1½ hours or until doubled. Knead on floured board. Divide in half; shape into balls. Let rise for 10 minutes. Shape into loaves. Let rise until doubled. Bake at 400 degrees for 10 minutes. Reduce heat to 375 degrees and continue baking for 40 minutes. Yield: 2 loaves.

Kringle

2 cups flour
½ lb. butter

1 teaspoon almond extract
3 eggs

Mix 1 cup flour, ¼ pound butter, and 1 tablespoon water as for a pie crust. Pat into two 8 × 10-inch rectangles on ungreased cookie sheet. Bring 1 cup water and ¼ pound butter to a boil. Add almond extract and 1 cup flour; mix well. Add eggs, one at a time, mixing well after each addition. Spread over crust. Bake at 375 degrees for 45 minutes. The top layer will puff somewhat. Dust while warm with powdered sugar. Yield: 8–10 servings.

Kronans Kaka
(crown cake)

7 tablespoons butter
1¾ cups powdered sugar
3 eggs, separated

2 tablespoons grated potatoes
1½ cups ground almonds

Cream butter and sugar with 3 egg yolks, add grated potatoes, working mixture for 30 minutes. Add ground almonds and mix thoroughly. Finally, add whites of eggs, beaten to a stiff froth. Pour mixture into buttered cake pan, sprinkled with bread crumbs, and bake in 325 degree oven about 45 minutes. Let stand for 15 minutes before turning out. Serve with lemon cream (see below).

Citron-Kram
(lemon cream)

1 cup sugar
½ cup white wine
grated lemon rind

juice of 1 lemon
6 egg yolks

Mix sugar, wine, grated lemon rind, lemon juice, egg yolks and ½ cup water in a saucepan. Simmer, stirring continuously, until mixture begins to thicken. Remove from heat and continue stirring until lemon cream is cool.

Drinks

Swedish Glögg

3 whole cardamom seeds
8 whole cloves
1 stick cinnamon
1 4-inch strip orange rind
   (yellow part only)
¼ cup blanched almonds

½ cup golden raisins
1 bottle Bordeaux wine
1 bottle port wine
½ bottle cognac
sugar to taste

Tie cardamom seeds, cloves, cinnamon and orange rind in a cheesecloth bag. Place in 1⅓ cups water and bring to a boil. Simmer, covered, 10 minutes. Add almonds and raisins and simmer 10 more minutes. Add Bordeaux wine, port wine, and cognac and bring to a quick boil. Remove from heat immediately. Cool and store, covered, overnight. At serving time, remove spice bag. Heat *glogg* but do not boil. Add sugar to taste. Serve in heated mugs or glasses, with a few almonds and raisins in each glass.

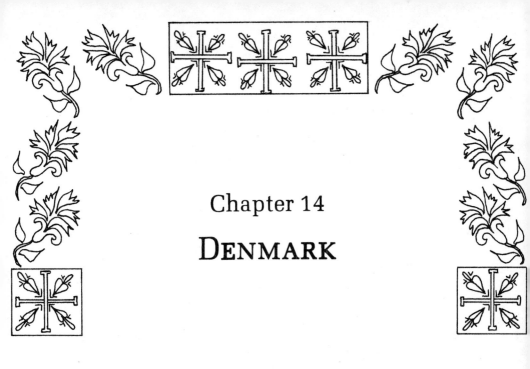

Chapter 14

DENMARK

Even in Elsinore, one of Denmark's oldest towns and the home of Shakespeare's Prince Hamlet, where you might expect to find at least one melancholy Dane, you will be happily disappointed. Danes throughout their country, one of the smallest and most popular in Europe, are a happy breed, and their gaiety is infectious.

Well-travelled tourists contend that Danish women are even more beautiful than Swedish, and that Danish men are the handsomest in Europe. They love good food, drink, dance, are cosmopolitan, carefree, thrifty, and prosperous. With all that and good looks too, why should they be melancholy!

The Danes are also among Europe's oldest-settled people. Evidence has been found that Stone Age hunters and fishermen moved to the north country after the Ice Age melted. Danes, a closely-knit people, have been good farmers since 2,500 B.C., so famine did not force them to leave their homeland.

Vikings from Denmark held power over Europe in A.D. 800 and even conquered England. After some centuries of rivalry with their neighboring Scandinavian countries, the Danes entered the twentieth century perhaps better prepared for modern times than other European nations, and this may be largely attributed to their sense of humor. Nothing seems to get a Dane down.

Denmark also is one of the most prosperous of Scandinavian

countries, and its social welfare programs are among the most advanced anywhere. Physically, there are no mountains or valleys, but there are magnificent meadows of flowers, ancient castles high on hilltops, quaint picture-postcard villages with medieval houses and inns, pastel-colored thatched cottages, and sparkling lakes and brooks amid cool, green forests. Nearly surrounded by the North Sea and the Baltic, Denmark points its way northward into the Skagerrak and Kattegat, bold and charming names for the straights leading to the coast of Sweden and the Norway fiords.

There is plenty of work to do in the summer and long, hard winter nights to endure. Danes make the best of it by having a good time. High on the list of ways to do this is to enjoy a good meal. Danes are known to be among Europe's biggest eaters, though they're active enough not to let it show.

Good food can be found throughout Denmark, in Dyrehaven with its summer resorts, Bellevue with its beaches and luxurious Strandhotel, Elsinore and Kronborg Castle, the Renaissance castles of Frederiksborg and Fredensborg, Traelleborg and its ten-century-old Viking fortress, the idyllic southland of Zealand, Funen and its capital of Odense, where Hans Christian Andersen was born, and Jutland, the only part of Denmark attached to the continent. But once you've eaten in Copenhagen, you may not care to leave.

Copenhagen, pronounced "hagen" with a long "a," is over eight centuries old and at the same time among the newest cities anywhere. It is a charming, gracious capital with enough to fascinate the most discriminating searcher after castles, palaces, museums, Viking lore, and other places historic and cultural.

Danes like to eat. Meals are hearty but on the bland side, except for curry used mildly, and pickled herrings and other fish. But there is a national passion for horseradish and mustard.

Denmark is a major dairy country, so milk, sweet butter, golden cream, and cheese are plentiful. Milk is used extensively in cooking, especially in soups and sauces. Danish hams, of course, are world-famous.

Danish cooking is strongly influenced by French, because in centuries past, Danes may have been on the throne in Denmark's castles, but French cooks worked in the castle kitchens. Still, the

Danes did not develop a French stomach for rich foods. Danish food is substantial and even unusual because of contrasting ingredients. Beef stews are made with bacon curls, kidneys with sausage; chicken may be boiled with shrimp and asparagus; and pork tenderloin will be served with prunes. Odd, you might say. But good.

Danes love sauces and potatoes, their favorite sauce being brown sauce, made plain with onions or fancy with Madeira. White sauce is enriched with whipped cream and flavored with mustard and horseradish.

The Danes love potatoes so much that they have them at every meal and often have more than one kind, such as boiled and browned, or browned and fried. But boiled potatoes are the favorite. And if you wonder why Danes love potatoes so, it's because their potatoes taste so much better than ours. They are more flavorful and are grown in greater variety than we are familiar with.

In Copenhagen, as elsewhere in Denmark, you don't just eat when you go to a restaurant. At Stephan a Porta, a waiter hands you the morning paper with your coffee and Danish pastry. In Oskar Davidsen's Sopavillonen, you'll meet dozens of happy diners as you make your way around the four-foot-long smorrebrod with over 200 varieties of open-faced sandwiches piled high with meat or fish garnished with eggs, pickled or fresh vegetables, or salads. Art lovers will talk paintings with you at the Glyptoteket across from the museum of that name. Journalists and artists will be found at the Bronnum having chestnuts in rum or eating Brunswick cookies and sipping coffee.

Copenhagen's favorite sidewalk cafe for dining is the Frascati, on the town hall square, where you can enjoy Chartreuse ragout and beer bread while watching a delightful passing parade of people walking or biking.

Perhaps the most fun of all is dining in Tivoli Gardens, Copenhagen's fairyland of summer excitement and carnival. A dinner of Danish ham with lemon sauce followed by a frozen cream with fresh strawberries and pineapple and you're ready for a ride on the double ferris-wheel. Tivoli and Copenhagen does that to you.

Appetizers

Smörrebröd
(open-faced sandwiches)

The Danish sandwich is an appetizer or a meal in itself, served on a large slice of thickly buttered rye bread. Stack the bread with slices of cold meat (Danes love cold roast veal), then slices of cucumber or a green salad. Variations are a whole fillet of sole topped with a thick layer of Russian salad or a liberal helping of smoked salmon covered with a thick layer of scrambled eggs.

Sild i Flode Melchior
(herring in cream Melchior)

1 whole salt herring or 1 jar
   herring fillets
½ cup sour cream
½ teaspoon sugar
1 tablespoon minced onion

1 tablespoon minced parsley
½ teaspoon salt
1 tablespoon vinegar or lemon
   juice

If whole salt herring is used, soak it overnight in cold water. Drain, remove the head, tail, skin, and bones and cut into 1-inch pieces. If jarred herring are used, drain them and cut into 1-inch pieces. Mix all ingredients together. (Reserve enough sour cream for topping or garnish.) Arrange drained herring on a plate and top with sour cream. Yield: 6 servings. (This dish was named after the famous Danish opera star, Lauritz Melchior.)

Soups

Kraasesuppe
(giblet soup)

giblets (from 1 or more
   chickens)
salt
3 carrots, sliced
2 stalks celery, diced

2 leeks, cut up
3 apples, sliced
6 prunes
2 teaspoons sugar
1 tablespoon vinegar

Clean giblets thoroughly and put in saucepan with enough cold water to cover. Season with salt to taste. Bring gradually to a boil, skim, and simmer 30 minutes, then add carrots, celery, leeks, apples, and prunes (previously soaked). Simmer until vegetables and fruit are tender, add sugar and vinegar and serve with flour dumplings (see index).

Ollebrod
(beer and bread soup)

½ pound whole wheat bread	¼ teaspoon salt
½ pound pumpernickel bread	1-inch stick cinnamon
4½ cups dark beer or ale	¼ lemon, peel only
6 tablespoons sugar	

Pour 4½ cups water over both breads and let stand overnight in covered pot. When ready to make the soup, set it on low heat and cook covered, stirring frequently, until it forms a thick paste. Stir in the beer, sugar, salt, and add the cinnamon and grated lemon peel. Let it come to boiling, then boil for a few minutes. Serve topped with spoonful of chilled cream or whipped cream on each bowlful.

Salads

Kjød Salat
(meat salad)

2 cups cooked lamb, veal or beef	*Dressing:*
10 boned and cleaned anchovies	¼ teaspoon dry mustard
	¼ teaspoon pepper
6–8 pickled onions, chopped	½ teaspoon salt
crisp lettuce leaves or romaine leaves	1 tablespoon vinegar
	3 tablespoons tomato puree
	3 tablespoons olive oil
	1 teaspoon chopped parsley

Cut meat in small cubes. Cut anchovy fillets in small pieces. Chop the onions. Combine all and chill. Mix the dressing: mix dry ingredients, add vinegar and tomato puree, stir well. Add 1 tablespoon of oil and beat for 1 minute. Add parsley and remaining oil and beat again 1 minute. Mix with the salad. Serve on crisp lettuce. Yield: 4 servings.

Grøn Salat med Ansjos Sovs
(Green salad with anchovy dressing)

1 small head lettuce
1 small bunch watercress
6 radishes, sliced
1 small bunch endive
6 spring onions, sliced
boiled ham or chicken,
    optional

Dressing:
⅓ cup whipping cream
⅓ cup mayonnaise
3 tablespoons anchovy paste
3 tablespoons wine vinegar or
    tarragon vinegar
1 tablespoon finely cut chives
1 tablespoon chopped parsley

Whip cream stiff. Fold in mayonnaise and anchovy paste. Add vinegar, chives, and parsley and let stand a few hours. Just before serving, pour dressing over greens and toss lightly until greens are well-coated with dressing. You may add boiled ham or chicken cut in thin slivers, or sprinkle them on top. Yield: 6 servings.

Vegetables

Voksbønner i Tomatsauce
(wax beans in tomato sauce)

1 pound wax or green beans
¼ cup butter
¼ cup flour
3 cups broth or bouillon

½ teaspoon salt
¼ teaspoon pepper
1 teaspoon sugar
½ cup tomato puree

Trim ends from beans, rinse, and cook in salted water until tender. Melt butter, add flour and stir until smooth. Add broth or bouillon, stirring constantly, and cook until thickened and smooth. If no broth or bouillon is available, use water in which beans were cooked. Add salt, pepper, sugar, and tomato puree. Drain beans and pour sauce over them, or add beans to the sauce just before serving. Yield: 4 servings.

Grönlangkaal
(stewed cabbage)

Remove outer leaves of cabbage and the coarse ribs. Blanch in salted water for 20 minutes. Drain thoroughly and mince the cabbage. Melt 2 tablespoons butter in a saucepan, stir in 2 tablespoons flour and add ⅛ cup hot milk gradually. When it is thick as cream, put in minced cabbage, season with salt and pepper, and simmer 20 minutes. Served with small potatoes browned in butter and 1 teaspoon sugar. Yield: 4 servings.

Perleløge
(pearl onions)

1 pound small white onions   ¼ cup sugar or brown sugar
2½ cups vinegar

Wash the onions; cover with boiling water and boil 5 minutes. Drain. Cover with cold water, drain again, then peel the onions. Cover with the vinegar and sugar and boil 5 minutes. Put onions in a jar or crock, pour hot vinegar over them. Serve with roasts as garnish on the platter. Yield: 4 servings.

Dumplings, Potatoes

Melboller
(flour dumplings)

4 tablespoons butter   1 tablespoon sugar
¾ cup flour   ½ teaspoon salt
2 eggs

Melt butter and add the flour, stirring continuously. Add 1 cup water and stir over a rapid fire until mixture is easily detached from sides of the pan and from a spoon. Remove saucepan from heat and work mixture for 10 minutes. Add 1 egg and work well another 10 minutes. Mix in the other egg and lastly stir in the sugar and salt. Drop one teaspoon of the dough at a time into boiling water and poach until the dumplings rise to the surface. Put in a strainer and pour cold water over them.

Brunede Kartofler
(sugar-browned potatoes)

12 small new potatoes	2 tablespoons butter
1 teaspoon salt	3 tablespoons sugar

Cook potatoes in boiling salted water until tender. Drain and peel. Melt butter in skillet. When hot, stir in sugar. Cook, stirring constantly, until sugar is browned. Add boiled potatoes and cook until browned on all sides, shaking skillet frequently. Do not scorch. Sprinkle with salt and serve with meats, fowl, ham, or as part of a vegetable platter. Yield: 6 servings.

Kartoffelmos med Aebler
(potato and apple puree)

½ cup butter	2 cups thick unsweetened
2 cups hot mashed potatoes	applesauce from tart ap-
2 tablespoons sugar	ples
½ teaspoon nutmeg	

Beat butter into hot potatoes. Add all other ingredients and check for taste. Add more sugar and salt if necessary. Cool. Place in buttered baking dish and swirl mixture into peaks with a spoon. Bake in 400 degree oven for 30 minutes or until top is lightly browned. Yield: 4 servings.

Fish

Stegte Rodspette Filleter
(fried fillets of flounder)

2 pounds flounder fillets	1 egg
salt	½ cup butter
flour	1 thinly sliced lemon
2 slices zwieback, grated	1 tablespoon minced parsley

Sprinkle fillets with salt and let them stand in refrigerator for 1 hour. When ready to fry, drain them, dry well, and dredge with flour. Dip each in beaten egg, then in zwieback crumbs. Melt the butter in a deep skillet. When butter is very hot, lay fillets in and cook until browned and the coating is crisp. Turn out onto a warmed platter. Serve garnished with lemon slices and parsley. Yield: 4 to 6 servings.

Kogt Torsk
(boiled codfish)

1 cod

salt

melted butter

chopped raw onions

chopped pickled beets

chopped hard-boiled eggs

chopped parsley

Scrape and rinse fish thoroughly, rub with salt inside and out and let stand for about 1 hour. If fish is to be served whole, place in cold water to cover and bring to a boil. If cut up, drop pieces in boiling water. Cook slowly, uncovered, only until tender. Remove and drain. Serve with plenty of melted butter. Serve chopped onion, beets, eggs, and parsley in separate dishes or arranged around fish. Yield: 4 servings.

Poultry

Kylling Bryste Sauté à la Royale
(breast of chicken sauté à la royale)

1 leek

1 medium carrot

1 medium onion

2 stalks celery

2 slices bacon

½ cup butter

10 single breasts of chicken

salt, pepper and paprika

1 cup dry vermouth

½ pound button mushrooms

2 teaspoons tomato paste

2 cups heavy cream

20 medium shrimp

1 sprig fresh dill

3 sprigs fresh parsley

Peel and slice leek, carrot, and onion Mix with cut celery, parsley, and bacon, and saute in 1 tablespoon of butter. Season chicken breasts with salt, pepper, and a dash of paprika. Brown chicken in 2 tablespoons of butter and place on top of vegetables in a large roasting pan. Add vermouth and cover. Bake in 450 degree oven about 40 minutes. Remove chicken and vegetables and cook mushrooms in the stock. Place chicken in deep casserole after removing bones. Remove mushrooms from pan and add tomato paste and heavy cream. Cook until smooth. Whip in rest of butter; add cooked shrimp and mushrooms. Pour over chicken breasts in casserole and serve, 1 breast per serving, garnished with dill and parsley. Yield: 10 servings.

Meat

Frikadeller
(meat balls)

2 pounds lean pork, ground fine	1 teaspoon salt
½ cup flour	½ teaspoon pepper
1 egg	½ cup club soda or water
1 tablespoon grated onion	4 tablespoons butter
1 teaspoon grated lemon rind	½ to ¾ cups sour cream

Combine pork, flour, egg, onion, lemon rind, salt and pepper. Blend thoroughly. Stir in club soda gently (to make meat balls light). Shape meat into small balls, using hands. Heat butter in skillet. Brown pork balls on all sides. Lower heat and cook about 20 minutes or until done. Remove to a hot serving dish and keep hot. Add sour cream to pan juices and bring to a quick boil, stirring constantly. Pour over pork balls. Serve with boiled or browned potatoes and pickled beets. (Can be eaten cold, but omit gravy.) Yield: 4 servings.

Svinemorbrad
(spareribs of pork)

Flatten spareribs of pork and place dried plums that have been washed and soaked and pieces of apple between two of them. Tie the two ribs together and roast for 30 minutes. Baste with a little milk.

Bankeköd
(stewed beef)

Cut lean beef into slices about 1 inch thick, brown in butter, sprinkle with a little flour, and season with salt, peppercorns, and bay leaves. When browned, put meat in a saucepan with enough water to cover and simmer for 1½ hours.

Chartreuse Ragout

1 medium head cabbage	2 cups ragout of meat, chicken
2 carrots	or poultry
salt and pepper	½ cup melted butter

Precook cabbage and carrots until they are half cooked. Butter a deep casserole. Cut carrots into small pieces and place on bottom and around sides of the mold to make a pattern. Drain the cabbage, chop coarsely, and sprinkle with salt and pepper. Put a 1-inch thick layer of cabbage in bottom and around sides of casserole. Put in the ragout, without any sauce. Cover with another layer of cabbage. Pour melted butter over it. Set in a shallow pan of hot water and bake in 350 degree oven for 1 hour. Turn out carefully onto a warmed platter. Serve with Brown Sharp Sauce (see below). Yield: 6 servings.

Brun Skarp Saus
(brown sharp sauce)

4 tablespoons butter	⅛ teaspoon cayenne
4 tablespoons flour	¼ to ½ teaspoon salt
3 cups stock or bouillon	3 tablespoons sherry
3 tablespoons wine vinegar	

Melt butter, stir flour smoothly into it, and continue to stir until mixture is well browned. Add about half the stock, stir continually. Gradually add vinegar and remaining stock, continuing to stir. Let boil 15 minutes over low heat. Add the cayenne, salt, and sherry. Mix and remove from heat. Serve hot. Yield: 12 or more servings.

Kogt Skinke Medeira Vin
(Danish ham in Madeira wine)

1 smoked ham	8 whole cloves
3 bay leaves	1 bottle Madeira wine
7 peppercorns	

Wash ham and soak in cold water overnight. Drain. Cover with boiling water, add bay leaves, peppercorns, and cloves and cook slowly for 2½ hours or until tender. Drain. Cover with Madeira and simmer another ½ hour. The ham may be served with a sauce made by thickening 2 cups of the wine liquid with balls of butter and flour or with a thin paste of flour and water. Yield: 12 servings.

Flaesk med Svesker
(pork tenderloin stuffed with prunes)

1 pork tenderloin	1 teaspoon salt
12 pitted prunes	⅛ teaspoon pepper
¼ cup butter	

Wipe meat with a damp cloth. With sharp knife, cut a slit in the meat, lengthwise and deep enough to insert pitted prunes. Close meat opening with skewers or tie with string. Heat butter in skillet or kettle and brown meat on all sides. Sprinkle with salt and pepper, add about ½ cup water, cover and cook slowly 1½ to 2 hours or until tender, adding water as needed. To serve, slice through meat and prunes. Skim all fat from liquid and serve juice with the meat. Yield: 6 servings.

Desserts, Pastries

Marzipan

1 pound shelled almonds	3¾ cups powdered sugar
¼ pound bitter almonds	2 tablespoons rum

Scald and peel the almonds. Let them dry; then put twice through a grinder, using the finest knife. Add half the sugar and grind twice again. Then work in the rest of the sugar and the rum. Roll mixture in waxed paper and put in refrigerator; let stand 24 hours. Make into small potatoes or any small figures, roll in powdered chocolate or cocoa, or decorate with colored icing. Let stand in cool place about 2 days before serving. Yield: about 3 pounds of marzipan.

Öllebröd
(beer bread)

½ loaf of rye bread
2 pints pale ale
sugar

lemon peel
cream

Cut bread into dice and soak for 12 hours in ½ cup water and one pint of ale. Put in a saucepan and simmer for 20 minutes. Rub through a sieve and put this puree in a saucepan on a slow flame and thin with the other pint of ale. Add sugar to taste and a little lemon peel. Serve with thick cream.

Jule Kage
(Christmas bread)

1 cup lukewarm milk
½ cup sugar
½ teaspoon salt
½ teaspoon powdered
   cardamom
1 cake yeast

1 small egg
4 tablespoons soft shortening
3½ cups sifted flour
¼ cup chopped citron
½ cup raisins

Combine milk, sugar, salt, and cardamom. Crumble in yeast; stir until dissolved. Add egg and shortening. Stir in mixture of flour, citron, and raisins. Knead. Let rise. Punch down. Let rise. Shape into round loaf and place in greased 9-or 10-inch round layer cake pan. Cover. Let rise for 45 to 60 minutes or until doubled. Bake at 350 degrees for 30 to 40 minutes or until browned. Cool. Frost with powdered sugar icing; decorate with walnuts, candied cherry halves, and candied pineapple pieces. Yield: 12 servings.

"Bondepige med Slör"
("peasant girl with veil")

4 to 6 apples
4 to 6 slices day-old rye
   bread
2 tablespoons sugar

1 teaspoon butter
chocolate
whipped cream

Peel and core the apples and stew until reduced to a pulp. Mix grated rye bread, sugar, and butter and cook until set and almost dry. Put a layer of this mixture on a dish, cover with stewed apples, place another layer of the rye bread mixture over this, and finally sprinkle with grated chocolate. Cover with whipped cream.

Wienerbrød
(Danish pastry)

1½ yeast cakes
¼ cup lukewarm milk
1½ cups milk
1½ teaspoons salt
6 tablespoons sugar
6 tablespoons butter
2 small eggs
½ teaspoon grated nutmeg

½ teaspoon lemon extract
¼ teaspoon almond extract
7 cups sifted flour
¾ cup butter
fillings of your choice
1 egg, beaten
chopped pecans or almonds

Mash yeast in lukewarm milk and set aside. Heat 1½ cups of milk, dissolving the salt, sugar, and 6 tablespoons butter in it. Let it cool to tepid, then add it to yeast mixture. Beat eggs, add nutmeg and flavoring and stir into the other mixture. Gradually work in 2 cups of flour. Beat well 5 or 6 minutes. Add remaining flour, a little at a time. When dough is well mixed, remove it to a floured board and knead with floured hands until dough is very smooth. Then turn dough into a warm, buttered bowl, cover lightly with a light cloth, and set bowl in warm but not hot place. When it has doubled in bulk, return it to the board and roll it to about ½-inch thickness. Spread softened butter over half of it, fold dough in half, spread again with butter and fold in half, then roll out to its original size. Spread half of remaining butter on it, fold in half and roll out again. Spread the remainder of the butter on the dough, fold again, and roll out for the final time. Cut into rounds, triangles, or squares. Add a little cottage cheese, jam, or cooked apples to each piece and fold pastry over, letting a little of the filling show. Brush pastry with beaten egg and bake in 450 degree oven 15 to 20 minutes.

If you wish, when pastries are cooled, frost them with icing made of ½ cup powdered sugar mixed with 1 tablespoon of water, then sprinkle with chopped nuts. Yield: 3 dozen small pastries.

Frossen Fløde
(frozen cream)

2 cups heavy cream
½ teaspoon vanilla
ice
salt

1 pineapple
2 tablespoons sugar
½ cup candied cherries or
    fresh strawberries

Whip the cream until stiff, then add vanilla. Pack in a mold, surround with ice and salt and freeze for 2 hours, or pack in the freezing tray of your refrigerator and freeze until firm. Pare and slice the pineapple, removing dark eyes and core. Arrange pieces in a serving dish and sprinkle with sugar. Dip a large serving spoon in cold water, then scoop out large ovals of the frozen cream. Arrange ovals of frozen cream around the pineapple. Decorate with the cherries or strawberries. Yield: 6 servings.

Ingefaer Brød
(gingerbread)

2 eggs
1 cup sugar
1¾ cups sifted flour
½ teaspoon salt

1 teaspoon baking powder
1 tablespoon ground ginger
⅔ cup milk or cream

Beat eggs and sugar together. Sift dry ingredients and add alternately with the cream, beating well after each addition. Pour into buttered loaf pan and bake in 350 degree oven 45 minutes. Yield: 1 loaf.

Brunsviger Kager
(Brunswick cookies)

¾ cup butter
¾ cup sugar
2 eggs, separated
1 teaspoon lemon extract
½ cup chopped almonds
1 cup sifted flour

Topping:
3 tablespoons powdered sugar
3 tablespoons dried currants
3 tablespoons chopped
  almonds

Cream butter and sugar together. Beat yolks of eggs and add the lemon extract and nuts. Combine butter mixture and eggs. Gradually add sifted flour, beating well. Whip egg whites stiff and fold in. Spread the dough abut ⅛ to ¼ inch thick on a buttered cookie sheet. Sprinkle it with the sugar, almonds, and currants. Bake in a 350 degree oven for 8 to 12 minutes. Remove from oven, leave in the pan, and when slightly cooled, cut into small squares. Yield: 2 to 3 dozen cookies.

Braendende Kastanier
(chestnuts in rum)

1 pound chestnuts
½ cup rum

1¼ cups powdered sugar

Chestnuts should be steamed or roasted until soft. Shell them and arrange nuts on a flat silver dish and sprinkle them thickly with sugar. Pour rum over and light it with a match. Flame the chestnuts well; serve. Yield: 2 or 3 per person.

Kastanjer Purée
(chestnut puree)

Cook shelled and skinned or blanched chestnuts in a little stock, adding 1 or 2 pieces of celery as flavoring. When nuts are tender, drain and force them through a sieve. Stir well. For each pound of nuts add 2 tablespoons butter, 2½ tablespoons of thick cream, ¼ cup thin cream, and salt and sugar to taste. Beat well in upper part of a double boiler over boiling water. Serve hot.

Chapter 15

NORWAY

If you were in Norway in Maytime, on a steamer out on the Sognefjord, longest and most spectacular of the thousands of narrow inlets on the Atlantic coast, surrounded by towering snow-capped mountains lined with groves of apple trees and cherry trees in full bloom, you might wish that spring could last forever.

Norway's other major attraction lies farther north, within the Arctic Circle. After three days of cruising through some of the world's most magnificent scenery, you reach Hammerfest, northernmost city in the world. From the North Cape, May 15 until August 1, the sun stays above the horizon all night to give the area its name "The Land of the Midnight Sun." The aurora borealis (northern lights) are another spectacle to behold.

Less than four million people, almost pure Nordic, live in this long, thin country only sixty miles wide and about the size of New Mexico. The sea penetrates the west side with *fjords*, which provide the 1,100-mile-long country with 12,000 miles of coastline and 150,000 islands.

This is the land of the Vikings, Leif Ericson, Thor Heyderdahl, Edvard Grieg, and Henrik Ibsen. Seven-tenths of Norway is bare rock and mountainous, with only four percent of the soil good for farming. So Norwegians for more than 14,000 years have been fishermen, earning a living from the sea. They are hard-working, robust, persevering, blond, muscular, handsome and healthy people with a good sense of humor. Come to Norway and you'll soon be eating and drinking with some of Europe's friendliest people.

Norway was settled soon after the glaciers withdrew to the central highlands. Its earliest inhabitants were Germanic in origin whose territories were variously ruled by Sweden, Denmark, and France. Norway was united with Sweden in 1814 and it was not until 1906 that the King of Sweden relinquished the crown of Norway.

During both world wars, Norway joined its neighboring Scandinavian countries in neutrality, but was occupied by Germany from 1940 to 1945, despite strong and courageous home front resistance. In postwar years, Norway has grown prosperous, so rich in hydroelectric power from its mountain streams that it is the most electrified country in the world, a democracy with advanced social security benefits for its people.

Because of the *fjords* and such easy access to the sea, Norwegians catch and eat more fish than any other country, so it is no wonder that their food includes so many fish dishes. Only those who live close to the sea know how good fresh-caught fish can taste, and Norwegian fish is so fresh it is without any fishiness in the taste. Norwegians also are the world's greatest whalers, and whale meat, dark red in color and tasting like beef, is eaten by many because it is plentiful and inexpensive.

Norwegians even eat fish for breakfast, which is always a large meal including porridge, cheese, eggs, bread, and jam. Lunch is usually *kold bord,* the Norwegian version of *smorgasbord,* a cold table of open-faced sandwiches, and the evening dinner is a hearty meal of cod, salmon, herring, trout, and shellfish or chicken served in one of a variety of ways. Many Norwegians raise their own chickens, so they also have an ample supply of eggs.

Meat is expensive and seldom eaten more than once a week. Pork, lamb, mutton, and reindeer are popular. Smoked reindeer tongues are considered a great delicacy.

Norwegian food is plain and plentiful, housewives using large quantities of home-grown produce to make soups and stews. Dairy farms provide a delicious variety of cheese, which is almost a food staple.

Evening meals are topped off with a dessert of pancakes, rice puddings, fruit, or Norwegian berries that grow in great abundance. Norway's national cake is the *kransekake,* a rich almond-paste confection baked in layers to form a tower.

Norwegians love *hors d'oeuvres,* dainty and unusual treats served at a side table, as in Russia. Smoked salmon, salted herrings, anchovies, and shellfish are served in imaginative ways, often with delicious Norwegian rye bread cut in small, attractive shapes to whet the appetite, which in Norway is always considerable anyway.

Appetizers

Smørgaas
(hors d'oeuvres)

Norwegians serve a great variety of *hors d'oeuvres* both delicious to eat and attractive to set on a table. Some of the favorites are the following:

One *smorgaas* consists of hard-boiled eggs cut in half crosswise. The yolk is carefully removed and a small slice cut from the bottom of each white of the egg, so it will stand. Shrimps are hung by their tails all around the whites of egg, the egg itself is filled with the pounded yolk, mixed with pounded anchovies, and a little butter.

Another egg *hors d'oeuvre* is made with hard-boiled eggs, left whole, with only a small slice cut from the bottom of each egg so it will stand upright. Half a tomato with a little of the pulp removed is placed on top each egg so it looks like a giant mushroom.

Simple but delicious *hors d'oeuvres* are made with rounds of buttered rye bread with a slice of hard-boiled egg in the center, ringed by anchovies previously skinned and boned.

A favorite open sandwich is buttered white bread cut in various shapes and garnished with shrimps in aspic.

Sur Sild
(sour herring)

Put three large salt herrings in cold water and soak for 12 hours. Dry the fish, skin, and bone them, and cut into 1-inch lengths. Put a layer of fish in a glass dish, cover with layer of sliced onions, and put alternate layers of fish and onions until dish is full. Cover with liquid consisting of ⅔ of vinegar to ⅓ of water and stand in cool place for 12 hours or even longer. To serve, remove fish from vinegar and garnish with a little sliced onion. (Will keep for several weeks.)

Soups

Sotsuppe
(fruit soup)

3 cups mixed dried fruits
7 cups mixed fruit juice and
    water
2 tablespoons tapioca
1⅓ cups sugar

1 cup mixed apples and
    oranges, chopped
1 lemon, sliced
½ teaspoon salt
2 or 3 cinnamon sticks

Mix ingredients and cook covered for 30 to 40 minutes or until tender. Serve hot or cold as a main dish, meat accompaniment, appetizer, or frozen dessert served with cream. Yield: 8 servings.

Byggsuppe
(barley soup)

½ cup barley
1 quart pork broth
3 green or 1 small dry onion
2 parsnips
2 stalks celery

1 small rutabaga
1 tablespoon chopped parsley
1 quart milk
salt and pepper to taste

Soak barley in water to cover for a few hours and cook until nearly done. Drain and finish cooking with the vegetables in the pork broth. Add milk and season to taste. Let simmer a few minutes and serve. Yield: 8 servings.

Salads

Reker Salat i Forme
(shrimp salad mold)

1 package lemon gelatin
½ cup mayonnaise
½ cup cream
1 glass pimento cream cheese
1 tablespoon green pepper, chopped

3 hard-boiled eggs, chopped
1 can shrimp
½ teaspoon salt
1 cup celery, chopped
parsley

Mix gelatin with 1 cup boiling water and let congeal slightly. Beat cream cheese and mayonnaise together. Mix cream into slightly congealed gelatin, add cream cheese and mayonnaise mixture and remaining ingredients. Put in ring or fish-shaped mold greased with mayonnaise. Refrigerate 2–3 hours until stiffened. To serve, unmold on lettuce leaves and garnish with parsley. Yield: 6 servings.

Hummer Salat
(lobster salad)

1 boiled lobster
2 hard-boiled egg yolks
1 raw egg yolk
½ teaspoon salt
6 tablespoons oil

1 tablespoon vinegar
1 tablespoon white wine
1 cup cooked macaroni
lettuce leaves

Remove meat from the lobster, cut in small pieces, and chill. Make the dressing: mash cooked egg yolks with raw yolk smoothly. Add salt and beat until thick. Add oil drop-by-drop, beating continually. Then add vinegar and wine, a little at a time, beating continually. Mix lightly with chilled lobster meat and macaroni. Serve in salad bowl garnished with crisp lettuce. Yield: 4 servings.

Vegetables

Fylte Lok
(stuffed onions)

6 large onions
2 tablespoons butter
1 pound beef, ground

1 teaspoon salt
⅛ teaspoon pepper
beef stock

Peel onions and cut slice from top for a "lid." Hollow out centers from onions and chop fine. Melt butter and brown chopped onion. Add to the ground beef with salt and pepper. Mix well and stuff centers of onions with meat. Put on "lid" and fasten with toothpicks to hold together. Put onions in baking dish, pour a little beef stock over them, and bake in 375 degree oven until onions are soft. Baste a few times with beef stock. Yield: 6 servings.

Spinatpudding
(spinach pudding)

4 eggs
2 cups milk
½ cup cracker meal
½ teaspoon salt

⅛ teaspoon pepper
⅓ cup butter
1 cup cooked, drained, and
    chopped spinach

Beat eggs, add milk in which cracker meal has been softened. Add salt, pepper, and melted butter to chopped spinach, and add to the egg, milk, and cracker meal mixture. Bake in buttered baking dish in 350 degree oven for 1 hour. Yield: 4 servings.

Surneper
(pickled turnips)

2 pounds turnips
1 teaspoon salt
2 teaspoons caraway seeds
1 tablespoon flour

1 tablespoon butter
1 teaspoon sugar
1 tablespoon vinegar

Peel and dice turnips. Place in 1 quart boiling water to which salt and caraway seeds have been added. Work flour and butter together, add a little turnip stock, add to turnips, and simmer for 10 minutes. Add sugar and vinegar. Yield: 4 servings.

Potatoes, Dumplings

Lefse
(pastry potato)

4 cups hot mashed potatoes ¼ teaspoon salt
¼ cup shortening 2 cups flour

Combine hot potatoes with shortening and salt. Cool and add flour. Roll out a small portion of dough on pastry cloth until very thin. Bake on grill or cookie sheet until light brown on both sides. Cool. Fold each *lefse* over twice and wrap in a cloth or waxed paper to keep soft. Serve with butter; sprinkle with granulated or brown sugar.

Potetes og Fisk Kumler
(potato and fish dumplings)

2 pounds fresh or salt fish salt and pepper to taste
3 large raw potatoes ½ teaspoon ginger
½ boiled potato 4 tablespoons barley flour or
⅛ pound suet other flour
2 slices onion

Clean fish, remove all skin and bones. Grind fish, potatoes, suet, and onion twice in meat grinder. Add salt, pepper, ginger, and the flour. Form into round balls, place in boiling water, and let simmer covered for half an hour or until done. Serve with fish soup or with melted butter or a white sauce. When cold, dumplings may be sliced and fried. Yield: 6 servings.

Fish

Laks
(boiled salmon)

Clean salmon without cutting along the belly, wash and dry
well. Use an oblong fish pan or kettle with removable perforated
rack to cook the salmon. Lower rack into 3 quarts boiling salted
water and simmer fish gently. Allow 15 minutes cooking time for
every 2 pounds for a large, thick salmon. Remove fish on the
rack, drain, and transfer to a serving dish. Serve with parsley,
butter, and cucumber salad.

Rokelax i Vand Sas
(smoked salmon in water sauce)

Take 3 pounds fresh salmon, cut from the thick middle part, and
fillet it. Wipe fish with a damp cloth, lay it on a dish, and cover
with salt and sugar. Let it stand in a cold place for 24 hours.
Carefully remove all salt from the fish and lightly smoke it. Cut
the smoked salmon in thick slices, dip lightly in flour, put in an
earthenware casserole, and cover with cold water. Add a few
pieces of butter and sprinkle with parsley. Bring to a boil and
simmer slowly until fish is tender. Remove fish from casserole
and let the sauce reduce until it begins to thicken. Season with
salt and a little sugar, put fish back in casserole, and serve.

Prinsefisk
(prince fish)

codfish fillets	⅛ teaspoon salt
2 tablespoons butter	½ cup sour cream
2 tablespoons flour	3 or 4 egg yolks
1 cup milk	asparagus

Remove skin and bones from fresh or frozen cod fillets. Wash
and simmer gently in boiling salted water until done. Prepare a
white sauce by melting butter, adding flour and milk gradually,

stirring vigorously over low heat until thickened. Add salt and sour cream and heat to boiling point. Remove from heat and beat in the egg yolks, slightly beaten. Place the well-drained fish on a serving dish, put hot cooked asparagus over and around the fish, and cover with the sauce. Serve with hot boiled potatoes. Allow 1 or 2 cod fillets per serving.

Poultry

Kylling
(chicken)

Stuff chicken with generous amounts of butter and parsley and put in an iron pan and cook until brown in butter. Turn the chicken while browning so the color will be even. Add a little water and slowly simmer for 2 to 3 hours, according to size. Just before serving, add a little hot water to the pan so the thick part of the bastings will be detached. The thick and clear sauce (without adding flour) is served with the chicken.

Meats

Far i Kal
(mutton and cabbage)

2 pounds lamb or mutton breast and/or shoulder	2 tablespoons butter flour
4 pounds white winter cabbage	1 teaspoon peppercorns

Cut meat into serving pieces. Prepare cabbage by removing the thick stalk and cutting it into rough cubes about an inch thick. Allow twice as much cabbage as meat. Melt butter in a large, thick-bottomed saucepan, sprinkle with flour, and add cabbage and mutton in alternating layers. Sprinkle each layer with salt and a little flour and add a few peppercorns. Pour on boiling water until it covers about ⅓ of the contents of the pan. Simmer slowly for 2–3 hours, stirring occasionally. Yield: 4 to 6 servings. (Tastes very good the next day.)

Benlöse Fugle
(beef birds)

1½ pounds sirloin of beef
1½ teaspoons salt
½ teaspoon pepper
¼ teaspoon ground ginger
¼ teaspoon ground cloves
¼ pound ground beef

¼ cup marrow or kidney suet
parsley
2 tablespoons flour
4–5 tablespoons butter
3 cups hot meat stock or water

Have butcher cut beef in very thin slices. Wipe with clean, wet cloth. Pound each slice thin and cut in pieces about 3 inches wide and 4 or 5 inches long. Sprinkle each with salt, pepper, ginger, and cloves. Put 1 tablespoon of the ground meat, a little of the finely chopped marrow or suet and a little chopped parsley on each. Roll and tie with string dipped in hot water. Sprinkle each with flour. Brown in melted and browned butter. Turn birds so they brown on all sides. When browned, pour in hot stock or boiling water, enough to cover. Cover the pan and simmer slowly for 30 minutes. Uncover and continue cooking another 30 minutes. Lift cooked birds out, cut and remove strings, place meat on a warmed serving dish. Boil the gravy for a few minutes. Pour over birds or serve separately. Yield: 4 to 6 servings.

Svinekam Piquant
(pork roast piquant)

¼ cup prepared mustard
1 tablespoon prepared
   horseradish
1 teaspoon anchovy paste

1 tablespoon sugar
1 pork loin (3–4 pounds)
⅔ cup fine dry bread crumbs
2 cups dry white wine

Combine mustard, horseradish, anchovy paste, and sugar. Blend into a smooth paste. Trim excess fat off the meat. With a brush, spread meat on all sides with mixture. Place on rack in baking pan. Cover top and sides with bread crumbs. Roast 35 to 40 minutes to the pound in a preheated 325 degree oven or until meat thermometer reaches 185 degrees. After 1 hour of roasting, pour 1 cup boiling wine into pan. Do not let wine touch the meat. When wine has evaporated, pour remaining wine into pan.

Serve on a platter with alternating mounds of tiny buttered peas, carrots, and small browned potatoes. Yield: 4 to 6 servings.

Nyrer i Hvitvin
(kidneys in white wine)

4 veal kidneys
¼ cup butter
1 tablespoon chopped parsley
½ pound mushrooms, sliced
thin

2 tablespoons flour
1 cup dry white wine
½ cup beef bouillon
salt and pepper to taste

Trim kidneys and cut into thin slices. Place in cold water and let stand half an hour, changing water twice. Drain and wipe kidneys dry. Heat butter in skillet, and brown kidneys rapidly on all sides. Sprinkle with parsley and add mushrooms. Cook 1 minute, stirring constantly. Sprinkle with flour and add white wine and bouillon. Cook over medium heat for 5 minutes, stirring constantly. If too thick, add a little more bouillon. Serve with steamed potatoes. Yield: 4 servings.

Pastries, Desserts, Breads

Kringles

1 cup sugar
2 tablespoons butter
1 cup sour cream
1 egg yolk
½ teaspoon salt

1 teaspoon soda
1 teaspoon baking powder
3 cups flour
½ cup sour milk

Cream sugar and butter, add sour cream that has been combined with egg yolk. Sift dry ingredients together, add alternately with sour milk to creamed mixture. Refrigerate 2 hours or overnight. Turn out on a floured board. Cut off small pieces of dough and roll with hands until pieces are the size and length of a pencil. Form into figure eights; place on greased cookie sheet and bake at 400 degrees for 8 to 10 minutes. Store in a tight container. Serve buttered with coffee. Yield: 3½ to 4 dozen.

Flatbrod
(flat bread)

½ cup shortening
1 teaspoon salt
1 cup quick-cooking oatmeal

2 cups buttermilk
1 teaspoon soda
4 cups flour

Combine all ingredients and roll out quite thin. Divide dough and bake in 2 buttered 13×9×2-inch pans at 400 degrees for about 8 minutes.

Rommegrot
(cream pudding)

2 cups thick cream, slightly
  soured
½ cup sifted flour
½ teaspoon salt

sugar
2 cups hot milk
cinnamon

Simmer cream and ½ cup water for 45 minutes to 1 hour, stirring occasionally. Combine flour and salt. Sift into hot cream, beating until smooth. Cook until mixture is thick and butterfat rises to the top. Remove fat and save. Stir in hot milk and beat well. Pudding should be very smooth and creamy. Pour into a bowl. Make depressions on top for butterfat. Serve hot in dessert dishes with sugar and cinnamon sprinkled on top. (Pudding is not a success unless butterfat rises to the top after flour is added.) Yield: 6 to 8 servings.

Kranserkake
(ring cake)

1 pound ground sweet
  almonds
about 25 ground bitter
  almonds

icing (see below)
1 pound powdered sugar
3 egg whites

Mix together ground almonds and all but ⅓ cup powdered sugar and add 1 egg white. Set mixture over a low heat until it is tepid, then stir in other 2 egg whites, one at a time. Put mixture in a forcing bag fitted with a fluted biscuit nozzle, the thickness of a finger. Squeeze in rings onto greased baking trays. The diameter of the largest should be about 10 inches and each additional ring should be ¼ inch less in diameter, down to the smallest of 2 inches in diameter. Bake in a 300 degree oven until light golden brown. Remove rings and while still warm, mount one upon the other, forming a tower. Decorate by piping a thin line of white glacé icing in zig-zag lines all over the cake in an irregular design.

Icing

Make icing by mixing ⅓ cup powdered sugar, ½ egg white, and ½ teaspoon lemon juice.

Affix miniature crackers, marzipan flowers, or candy to the cakes by dipping them in lightly browned caramel. Top cake with a small national flag or with marzipan flowers.

Solskinnkake
(sunshine cake)

6 eggs, separated
pinch of salt
1 teaspoon cream of tartar
1¼ cups sugar

2 teaspoons lemon juice
grated rind of ½ lemon
1 cup cake flour
powdered sugar

Beat egg whites until frothy and add salt and cream of tartar. Continue beating until stiff. Beat egg yolks until thick and light. To egg whites add sugar, folding it in slowly and carefully. Fold in beaten yolks of eggs and lemon juice and grated lemon rind. Lastly fold in flour which has been sifted four times. When well blended, pour into ungreased form or tube pan. Bake in 325 degree oven for about 1 hour. When cool, remove from pan by running a knife around edge, turning pan over serving plate, and gently shaking until cake is released.

Icing

Mix cream, lemon juice, and grated lemon rind and enough powdered sugar for icing consistency.

Fyrstekake
(Prince's cake)

¾ cup butter
2 cups flour
2 teaspoons baking powder
¾ cup sugar
1 egg yolk
2 tablespoons milk
½ cup powdered sugar

1¼ cups almonds, blanched
and ground or chopped
¼ teaspoon almond extract
½ teaspoon ground cardamom
½ teaspoon cinnamon
1 egg white, beaten slightly

Mix butter with flour as for pastry. Add baking powder, sugar, egg yolk, and milk. Roll out about two-thirds of the dough and cover bottom of a baking dish. Mix the remaining ingredients with 6 tablespoons water and spread over the dough. Roll out the rest of dough and cut into wide strips with a cookie wheel or knife and place crosswise over filling. Bake in 300 degree oven for 45 minutes.

Chapter 16

FINLAND

Finland has had forty-two wars with Russia and, despite the heroic one hundred day "Winter War" of 1939–40 in which they taught the Soviets lessons in how to fight in the cold and snow, lost them all.

Finnish determination in refusing to give up their freedom is a David and Goliath story unparalleled in the history of nations. Such resolve is indicative of the people of Finland who are courageous, handsome, stubborn, and very healthy.

Perhaps some of their good health comes from their national pastime, the sauna. In a backwoods sauna, you go to a log cabin by a frozen lake, strip naked, and sit in a Hades-hot room where cold water is splashed over hot stones to create stifling steam. You beat yourself with birch branches to increase your circulation, then rush outside and chop a hole in the ice and jump in the lake.

Almost every Finnish home has a sauna of some kind, and more civilized versions of the backwoods sauna are offered in most Finnish hotels.

Finland is the most northerly republic in the world, with one-third of its area above the Arctic Circle. There are 60,000 lakes and 200,000 islands in this low-lying northlands paradise of water, forests, and sky. But despite its northern latitudes, Finland is not extremely cold because it is warmed by gulfstream waters.

Finland also is a land of the Midnight Sun. In Helsinki midsummer days last nineteen hours. In Lapland's northern tip, there is daylight for seventy-three continuous days. But there also is darkness for fifty-one continuous days.

Helsinki, which is as far north as Oslo and Leningrad, is the capital city and focal point of the nation. It is distinctly different from other Scandinavian capitals, called "The White City of the North" because of its new, light-colored buildings. Unlike Copenhagen, Oslo, and Stockholm, Helsinki does not cherish the past. Its architecture and personality are much more of today. And its hard-working, inwardly somber or at the very least contemplative people, throw off their cares at night and paint the town. Finland, for all its Scandinavian discipline, has one of the world's greatest drinking problems. Perhaps this comes from David living with the ever-present threat of a forty-third war with Goliath.

Modern as Helsinki is, Finland is not without its history. Old castles and forts throughout the country date back to a time when Finland was part of Sweden.

Forestry is Finland's main industry. Little of the land is suitable for farming, but the sea is close at hand for fishing, so it is no wonder that fish, especially smoked or fried, figures prominantly in the nation's food. But of the four basic foods of Finland—fish, bread, meat, and potatoes—bread is the most important, for it is bread that kept the Finns alive during the years in and between wars. Finnish housewives excel in baking rye bread. A slice of *Hapanleipa*, the traditional flat round bread loaf with a hole in the middle (stored on poles suspended from the kitchen ceiling), some cheese and cold milk and you know why bread is among the favorite foods.

Finnish food is similar to Swedish food, though less sweet. Dumplings, heavy soups, and cereal porridges of barley, rye, and rice are popular as one-dish meals, often eaten with berry preserves and milk.

Superb fish, from the sea and lakes and streams, are carefully cooked and are a cornerstone of daily eating. Fish, meats, and vegetables are blended into stews and casserole dishes, of which the Finns seem fonder than their Scandinavian neighbors. Clabbered (curdled) milk, homemade cheeses (one is baked in the oven), and many cheese dishes are relished.

Pancakes, both sweet and nonsweet, are a popular staple of Finland. Simple puddings are numerous, and the Finns eat a good deal of rice. On the whole, Finnish food is more simple though more varied than elsewhere in Scandinavia.

Finnish mushrooms and berries, picked by families on outings in the forests, are enjoyed by all, served fresh and preserved, or made into fruit wines and cordials.

Despite the Finns' abhorrence of being under Russian domination, they have allowed some Russian culinary influences to creep into their native foods, most notably the pastries filled with fish or meat, and some soups.

Most Americans get some feeling for Finland from the music of its most noted composer, Jean Sibelius. His Second Symphony and best-known work, *Finlandia,* evoke images of this vast, lonely, fiercely patriotic northlands country.

Appetizers

Voileipäpöytä
(bread and butter table)

Start with bread (especially rye) and butter and build with things that go well *on* bread, including meats, cheeses, fish. Then add things that go well *with* bread, such as meat balls, boiled potatoes, salads, egg dishes, fruits, and relishes. (A delicious snack is to spread hot mustard on a small square of rye bread, sprinkle with salt and pepper, and top with grated Parmesan cheese.)

Soups

Pinaattikeitto
(spinach soup with milk)

½ pound spinach	5 cups milk
2 tablespoons butter	½ teaspoon sugar
3 tablespoons flour	½ teaspoon salt

Rinse spinach in cold water and cook in its own juice until soft. Chop fine or put through a vegetable mill. Melt the butter, add flour and stir until smooth. Add milk gradually, stirring constantly. Simmer a few minutes and add chopped spinach, sugar, and salt. Spinach soup is served with hard-boiled or poached eggs. Yield: 8 servings.

Porkkanakeitto
(carrot soup)

4 or 5 large carrots	salt
2 tablespoons butter	sugar
2 tablespoons flour	parsley
10 cups milk	

Wash and scrape the carrots. Cook until soft in slightly salted water. Keep the carrot stock, strain and mash the carrots. Melt butter in saucepan and add flour, stirring until smooth. Add boiling milk gradually, stirring constantly. Simmer for 10 minutes, then add stock and carrot puree. Season to taste with salt and sugar and add chopped parsley. Yield: 8 servings.

Kesäkeitto
(Finnish summer vegetable soup)

1 tablespoon salt	½ cup chopped spinach
1 cup green string beans	2 to 3 tablespoons flour
1 cup sliced carrots	4 cups milk
1 cup cubed peeled potatoes	3 tablespoons butter
1 cup fresh peas	¼ cup chopped parsley
1 cup cauliflower buds	

Bring 1 quart water and salt to a boil in a deep pot. Add string beans, carrots, and potatoes. When half-cooked, add peas, cauliflower, and spinach. Cook until vegetables are just tender, but do not overcook. Mix flour with a little of the cold milk to a smooth paste (2 to 3 tablespoons flour depending on thickness of soup desired). Stir into hot soup. Add remaining milk and simmer soup for 10 minutes. Remove from heat and stir in butter and parsley. Yield: 6 to 8 servings.

Salads

Sillisalaatti
(herring, beet, carrot, and apple salad)

1 salt herring
1½ cups diced cooked beets
½ cup diced cooked potatoes
carrots
½ cup diced cooked meat
    (beef, pork, veal)
2 diced apples
1 sliced dill pickle
2 hard-boiled eggs, chopped

pepper
1 cup sour cream
3 tablespoons vinegar
1 tablespoon prepared mustard
2 tablespoons sugar
½ teaspoon salt
parsley to garnish
hard-boiled eggs to garnish

Wash herring and soak overnight in cold water. Drain, cut off head and tail and remove bones. Cut fillets into small pieces. Mix lightly with diced vegetables, meat, apples, pickle, and chopped eggs and season to taste with pepper. Combine sour cream, vinegar, mustard, sugar, and salt for dressing. Add dressing to salad and toss until blended. Garnish with parsley and slices of hard-boiled egg. Yield: 8 servings.

Sienisalaatti
(mushroom salad)

2 cups mushrooms,
    fresh or canned
1 tablespoon chopped chives
    or grated onion

1 teaspoon sugar
2 tablespoons cream
salt and pepper to taste

If using fresh mushrooms, boil them, after washing carefully, for 5 to 8 minutes in salted water. Cool and slice thin through stem and cap. Chop the chives, or if onion is used, grate it. Combine sugar to cream and add to mushrooms and onions or chives. Season to taste with salt and pepper. Serve in small lettuce cups. Yield: 4 servings.

Vegetables

Sienimuhennos
(stewed mushrooms)

2 cups fresh or canned mushrooms
3 tablespoons butter
1 chopped onion

4 tablespoons flour
1½ cups thin cream
salt and pepper

If fresh mushrooms are used, wash carefully in cold water, cutting off any dark spots, and boil in salted water for 5 to 8 minutes. Slice mushrooms either before or after cooking. Add mushrooms to melted butter in a frying pan and brown, stirring well. Add chopped onion, stirring until onion is lightly browned. Add flour and then gradually add the cream. Simmer slowly for about 30 minutes and season to taste with salt and pepper. Yield: 4 servings.

Porkkanalaatikko
(baked carrot custard)

1½ pounds carrots
1 cup bread crumbs
1 cup milk

3 tablespoons melted butter
3 eggs, separated
1 teaspoon salt

Wash the carrots, scrape them, cover with salted boiling water and cook until tender. Let them cool, then grate or chop fine. Mix crumbs and milk in a bowl, beat in butter, egg yolks, and salt. Combine with the carrots. Whip egg whites stiff and fold in. Pour into buttered baking dish and set in a shallow pan of water. Bake in 350 degree oven for 30 to 45 minutes or until risen, set, and lightly browned. Yield: 6 servings.

Perunarieska
(potato scones)

4 to 6 peeled and sliced potatoes

½ teaspoon salt
2 cups barley flour

Cook potatoes in salted water about 20 minutes or until soft. Drain and keep the potato water. Mash the potatoes. Add 1 cup potato water, mix well, and set aside to cool. Add salt and enough barley flour to make a stiff dough. Shape dough into thin rounds on a floured baking board and bake on greased baking sheet in a 425 degree oven until they begin to turn brown (5 to 10 minutes). When scones are baked, split and butter them. Cover with greaseproof paper and a cloth. Serve hot as a bread with meals or for tea. Yield: 16 scones.

Fish

Sillipyörykat
(Herring fish balls)

2 salt herring	½ tablespoon potato flour or
2 cups cold boiled potatoes	cornstarch
1 cup minced cooked meat	½ cup bread crumbs
½ onion	fat for frying

Soak fish in cold water to remove surplus salt. Clean and remove skin, viscera, bones, head, and tail. Chop herring fine with the potatoes and meat. Add chopped onion and potato flour. Mix thoroughly and work until smooth. Form into little balls, roll in the bread crumbs, and fry to a golden brown. During frying, the pan should be shaken so that the fish balls are cooked evenly all over. Yield: 6 servings.

Uunissa Paistettu Hauki
(baked stuffed pike)

1 three-pound pike	⅔ cup fine dry bread crumbs
1 tablespoon salt	⅔ cup hot water
¼ cup butter	

Preheat oven to 350 degrees. Rub fish with salt inside and out. Stuff with stuffing (see below) and sew up or fasten with skewers. Melt butter in baking dish. Place fish in dish and spoon melted butter on all sides. Sprinkle with bread crumbs. Bake for 5 minutes. Pour hot water into baking dish around fish. Cook about 30 to 35 minutes or until fish tests flaky. Baste fish occasionally after it has browned.

Stuffing

⅓ cup rice
½ pound spinach or 1 package
    frozen chopped spinach

1 teaspoon salt
½ teaspoon pepper
2 egg yolks, beaten

Cook rice. Cook spinach and chop fine, or cook frozen spinach according to directions. Combine rice and spinach, season with salt and pepper. Blend in beaten egg yolks.

Paistettu Siika
(baked stuffed whitefish)

1 3-pound whitefish or large
    lake trout
salt
vinegar

½ teaspoon salt
¼ teaspoon white pepper
1 tablespoon lemon juice

Stuffing:
1½ tablespoons butter
3 tablespoons chopped dill
2 tablespoons chopped parsley
1 tablespoon chopped onion
4 medium tomatoes, peeled
    and chopped

Topping:
1 beaten egg
bread or cracker crumbs

Basting ingredients:
¼ cup melted butter
½ cup boiling water
1 cup light cream

Clean the fish, removing the scales, fins, and bones, but do not remove skin or separate the two fillets. Sprinkle lightly with salt and rub with enough vinegar to coat the whole fish lightly inside and out. Let stand 20 minutes. To make stuffing, combine the butter, dill, parsley, onion, tomatoes, salt, pepper, and lemon juice. Fill the fish with this mixture and truss or fasten with string or toothpicks. Lay the fish in a buttered casserole, brush with the egg, and cover with the crumbs. Bake in 350 degree oven for 10 minutes, then brush with melted butter. Bake another 10 minutes and baste with the boiling water. Bake for another 10 minutes and pour the light cream over it. Continue baking until the fish flakes when probed with a fork (about 20 minutes more). Serve hot. Yield: 4 to 6 servings.

Paperissa Savustettu Kala
(fish smoked in newspaper)

1 whitefish or other fish suitable for baking	butter
	pepper
salt	lemon

Scale and clean the fish. Remove as many bones as possible. Leave head and tail on. Rub salt inside and out and let fish stand in refrigerator 30 minutes before baking. To prepare outdoors or on a grill, rub waxed paper with butter and wrap fish loosely, buttered side next to the fish. Roll this in many layers of newspaper. Place on smoldering ashes. The fish cooks inside the paper. When newspaper is burned away and only the waxed paper is left around the fish, remove it from the coals, split the paper, season the fish with salt, pepper, and butter and serve. Garnish with lemon. Yield: 2 to 4 servings.

If prepared in the kitchen, use buttered parchment paper or waxed paper only, no newspaper wrappings. Bake on a pan in a 350 degree oven for 30 minutes or longer, depending on size of the fish. When done, place on a warmed plate and tear the paper wrapping open. Season the fish and garnish it with lemon.

Meats

Karjalanpaisti
(Karelian hot-pot)

½ pound pork	1 pound mutton or lamb
1 pound beef	salt to taste

Wash meat well and cut into small pieces. Put meat into an ovenproof casserole and add enough water to cover. Add salt. Bake at 300 degrees for about 1½ hours. Add more water when needed. Serve with potatoes. Yield: 4 servings.

Maksalaatikko
(liver and rice pudding)

1 cup rice
5 cups milk
1 egg
1 onion
2 tablespoons butter
4 tablespoons molasses

½ teaspoon ground marjoram
¾ cup seedless raisins
1 tablespoon salt
½ teaspoon white pepper
½ pound chopped veal or beef
　liver

Wash the rice and cook covered in 1 cup water and milk until nearly soft. Let the rice porridge cool. Beat the egg. Saute chopped onion in butter. Add the onion, egg, molasses, marjoram, raisins, salt and pepper and the liver to the rice porridge. Mix well. Pour into greased casserole and bake in 325 degree oven for 1 hour. Serve melted butter with the hot pudding. Yield: 6 servings.

Kallalaatiko
(pork casserole)

4 pork chops
2 fresh herrings
4 medium potatoes
4 onions
butter

2 eggs
2 cups milk
⅛ cup flour
salt and pepper to taste

Trim the pork chops; split and bone the herrings, and cut off the heads and tails. Peel the potatoes and onions and slice fairly thin. Butter an ovenproof dish, put in a layer of potatoes, a layer of onion, then 2 pork chops, next 2 herring halves and then another layer of potato and onion. Add remaining pork chops and herring, fill in round the sides and cover the top with the rest of the onion and potato. Put a few pats of butter over the top. Cook uncovered in 350 degree oven for 1 hour.

　　Beat the eggs with the milk, add the flour and seasonings and mix well to make a smooth paste. then pour over the mixture in the casserole. Return the dish to the oven and cook another 1/2 hour until the custard topping is set. Yield: 4 servings.

Sianlihakastike
(pork sauce)

½ pound salt or fresh pork,   3 tablespoons flour
    sliced   1 medium onion, chopped

In hot skillet, brown meat quickly on both sides until crisp. Remove and keep hot. Stir flour into pan drippings. Cook until browned, stirring constantly. Add onions and continue cooking until onions are browned. Do not burn. Stir in 3 cups hot water a little at a time. Cook until sauce is thick and smooth. Return meat to sauce. Check for seasoning. Salt is needed when fresh pork is used. Cook over low heat about 20 minutes, stirring occasionally. Serve hot with boiled potatoes. (The sauce can be seasoned with mustard, paprika, tomato puree, or a little cream.)

Pastries, Desserts, Breads

Hapanleipä
(rye bread)

2 cakes yeast   3 tablespoons salt
9 pounds rye flour

Dissolve yeast in a little warm water, then add to 12 cups cold water. Work in half of the flour and beat until it is of a thick consistency. Cover and leave overnight to leaven in a warm place. Then add salt and the rest of the rye flour to the dough. Beat until stiff and allow to rise until almost doubled in bulk. Turn out the dough onto a baking board and knead well. Make into round loaves or flat round loaves with a hole in the center. For the former, the dough can be more stiff than for the latter. Remove the plain round loaf so that it rises to form a cone in the middle, and press the point down firmly. The other type of loaf is patted flat until it is about 1/4 inch thick, and the middle is cut out. Cover the loaves with a baking cloth and let rise. Prick the loaves with holes in the middle before baking. Bake in 400 degree oven for 1 hour. When baked, the loaves should be covered with a baking cloth and left to cool. Makes several loaves.

Viipurin Rinkeli
(viipuri twists)

4 eggs
1¾ cups sugar
3 cups milk
3 cakes yeast, dry or com-
    pressed

1 teaspoon ground nutmeg
2 teaspoons ground cardamom
1 teaspoon salt
16 cups flour
½ cup butter

Beat eggs and sugar well, add lukewarm milk, yeast dissolved in a little warm water, the spices, salt, and some of the flour. Beat well, then add the rest of the flour and the well-creamed butter. Knead dough and set aside in warm place to rise. When about double in bulk, place on baking board and work until very elastic. Divide into four parts, each of which will make one twist. Roll each part into a sausage shape, thicker in the middle than at the ends. Twist like a pretzel. Sprinkle with boiling water either immediately or after it has been left to rise. Place in oven and moisten again while baking and once again when the baked twist has been removed from the oven. Twists are baked at 400 degrees for 20 to 30 minutes depending on thickness. (They taste good hot or several days after making.) Yield: 4 twists.

Mansikkalumi
(strawberry snow)

2 cups strawberries
sugar to taste

4 egg whites
¾ cup whipping cream

Crush strawberries with the sugar. Beat the egg whites until stiff and add the crushed strawberries. Fold in whipped cream, mixing carefully. Pour into dessert bowls and decorate with whole strawberries. Yield: 6 servings.

Vehnäkorput
(wheat rusks)

3¾ cups sifted flour	¾ cup butter
2 teaspoons baking flour	½ cup sugar
1 teaspoon ground cardamom seeds	1 egg
	⅝ cup cold milk

Sift flour, baking powder, and cardamom together. Cream the butter and sugar smoothly together. Beat egg and combine with butter mixture. Add flour and milk alternately, mixing well after each addition. Take small amounts of dough and shape into small balls about size of a large walnut. Place balls on greased baking sheet and bake in 400 degree oven for 15 minutes. While still hot, cut them in half. Set the pan back in the oven with the cut side of the rusks up. Reduce heat to 250 degrees and dry out the rusk. Serve with coffee or fruit soup. Yield: 2 dozen rusks.

5

The British Isles

England, Ireland, Scotland

British cooking is wholesome and on the plain side, not as rich or spicy as the fare favored by their neighbors on the continent. But this is not to say British food is dull. Often the simple style of preparation allows the natural flavors of the food to come through.

The peoples of the British Isles eat large amounts of meat, and this is no wonder because of the excellent Scottish and English beef and mutton and Welsh lamb and mutton. English pork pies and York hams are known worldwide. Their roast beef, dredged with flour and served with Yorkshire pudding, horseradish sauce, or brown gravy, is also famous. Boiled beef is another favorite, especially the brisket, well-skewered and tied, then braised, and finally boiled with carrots and turnips.

The Scots enjoy minced collops (coarsely minced or chopped meat), haggis (a sheep's paunch, browned with oatmeal, suet, and onions), and other interestingly-named meat dishes such as hotch-potch and inky-pinky. The Irish, of course, have their well-renowned stew.

Vegetables are not among the Britons' favorite foods, while the Scots like turnips and beetroots, and the Irish enjoy colcannon (cabbage with mashed potatoes) and various root vegetables served with bacon.

Among soups, British favorites are gravy soup, mock turtle, and a distinctive concoction called mulligatawny. The Irish, least affluent of the countries of the Isles, make soup of just about anything, and the Scots have both Scotch broth and cock-a-leek-ie soup.

Fish is, of course, just a short fly cast away from most places in the British Isles, and each country has its specialty. Besides Dover sole, the British are known for their way with boiled cod, whitebait, dressed crab, and that institution of fish and chips. The Irish have no distinctive fish dish though they enjoy many of the same fish dishes as their neighbors, while the Scots have their crab pie and finnan haddie, smoked haddock.

Desserts, pastries, and breads of the British Isles can hold their own against those on the continent, yet they are not as rich. In England the champions are puddings (notably plum and roly-poly), mince pies, trifles, crumpets, various biscuits, and hot cross buns. The Irish have soda bread and potato cake, and the Scots are known for their shortbread fingers and marmalades.

Plain and simple are the words for cooking of the countries of the Old Sod. The distinction lies in attention to detail, for often the simplest dishes are the most difficult. To prepare them well calls for allowing the natural flavors to assert themselves.

Chapter 17

ENGLAND

"There'll always be an England," so the song goes, and if some day there isn't, I for one will be sorely sorry. England has no mountains, its lakes are pretty but I can do without them, its towns are on the dreary side, and London is cold in the rain and fog. You can't ski there, it's hard to find a place to swim, I've never had what I'd call a great meal there, but I love England.

England, how do I love thee? Let me count the ways. You are noble, majestic. Your people are so polite. You are a people alive, full of life, and yet so enviably reserved. You have courage and when you fight, you fight with style. You have been your brothers' keeper and you are paying the price for it, also with style.

Your countryside is idyllic, your Shakespeare country all it takes to bring out the poet in us all. Your cathedrals and museums house the bones of some of the world's greatest men and women—saints and soldiers, writers and statesmen, kings and bishops who peopled our history and literature.

England underwent a long and heart-breaking period of decline as a world power following World War II. It lost most of its colonies to independence, other nations in the Common-wealth began exerting more home rule, and both its economy and stature in the world of diplomacy declined. Happily, since 1969 England has been on the upswing. With higher exports, lower imports, the pound devaluated but steady, and most of all with a new sense of confidence in her future, England is again prospering.

Conservative England is dying, with its old school system revolutionized, more liberal divorce laws, abortion legalized, and theater censorship relieved. Many problems remain, of course, including often unmanageable labor disputes, racial problems (though only 2 percent of England is black), and ever-present problems of how to deal with the other nations of the Commonwealth, especially the long-standing unrest in Northern Ireland.

But time has always been on the side of the patient British, and time, the great enemy, also can be the great friend. The Forsythes lived through their England and their grandchildren will live through theirs.

Most of us think only of London when we think of England, but that is only because London is in fact one of the most fascinating cities of the world. Spend a day touring Westminster Abbey, strolling Victoria Embankment along the Thames, seeing the crown jewels, admiring the Greek and Egyptian antiquities in the British Museum, watching the changing of the guard at St. James and following a horse troop to Buckingham Palace, ambling along The Mall up past Wellington Arch to Hyde Park, then seeing *Carmen* at Covent Garden or hearing a symphony in acoustically incredible Royal Festival Hall, and looking around you at night from Waterloo Bridge, feeling the glory of the ages sweep over you. Then hurry to Grosvenor Square and have trifles, a dessert nightcap, at Pam Pam's.

But England is also Windsor Castle, the old school at Harrow, villages and thatched-roof cottages of the Thames country, Oxford and its university founded in 1249, Canterbury where Becket was murdered, Sussex where William the Conqueror defeated Harold in 1066 and changed the course of world history, Winchester which was the capital of Alfred the Great and where stands King Arthur's Round Table, Dorset in the southwest where the old country England of Thomas Hardy remains virtually untouched, the midland shires of Shakespeare's Stratford-on-Avon, and the brooding northern hills of *Jane Eyre* and *Wuthering Heights*.

With all that sightseeing and history to absorb, you'll be wanting to start the day on a full stomach. That's always been how the British start their day. An English breakfast is *the* meal of the day, with porridge, bacon and eggs, grilled tomatoes, grilled kidneys, fish (fried sole or grilled herrings), toast and marmalade, breakfast scones, fresh or stewed fruit, and tea or coffee.

In the brisk country air or after pounding cobblestone pavements all day in search of history and culture, you may stop at an inn for some gravy soup or mulligatawny, a mutton or chicken and curry soup based on an East Indian dish. After that it's a short step to ordering Toad-in-the-hole, steak baked inside dough. Or a steamed pudding, a Lancashire hot pot or Cornish pasty.

For dinner, a dish of beef, boiled, roasted, or pressed, with Yorkshire pudding, leeks in white wine, salmagundy salad, plum pudding with hard sauce or crumpets followed by a savory of "angels on horseback," an oyster seasoned with lemon juice, wrapped in a slice of bacon, then baked and served on fried bread, washed down with rhubarb wine or a glass of old country mead.

England, how do I love thee? These are some of the ways.

Appetizers

Kippered Herrings

Place fresh kippers in hot water for 1 or 2 minutes and wipe dry. If they are dry or over-smoked, they should be soaked for about an hour. Kippers also may be fried in a little hot butter, but this changes the natural flavor of the old method of preparing them. Bloaters, unsplit kippered herrings, are cooked in either of the above ways, but just before serving spread with a little cold butter. (Normally a breakfast dish, kippered herrings can be enjoyed anytime.)

Deviled Kidneys

8 sheep's kidneys	4 tablespoons butter
1 teaspoon Worcestershire sauce	salt and pepper
1 tablespoon dry mustard	4 pieces toast

Skin the kidneys, cut them in half, and core them. Mix the sauce and mustard together. Heat butter in a saucepan, add the kidneys, season with salt and pepper, brown quickly for 2 minutes. Lower the heat and cook very gently for 6 minutes with the pan covered. Add the mustard mixture, stir well, and cook slowly another 2 minutes. Stir and serve on hot toast.

Cheese Straws

4 tablespoons unsalted butter	⅛ teaspoon cayenne pepper
4 tablespoons grated sharp Cheddar cheese	¼ teaspoon salt
¾ cup flour	1 egg yolk
	2 tablespoons ice water

Chill butter and cut into ¼-inch pieces. In a large, chilled mixing bowl, combine butter, cheese, flour, cayenne pepper, and salt. Rub ingredients together with fingers until mixture looks flaky. Break up egg yolk in separate bowl with a fork, stir in ice water, and pour over the flour mixture. Toss together until well mixed, then gather the dough into a ball, dust it lightly with flour, and wrap in wax paper. Refrigerate about 1 hour. Preheat oven to 400 degrees. Place ball of dough on lightly floured surface and shape into rectangle about 1 inch thick. Dust a little flour over and under it, and roll it into a rectangle about 4 inches wide, 14 inches long, and ¼ inch thick. With a sharp knife or pastry wheel, trim edges neatly. Cut dough crosswise into strips about ½ inch wide and 4 inches long. Transfer strips onto an ungreased baking sheet and bake in the middle of the oven until they are firm and lightly colored. Be careful not to let them brown too much. Using a spatula, transfer the straws to a wire rack to cool before serving. Yield: about 30 straws. (The straws keep up to two weeks if they are refrigerated in a covered container.)

Soups

Gravy Soup

¾ pound shin of beef	1 sprig thyme
butter	½ a bay leaf
1 stick celery	1 sprig of parsley
1 or 2 carrots (small)	peppercorns
1 or 2 onions	salt
5 to 6 cups beef stock	flour

Chop the meat, and cook until brown in a saucepan in a little butter. When meat begins to brown, add sliced celery, carrots, and onions and cook until also browned. Add warm stock, bring to a boil, and skim carefully. Add herbs and seasoning and simmer for about 3 hours. Strain soup through a cloth and replace in saucepan, bring to a boil, and thicken with a little flour worked with butter (about one ounce of flour is sufficient). Stir a few minutes before serving. (Sherry also can be added to the soup.)

Mulligatawny Soup

1 2-pound stewing chicken	salt
7 cups white stock	butter
2 onions	flour
1 small carrot	1 tablespoon curry powder
1 tablespoon chopped much-	½ cup cream
room	parsley
1 stick celery, chopped	cooked rice

Joint the chicken in 8 or 10 pieces and put in a saucepan with the stock, one shredded onion and carrot, mushroom, celery, and a little salt. Bring to a boil and skim. Simmer gently, covered, for about 2 hours. Chop the other onion finely and brown in a little butter, sprinkle with the flour and curry powder, and stir until smooth. Strain and put back in the same pan, and stir in the cream. To serve, put the pieces of chicken, skinned, into a soup tureen, strain the stock over them, and stir in cream and curry mixture. Add cooked rice to the soup and sprinkle with chopped parsley.

Salad

Salmagundy

This is an old English salad in which the ingredients are placed on an inverted saucer which rests on a serving dish. The ingredients are set down in a ring, each layer slightly smaller in diameter than the preceding one, so a pyramid is built. Use white meat of a cold chicken or cold roast veal, 4 hard-boiled eggs, some anchovy fillets or 2 pickled herrings, and some olives, sliced beetroot, pickled red cabbage and other *hors d'oeuvres* of your choice. Thin slices of cold ham or tongue also add to the salad. Try to vary the colors of ingredients as you build your pyramid. Garnish with lemon slices and top with parsley.

Vegetables

Green Peas with Mint

Boil peas with a sprig or two of mint, or add mint to the peas after they have been boiled.

Potatoes with Mint

Either boil potatoes with mint, or garnish them with mint.

Leeks Braised in White Wine

10 leeks	salt
3 slices bacon, diced	pepper
1 cup white wine	

Wash and soak leeks, trimming to leave about 3 inches of the green part on. Cut a cross on the edge of the green part and let leeks stand, green part down, in cold water for about 1 hour to make sure all the dirt is out, then drain them well. Cut leeks crosswise in two and put in a casserole with diced bacon. Season well and add wine and ½ cup water to about halfway. Cover and braise in 325 degree oven for about 1½ hours. Yield: 4 servings.

Dumplings

Suet Dumplings

Put 3 cups of flour in a bowl with 1 teaspoon baking powder, a pinch of salt, and mix with ⅓ pound of finely chopped suet. Gradually add enough water to make a stiff dough. Shape into small dumplings and add to stock of boiled salt brisket about ½ hour before beef is served.

Fish

Boiled Cod

2 teaspoons salt	1 bay leaf
1 teaspoon vinegar	juice of 1 lemon
1½ pounds cod cutlets	2 tablespoons butter
1 medium onion, chopped	parsley
2 peppercorns	

Put 1½ teaspoons salt and 1 teaspoon vinegar in 4 cups of water. Add the fish and let set for 3 hours. Add onion, peppercorns, bay leaf, and ½ teaspoon salt to 3 cups water. Bring to a boil and simmer for 20 minutes. Put fish into boiling water, then lower heat and simmer for 10 minutes or until tender. Drain and place on a hot dish, squeeze a little lemon juice on each cutlet, dab with butter, and garnish with parsley. Serve with boiled potatoes and any of the following three sauces:

Parsley Sauce

Melt 2 tablespoons butter in a saucepan, stir in 2 tablespoons of flour and add 1 cup of fish stock or water. Stir and simmer for a few minutes until sauce begins to thicken, then season with salt and pepper. Before serving, add 1 tablespoon finely chopped parsley. (The same sauce can be used for boiled chicken or veal by substituting chicken or veal stock for fish stock, and by adding ½ cup of hot milk.)

Egg Sauce

Melt 2 tablespoons butter in a saucepan, stir in ¼ cup flour and gradually add 1 cup boiling milk, stirring constantly. Season with a little salt and pepper, bring to a boil, and simmer about 5 minutes. Before serving, add 2 hard-boiled eggs, coarsely chopped.

Anchovy Sauce

Follow recipe for egg sauce, but substitute ½ cup milk and ½ cup fish stock for the milk. Omit eggs. Flavor with 1 teaspoon of anchovy essence, and color with a few drops of carmine.

Dover Sole

Wash and dry the fish, dip it in flour, and brush with beaten egg yolk, coat with bread crumbs, and fry in a pan of deep fat to a light golden color. (Or cook it for 7 to 10 minutes under a very hot grill, lowering heat after the first 2 or 3 minutes and turning the sole to brown both sides.) Garnish with lemon and parsley and serve with melted butter sauce.

Dressed Crab

Remove meat from the shells and claws and shred it. Put soft, creamy parts of the crab in a bowl and mix with oil and vinegar in equal quantities, a little prepared mustard, and season with salt and pepper. Add crab meat, mix all well, and put mixture back in the cleaned crab shell. Garnish with yolk of a hard-boiled egg rubbed through a sieve, coarsely chopped egg white, thin slices of lemon, and sprigs of parsley.

Fish and Chips
(deep fried fish and potatoes)
Batter

1 cup flour
1 egg yolk
2 tablespoons beer
¼ teaspoon salt

3 tablespoons milk mixed with
3 tablespoons cold water
1 egg white

Pour flour into large mixing bowl, make a well in the center, and add the egg yolk, beer, and salt. Stir together until well-mixed, then gradually pour in combined milk and water and stir until batter is smooth. Beat egg white until it forms peaks on the beater, then fold it into the batter.

Chips

Vegetable oil or shortening   2 pounds baking potatoes

Peel potatoes, slice lengthwise into strips ½ inch thick and ½ inch wide. To cook the chips and fish, heat 4 or 5 inches of oil or shortening in a deep-fat fryer to 375 degrees. Preheat oven to 250 degrees and line a large shallow roasting pan with paper towels. Dry potatoes and deep fry in 3 or 4 batches until they are crisp and light brown. Transfer to lined pan to drain and place in oven to keep warm.

Fish

2 pounds fresh white fish fil-
    lets (sole, haddock, flounder)

Skin and cut fish into 3-by-5-inch serving pieces. Wash under cold water and pat dry with paper towels. Drop 2 or 3 pieces at a time into batter (see above) and, when well soaked, drop into hot fat. Fry for 4 or 5 minutes until golden brown, turning pieces occasionally with spoon to prevent them from sticking together or to the pan. To serve, heap fish in center of large heated platter and arrange chips around them. Sprinkle both fish and chips with malt vinegar and salt. (The British eat fish and chips wrapped in newspaper, unwrapping the paper first, of course.)

Poultry

Boiled Chicken

Boil chicken in water with salt, peppercorns, herbs, and vegetables for 45 minutes to an hour, until tender. Serve with slices of bacon, accompanied by parsley sauce (see index).

Chicken Curry

1 chicken, 3–4 pounds, jointed	1 tablespoon mild curry powder
4 tablespoons cooking oil	2 small raw potatoes, grated
1 large onion, chopped	1 apple, grated
1 cup chicken stock (or chicken bouillon) (or milk from 1 coconut)	salt and pepper
½ coconut, grated	1 chicken liver

Bone and skin chicken and chop into large pieces. Heat oil in large skillet and fry chopped onion until light brown. Add chicken and fry on both sides about 15 minutes. Add coconut milk (or chicken stock or bouillon), grated coconut, curry powder, grated raw potatoes, apple, pepper, and salt. Cover and simmer slowly about 1 hour. Add stock if necessary. Fifteen minutes before chicken is ready, add chopped chicken liver. Serve with boiled rice and chutney. (Best rice to serve with a curry is long-grained Patna rice.) Yield: 4 to 6 servings.

Meats

Roast Beef

1 sirloin or middle rib   drippings
salt   pepper
flour (optional)

Sprinkle the meat all over with salt and pepper and rub in well. If meat does not have much fat, put 2 ounces of drippings on the fat side. Heat oven to 450 degrees, stand the roast beef in a roasting dish and cook for 20 minutes. Reduce to about 350 degrees and cook 16 minutes per pound for underdone beef, 22 minutes per pound for medium, and 30 minutes per pound for well done. (You may want to dredge the meat with flour or sprinkle flour on the meat shortly before the meat is done.) Baste with drippings periodically.

Serve with horseradish sauce, Yorkshire pudding, and potatoes, peeled (halved if too big) and cooked in the roasting dish with the meat for 30 to 45 minutes or until soft inside and brown outside.

Cold Horseradish Sauce

Add 2 tablespoons finely grated horseradish to 1 cup white sauce (see below) and add a little vinegar (about 1 teaspoon), sugar, salt, and cayenne pepper to taste.

Hot Horseradish Sauce

Put yolks of 2 hard-boiled eggs in a bowl, work into a paste with a wooden spoon, add 3 tablespoons vinegar gradually, and work into a cream. Add 2 tablespoons finely grated horseradish, 1 tablespoon cream, a little salt, and powdered sugar to taste.

White Sauce

Put 4 tablespoons butter and 4 tablespoons flour in a saucepan and dilute with a little less than 2 cups of either boiling water or boiling milk. Stir until thick, season with a little salt and pepper and simmer 10 minutes.

Yorkshire Pudding

¾ cup flour   1 teaspoon salt
2 eggs   1 cup milk
4 tablespoons beef drippings

Mix flour and salt in a bowl, add eggs and milk, beating batter all the time. Allow to stand in cool place for 1 hour. Pour beef drippings into an oblong shallow pan and heat. Then pour batter into pan and bake ½ hour in 450 degree oven. Cut into squares and serve with roast beef.

Boiled Beef

3 pounds brisket of beef   1 sprig parsley
3 carrots, sliced   1 bay leaf
2 turnips, diced   salt
3 onions   ½ teaspoon peppercorns
1 sprig thyme

Wash meat and place in pot with barely enough water to cover. Bring to a boil and cook for 20 minutes, removing any scum that forms on top. Add carrots, turnips, whole onions, thyme, parsley, bay leaf, salt, and peppercorns. Reduce heat and simmer until meat is tender. Serve with dumplings. Yield: 4 to 6 servings.

Pressed Beef

Wash salt brisket of beef and put in saucepan with enough warm water to cover. Bring to boil and skim. Add 1 or 2 onions, carrots, ½ turnip, sprig of parsley, sprig of thyme, 1 bay leaf, and a few peppercorns. Simmer until bones can be easily detached from the meat. Remove from stock and press meat between two boards or two dishes, placing a heavy weight over upper board or dish. Serve cold with your favorite sauce.

Toad in the Hole

1 pound steak
½ cup flour
1 cup milk
1 egg

2 tablespoons drippings
salt and pepper
kidneys and bacon

Cut steak into 1-inch pieces. Mix flour, milk, beaten egg, and ½ teaspoon salt to make a smooth batter and leave for 1 hour or longer. Heat the dripping in a flat tin or fireproof dish in a 400 degree oven. When smoking hot, pour in ¼ of the batter and bake until set, about 10 minutes. Now put meat in and season with salt and pepper. Pour over the rest of the batter and bake 25 minutes until crust rises. Lower the heat to about 350 degrees and cook another 20 minutes. Cut up pre-cooked kidney, small rolls of bacon, and add to the meat.

Shepherd's Pie

leftover cold mutton
mashed potatoes
butter or drippings
1 tablespoon chopped onion

salt and pepper
1 cup stock or gravy
egg yolk

Cut meat into thin slices and place in pie pan over a thin layer of mashed potatoes mixed with butter. Sprinkle meat with chopped onion, season with salt and pepper, add stock or gravy, cover with another layer of mashed potatoes, and either roughen the surface with a fork or smooth it with a knife so that it looks like pastry. Brush with egg yolk and bake in a 350 degree oven until lightly browned.

Beefsteak Pie

1 pound lean beef
¾ pound potatoes
1 tablespoon chopped onion

pinch of chopped parsley
salt and pepper
stock or water

Cut beef into slices about ½ inch thick and arrange around a pie pan. Put potatoes in center, cut either in thick slices or shaped into small balls, and sprinkle with onion and parsley. Season with salt and pepper and add enough stock or water to cover the meat. Cover with either puff pastry or short crust, press edges down firmly, moistening the pastry slightly, and decorate with pastry cut out in fancy shapes. Make a slight opening in the center of the pie, brush with beaten egg yolk, and bake in 250 degree oven about 2½ hours.

Lancashire Hot Pot

6 potatoes, peeled and sliced   1 large onion, sliced
1½ pounds lamb shoulder or   salt and pepper
   breast   2 tablespoons butter, melted
2 sheep kidneys (optional)

Butter a casserole and put a thick layer of sliced potatoes on the bottom. Then add meat, cut into cubes, and cover with the sliced onion. Season with salt and pepper. Add 1 cup water. Place layer of potatoes on top, covering meat completely. Brush with melted butter. Place in 350 degree oven and bake for 2 hours. Yield: 4 servings.

Cornish Pasties

½ pound beef or liver, diced   1 teaspoon baking powder
3 potatoes, diced   ⅛ teaspoon salt
1 onion, chopped fine   6 tablespoons butter or short-
salt and pepper   ening
1¾ cups flour

Mix diced beef or liver, potatoes, and onions together and season with salt and pepper. Set aside until ready to use. Sift flour, baking powder, and salt together. Cut in the shortening and when well-blended, add enough water to make dough. Place dough on a floured board and roll out ¼ inch thick. Cut into squares (or circles) and place a little of the meat mixture on ½ of the square. Fold dough and pinch edges together. Bake in 325 degree oven about 1 hour. Yield: 4 servings.

Pastries, Desserts, Breads

Crumpets

1 package or cake of active yeast or compressed yeast	½ cup milk
½ teaspoon sugar	1 egg
1 cup flour	5 tablespoons butter cut into
¼ teaspoon salt	¼-inch bits

Ideally crumpets are made in 3-inch-round flan rings (you'll need 5 or 6 of them) but they can be made with open-topped cookie cutters.

Sprinkle yeast and sugar over 2 tablespoons lukewarm water in a small, shallow bowl and let stand for 2 or 3 minutes. Then stir them together to dissolve the yeast. Set bowl in a warm, draft-free place such as an unlighted oven, for 4 or 5 minutes until yeast bubbles up and mixture almost doubles in size.

Sift flour and salt into large mixing bowl and make a well in the center. Pour in yeast mixture and milk and drop in 1 egg. Beat with large spoon and add 1 tablespoon butter, then beat until a smooth soft batter is formed. Place a towel over the bowl and set bowl aside in warm draft-free place for 1 hour or until batter has doubled in volume.

Melt remaining 4 tablespoons butter in a small pan without letting it brown. Skim off surface foam and spoon clear butter into a bowl, discarding milky solids at bottom of pan. With a pastry brush, coat bottom of a heavy 10- to 12-inch skillet and inside of the flan rings or cookie cutters with about half the clarified butter.

Arrange rings in skillet and place the pan over moderate heat. For each crumpet, drop about 1 tablespoon of batter into each ring. Batter will spread out and fill the ring. When crumpets start to bubble and their bottoms turn a light brown, remove the rings. Turn crumpets over with a spatula and cook another minute or so to brown on the other side. Transfer crumpets to a heated serving plate and cover with foil to keep them warm while you coat the skillet and rings with the rest of the clarified butter and cook the remaining batter. Serve crumpets with unsalted butter and syrups, jams, jellies, or marmalades. Yield: 5 or 6 crumpets.

Hot Cross Buns

6½ cups flour
4 cups sugar.
4 cups currants
1 teaspoon mixed spice

pinch of salt
1 ounce yeast
1 cup milk
½ pound butter

Mix 6 cups flour and sugar and add currants, mixed spice, and salt. Make a hole in center of flour and put in yeast dissolved in a little warm milk, making a light batter with the rest of the milk and ½ cup flour. Cover and let stand in warm place for about 1 hour until it rises. Then add melted butter and mix and beat thoroughly, making a soft paste with all the flour and a little warm milk if needed. Cover with a cloth and let stand in a warm place for another ½ hour until dough has risen. Then shape into buns about the size of an egg, place on buttered baking tins in rows three inches apart and leave to rise again for another ½ hour. Then make a cross on each bun with a knife and bake in a 400 degree oven for 15 to 20 minutes. Brush buns over with a brush dipped in milk as soon as they are taken from the oven.

Plum Pudding

2 cups seeded raisins
1 cup seedless raisins
¼ cup candied lemon peel,
   finely chopped
¼ cup candied citron peel,
   finely chopped
1 cup currants
1¼ cups flour
3 cups bread crumbs

1 cup brown sugar
1 teaspoon ground nutmeg
1 teaspoon mace
1 teaspoon salt
2 cups suet, chopped fine
6 eggs
1 cup molasses
½ cup brandy

Wash and seed the raisins and combine with the other fruits. Sift flour over the fruits and mix well. Combine breadcrumbs, sugar, nutmeg, mace, and salt, and mix. Add suet and work it in evenly. Mix in the beaten eggs, molasses and brandy and when well-blended, stir in the floured fruit. Pour mixture into well-buttered pudding molds, filling them about ⅔ full. Cover and steam about 5 hours. Serve with hard sauce (see below). Pudding may be reheated by steaming in top of double boiler ½ hour before serving.

Roly-Poly Pudding

¼ pound suet
2 cups flour
jam

pinch of salt
2 teaspoons baking powder

Chop suet finely and mix in a bowl with flour, salt, baking powder, and a little cold water. Put on floured board and roll out to a sheet of about ¼ inch thick. Spread with thin layer of jam, moisten the edges, roll lightly in shape of a long sausage, press down the edges to seal them tightly, wrap in a cloth, tie ends with string, and boil for about 1½ hours. If you prefer, bake the pudding for about ¾ hour or longer in a 350 degree oven.

Hard Sauce

Divide ½ cup butter into small pieces and work in 4 tablespoons powdered sugar, 4 bitter and 6 sweet almonds previously blanched, skinned, and pounded in a mortar, and brandy to taste. Beat all together with a wooden spoon, and keep in a cool place until used with plum or other pudding.

Mince Pies

Fill small individual pies with the following mixture: one pound each of very finely chopped suet, currants, raisins, stoned and quartered, peeled and cored chopped apples, powdered sugar, ½ pound sultana raisins, ¼ pound mixed candied peel, finely shredded, 1 lemon, a little cinnamon, mace, and grated nutmeg, ½ cup brandy. Lemon should be pared and the rind boiled until tender, then rubbed through a sieve and mixed in a bowl with all the other ingredients. Put in a jar with an air-tight lid and let stand for about 1 month before using.

Trifles

3 small sponge cakes
6 macaroons
3 tablespoons brandy
1 cup medium sweet sherry
strawberry jam
1 cup custard

½ cup cream
⅓ cup sugar
1 egg white
¼ cup blanched almonds cut
   in strips

Put sponge cakes and macaroons in a dish, pour over the brandy and sherry (keeping back 1 teaspoon of sherry), and leave to soak for 10 minutes. Cover with a thick layer of strawberry jam. Pour over the cooked custard. Whisk the cream, sugar, egg white, and 1 teaspoon sherry until fluffy, cover the cake and jam mixture. Stick almond strips all over the cream mixture. Serve cold.

Lemon Soufflé

1 cup confectioner's sugar
5 eggs

2 lemons

Sift the sugar. Separate the eggs and beat the whites until stiff. Grate 1 lemon and squeeze juice of both. Add the peel and juice to the egg yolks, stir in the sugar, and whip until creamy. Fold in the stiff egg whites. Put in a buttered soufflé dish and bake in a 375 degree oven for 20 minutes. Serve hot.

Savories

The British enjoy after-dessert meal-toppers they call savories. Some favorite savories follow:

Angels on Horseback

Season an oyster with a little lemon juice and cayenne pepper, wrap in a thin slice of bacon, secure with a toothpick, and either grill or fry in butter or bake in a hot oven until the bacon is crisp. Remove toothpick and serve on toast or fried bread sprinkled with a little more lemon juice and cayenne pepper.

Smoked Haddock on Toast

Chop a cooked smoked haddock finely, rub through a sieve, mix the puree with a little white wine, season and spread on rounds of toasted bread. Serve hot.

Sardine Toast

Skin and bone sardines and chop them coarsely. Cook in a little milk and butter with 1 or 2 egg yolks, a dash of essence of anchovy, and season with cayenne pepper. Stir mixture over a slow fire and when it begins to thicken, pour over hot buttered squares of toast and serve hot.

Toasted Cheese

Sprinkle grated Cheddar or Cheshire cheese liberally on slices of toasted bread cut ½ inch thick, season with cayenne pepper, and place in a hot oven until cheese melts. Serve on hot plates and eat with a little hot mustard.

Drinks

Mead

2 cups sugar	1 sprig rosemary
4 cups clear honey	1 small piece ginger root
2 lemons	1 ounce yeast
4 cloves	1 piece toast

Boil the sugar, 1 gallon water, and honey together and skim off any surface scum. Stand in an earthenware bowl and add juice of the lemons and the rind of one. Add cloves, rosemary, and ginger. When mixture has cooled, add yeast on a piece of toast. Cover with a cloth to keep out dirt or insects. Fermentation will continue for about a week, but remove lemon peel after 3 days. When liquid has stopped hissing, after about a week, strain and bottle. Cork tightly and leave at least 2 weeks before drinking. Mead will taste even better the longer it is aged. Yield: 1½ gallons.

Rhubarb Wine

4 pounds rhubarb	2 tablespoons dried hops
2 lemons	8 cups sugar

Clean and cut up rhubarb and put in a pan with sliced lemons and dried hops. Pour 1 gallon boiling water over and let stand for 9 days, then strain through a cloth. Add sugar and 1 quart boiling water. Stir until sugar is dissolved, then bottle but leave uncorked to ferment. Cover with a cloth to keep dust out. After about a week it will stop bubbling and hissing. Cork the bottles and let the wine age at least 2 months, the longer the better.

The Wassail Bowl

3 quarts beer	4 glasses sherry
2 cups sugar	3 slices lemon
1 grated nutmeg	3 slices toast with crust re-
1 teaspoon grated ginger	moved

Warm 1 quart of beer to comfortable drinking temperature, add sugar, nutmeg, and ginger. Stir until sugar is dissolved. Add sherry, remaining beer, and lemon slices. Warm again. Serve with toast floating on top.

Chapter 18

IRELAND

Everyone is at least a little Irish, especially on St. Patrick's Day, unless they don't have a soul for the land, comradeship, the old values, and a taste for Irish stew or Irish coffee.

Northern Ireland has been plagued by "The Troubles," a civil war between the Catholic one-third of the population and Protestant two-thirds off and on since the early 1920s. Despite the seriousness of the battles, the rest of Ireland is as tranquil as a pastoral scene from John Ford's exquisite movie, *The Quiet Man*.

Lovely red-haired, green-eyed colleens still walk the green hills of County Tipperary, O'Regans and O'Rourkes still down a pint and play darts in the pubs of Dublin, Ireland's fishing streams are not polluted, you can still take a cruise down the River Shannon, and it costs next to nothing to roll up and down the lake-filled hill country of Killarney in a pony-drawn trap. It isn't that the Irish resist change, they simply wouldn't know how to live without the old ways. And when we see what rapid change has done to so much of the world, we can wonder if the Irish don't have something we miss.

Ireland actually has had its "troubles" for more than 700 years, fighting to free itself from British rule. In 1921 a treaty recognized twenty-six counties in southern Ireland as a self-governing Free State now called the Republic of Ireland, while six counties in the north remained British. The province of Northern Ireland also is referred to by its ancient name, Ulster.

Its capital is Belfast, and its sights are many: the beautiful Antrim coast with its rolling glens and view to Scotland, Londonderry and its old city walls and seven gates, the lovely seaside resorts of County Down, and the hunting and fishing mecca of County Tyrone.

Ireland north and south never has been a productive land. During the famine years of 1846–47, millions of Irish emigrated, many coming to America. More than 20,000 Irish still leave the Old Sod each year, but new births are beginning to offset the outflow of population. The songs, traditions, and food of the Irish come with the emigrees to their new homes, and the fame of Ireland spreads.

The food of Ireland is simple and substantial. Beef, mutton, fresh fish, and potatoes are staples. Corned beef and cabbage is as Irish as Irish stew, and there also are crubeens (pig's feet), colcannon (potatoes mashed with cabbage), potato cake, soda bread, and of course, Irish coffee. Guinness stout, made in Dublin and enjoyed all over the world, is as popular in Ireland as Irish whiskey, and the two are often drunk together.

Sweet Molly Malone and Danny Boy have grown up and moved away, more's the pity. But Kathleen has come home again. I know because I saw her in the airport at Shannon when I first set foot on the emerald isle. A flame-haired, cat-eyed, long-stemmed Irish rose, working behind the counter at a duty-free gift shop. Alas, Irish lasses are always chaperoned, so all I was able to pick up was an address where I could buy a tweed sport coat.

The Irish eat many of the same foods as the English, with the following additions.

Vegetables

Colcannon
(mashed potatoes with parsnips and cabbage)

Mash together boiled potatoes and parsnips, moisten with a little milk, mix with boiled chopped cabbage, and simmer a few minutes with a little butter and season with salt and pepper before serving.

Swedes with Bacon

Place a layer of smoked ham, sliced thinly, in the bottom of a saucepan. Add a layer of cooked turnip, then another layer of ham and repeat. Add 2 tablespoons cold water and simmer until done.

Cabbage with Bacon

Cut a large cabbage in half and boil in salted water for 10 minutes. Take out of water and soak in cold water for a minute, then drain. Line bottom of a flat saucepan with thin layers of bacon. Place cabbage on top of bacon, season with salt and pepper, cloves, and allspice, then cover with cabbage stock and add another layer of bacon. Cover and simmer 1½ hours. Serve the bacon with the cabbage. (It also can be cooked in the oven at 350 degrees for about 2 hours.) Yield: 6 servings.

Champ

2 cups spring onions
1 cup milk
2 cups mashed potatoes

2 tablespoons butter
salt and pepper

Chop up onions and cook in 1 cup of milk. Drain and add to hot freshly cooked mashed potatoes. Beat them together, season to taste, and add enough milk to make them creamy. Put into a warm deep dish and make a well in the middle. Pour hot melted butter into the well and serve. (As a variation, chopped parsley, chives, and peas can also be used. If using peas, leave them whole and add them last.)

Potatoes, Dumplings

Farls
(soda scones)

3 cups flour	1 teaspoon baking powder
1 teaspoon cream of tartar	1 cup buttermilk
1 teaspoon salt	

Sift dry ingredients together and mix lightly with your hands. Make a hollow in the center and add enough buttermilk to make a soft dough. Turn onto a floured board and knead quickly and lightly until dough is free of cracks. Roll out and cut in scones (a flat, round cake). Place on a greased and floured tin and bake in 400 degree oven until thoroughly baked, about 15 minutes for medium-sized scones.

Stelk
(potatoes and onions)

Boil 2 pounds of potatoes until they are done. Simmer separately a medium bunch of spring onions, chopped, including the green part, in a little milk. When onions are cooked, mash the potatoes and cream them with the milk from the onions. Season with salt and pepper and finally add the green onion and 1 tablespoon of butter. Beat until mixture is a light green fluff. (Can be enjoyed as is or with a side dish of fried bacon.)

Poultry

Spatchcock
(split and boiled chicken)

1 young chicken, about 2½ pounds	1 tablespoon milk
salt and pepper	1 teaspoon dry mustard
4 tablespoons butter, melted	2 slices white bread made into bread crumbs

Split chicken in half through the breast. Beat each half well with the flat side of a heavy knife. Place in a broiler, without the rack, and season with salt and pepper. Pour half the melted butter over the chicken and broil for from 7 to 10 minutes. (Be careful not to have broiler too hot and burn the chicken.) Turn chicken over and broil same amount of time on the other side. Mix the mustard with the milk and brush the upper side of the chicken with the mixture, then sprinkle with fresh bread crumbs. Baste with the butter from the pan, put the chicken under the broiler again and let it color slowly. Serve with a lettuce salad or watercress.

Meat

Irish Stew

4 pounds neck of mutton	12 peeled potatoes
salt and pepper	1½ cups beef stock or water
8 small white stewing onions	

Divide mutton into 8 or 10 trimmed chops, cutting off all excess fat and rough bone. Season liberally with pepper and a little salt. Place chops in a deep saucepan with enough water to cover. Add onions, cover, and stew gently about 30 minutes. Then remove stew from the fire, pour the liquid in a bowl, remove any remaining fat from the meat, and pour liquid back over the chops. Add the potatoes and beef stock or water and boil gently about 45 minutes. To serve, put potatoes in center of serving dish, arranging meat around them, and pour the sauce and onions over the whole. Serve very hot. Yield: 6 servings.

Corned Beef and Cabbage

4–5 pound brisket of beef	1 garlic clove
3 onion slices	2 green pepper rings
4 cloves	1 stalk celery
6 whole black peppercorns	1 carrot
1 bay leaf	A few sprigs parsley
½ teaspoon dried rosemary	1 green cabbage

Place brisket in large, deep saucepan and cover with cold water. Add onion slices, studded with cloves, the pepper corns, bay leaf, rosemary, garlic, pepper rings, celery, carrot, and parsley tied in a bunch. Cover and bring to a boil, then reduce heat and simmer 4 to 5 hours until fork-tender. Wash the cabbage, cut into quarters, and trim off the core, leaving enough to hold cabbage together. About ½ hour before meat is done, skim off excess fat from top of water, arrange cabbage on top of meat and simmer, covered, for 25 to 30 minutes until cabbage is tender-crisp. To serve, slice the meat and put on a platter with cabbage around it. Yield: 8 servings.

Desserts, Breads

Fadge
(potato cake)

6 medium potatoes	salt
2 tablespoons butter, melted	flour

Peel and mash freshly boiled potatoes in a well-floured bowl, sprinkle with salt and add melted butter. Over this sift a layer of flour, work with both hands until flour is well blended, and continue dredging with flour and working it in until it is pliable enough to roll out. Add flour in small quantities, because too much flour and kneading will toughen the cake. Roll out to required thickness in a flat cake and cut into sections. Place on a hot griddle or in a frying pan and cook quickly until brown. Turn and cook upper side the same way. If served hot, butter the cakes as they come from the pan. Authentic Irish potato cake is buttered generously and served with sugar.

Boxty Pancakes
(potato pancakes)

Peel, wash, and grate some large potatoes, then drain. To each cupful of grated potato add 1 teaspoon salt, ½ cup flour, and enough milk to make a fairly stiff batter. Let stand 1 hour, then fry like pancakes in bacon drippings. Serve hot with butter.

Irish Soda Bread

3 cups flour	1 teaspoon baking soda
1 teaspoon salt	2 tablespoons fat
1 teaspoon cream of tartar	1 cup sour milk or buttermilk

Put dry ingredients through a sieve and rub in the fat. Make a well in the center and mix in enough liquid to give a soft, spongy dough. Turn out onto a lightly floured board and shape quickly into 1 or 2 round cakes. Place on a floured baking sheet and score with a knife. Bake in 425 degree oven for 30 to 40 minutes until well risen, lightly browned, and firm underneath.

Potato and Apple Cake

Boil and mash 4 potatoes and peel and slice 4 large cooking apples. Add ¾ cup drippings to 4 cups of flour and mix with potatoes, making a dough. Roll out to ½ inch thick. Line a greased pie dish with some of the dough and cover with a layer of apples. Sprinkle each layer with 1 tablespoon sugar. Repeat layers alternately, finishing with pastry. Bake in 350 degree oven for 1 hour.

Drinks

Irish Coffee

Heat a claret glass or goblet and put in 2 lumps of sugar. Pour in a jigger of Irish whiskey and fill ⅔ with hot, strong, black coffee. Dissolve the sugar, then carefully add some sweet cream, pouring it in over the back of a spoon so that it sits on top the drink. Do not mix, but drink the coffee and whiskey through the layer of cream.

Chapter 19

SCOTLAND

Bonnie Scotland—home of the highland fling, bagpipes, the poet Bobby Burns, heather on the hill, Scotch broth, marmalade, cock-a-leekie, Aberdeen Angus beef, Clydesdale draft horses, the Loch Ness monster, and Scotch whisky. A land of history and accomplishments as varied as its countryside.

Scotland's southern uplands are the brooding moors where shepherds tend their sheep and skilled ladies make beautiful woolen sweaters. The central lowlands are where most Scotsmen live, in Edinburgh and other industrialized cities. The highlands are mountainous and havens for tourists who can fish the bountiful streams for trout and salmon, hunt deer, grouse, ptarmigan, and hare in the forests, and swim or shop in Aberdeen and Inverness.

No poor country cousin is Scotland, one of the most prosperous members of the British Commonwealth. But prosperity has not gone to their heads. Scots are still a hard-working, thrifty people, friendly, quick to joke, and they are still very proper. Nightclubs are hardly known in Scotland, so Scots take their whisky at restaurants or at home.

Scotland has been tied to Britain since 1603, and though it has been politically united to England for more than three centuries, it remains nationalistically and culturally apart.

Edinburgh, home of the famous music festival each summer, is one of the most beautiful cities of the old country, often called

"The Athens of the North," blending old world charm with modern convenience. Edinburgh castle and Holyrood palace dominate the city. In between and along Princes Street are buildings and monuments memorializing Mary Queen of Scots and Sir Walter Scott. Gracious parks and gardens abound in the city.

Beyond Edinburgh and industrialized Glasgow are the famed Scottish Highlands with historic old villages and castles. Far out in the Hebrides are remote islands unspoiled by the passing of time.

Scots pay more attention to food than the British. Their food is more inventive and varied, though you may have to acquire a taste for some of their native dishes.

Haggis is not only a food it is a national institution, a combination of oatmeal, chopped meats, and spices ("haggis" means to chop or hack). Haggis is boiled in a sheep's paunch, and red-blooded Scots eat it with "gravy," straight Scotch whisky which is not poured over but drunk with the meat.

Scotch broth, cock-a-leekie soup (chicken with leeks), fresh fish including trout, salmon, cod, and sole are popular, and Scots are known for their crab pie and finnan haddie (smoked haddock). Hash and leftovers are blithely called hotch-potch and inky-pinky.

Marmalades were invented in Scotland, and favorite native baked goods include shortbread fingers, bannocks, and tea scones.

Once in Scotland, to quote the poet Robert Burns, and your heart is in the highlands.

Appetizers

Scotch Eggs

3 anchovy fillets
½ cup minced ham
¼ cup fresh bread crumbs
½ teaspoon pepper

1 beaten egg
4 hard-boiled eggs
fat for frying

Chop anchovies finely, add to minced ham, bread crumbs, and pepper, then stir in beaten egg. Dip hard-boiled eggs in mixture to coat, and fry in hot fat until brown all over. Cut in half and serve on toast. Yield: 4 servings.

Soups

Scotch (Barley) Broth

2 pounds lamb neck or shoulder
2 tablespoons barley
2 teaspoons salt
⅛ teaspoon black pepper
½ cup turnips

½ cup leeks
½ cup carrots
½ cup onions
½ cup celery
1 tablespoon chopped parsley

Place lamb in a heavy 4 or 5 quart casserole and add 2 quarts water. Bring to a boil over high heat, skimming off fat from surface. Add barley, salt and pepper, reduce heat to low, and simmer partially covered for 1 hour. Chop vegetables finely and add to the broth (including 2 inches of green of leek), partially cover again, and cook another hour or longer. Transfer lamb to a plate and cut meat away from the bones. Discard the bones, fat, and gristle, and cut meat into ½-inch cubes. Return meat to soup and simmer 2 or 3 minutes to heat throughly. Taste for seasoning. To serve, sprinkle with parsley. Yield: 6 servings.

Cock-a-Leekie Soup

1 small chicken
6 leeks
⅓ cup butter
salt and pepper

2½ quarts stock or water
a few sprigs thyme and
parsley tied together
2 tablespoons rice

Cut up the chicken. Wash the leeks and chop finely. Heat butter in a large saucepan and add chicken lightly seasoned with salt and pepper. Fry gently on all sides until brown, add leeks and fry another 3 minutes. Pour on the stock or water, add thyme and parsley, bring to a boil. Skim off fat if necessary and simmer 2 hours until chicken is tender. Add rice after 1 hour's cooking. Remove chicken, take out bones and chop the meat, return to the soup, remove the thyme and parsley. Add more salt and pepper to taste. (The soup tastes even better made 24 hours before eating.) Yield: 6 servings.

Vegetables

Turnip Purry

Peel young turnips carefully, boil in salted water until tender, rub through a sieve or mash with a wooden spoon through a colander. Put in a saucepan, season with salt and pepper, and add a lump of butter. Stir and when hot and smooth, put the puree in a hot dish and mark in diamond shapes.

Beets and Potatoes

oil for frying	salt and pepper
2 small onions, sliced	1 teaspoon fine sugar
1 tablespoon butter	1 tablespoon tarragon vinegar
1 tablespoon flour	2 medium beets, cooked
1 cup warm milk	4 cups cooked hot mashed
½ cup cream	potatoes

Heat a little oil and saute sliced onions in a skillet but do not let them brown. Melt the butter in a saucepan, stir in the flour, add warm milk and then the cream, stirring constantly. Season liberally. Add sugar and vinegar. Cook the sauce for a few minutes, then put sliced cold beets and sliced onion into it. Have the hot mashed potatoes ready and make a ring of them on a warm serving dish. Put beets and sauce in the middle and serve hot. Delicious with most cold meats. (Celery may be substituted for beets.) Yield: 4 to 6 servings.

Potatoes

Stovies

Peel potatoes and put in pan with just enough water to cover the bottom so they do not burn. Sprinkle with salt and put tiny bits of butter in, cover and simmer very slowly until soft. (Onions may be sliced and tossed in drippings and added with a little pepper, but the recipes for authentic stovies do not include onions.)

Fish

Herrings in Oatmeal

Prepare and bone herrings and dry well by letting them lie in the folds of a cloth for an hour or two. Then sprinkle with pepper and salt and dip each fish into coarse oatmeal, pressing it onto both sides. Put a little fat into a frying pan. When it is smoking hot, put herring in and brown nicely on both sides. Drain fish on paper and serve garnished with slice of lemon and parsley.

Finnan Haddie
(smoked haddock)

1½-2 pounds smoked haddock poached eggs (optional)
2 tablespoons fat parsley
½ cup milk

Wash and trim smoked haddock and cut in 2 to 4 pieces. Put fat and milk in a pan, bring to a boil and add the fish. Poach gently until cooked, then put on a hot dish. Boil the liquid for 2 or 3 minutes, add chopped parsley if desired, and pour over the fish. Serve finnan haddie topped with poached eggs if desired. Yield: 4 servings.

Partan Pie
(crab pie)

Scoop crab meat from shell, season with salt, pepper, and grated nutmeg and mix with some bread crumbs and a few small pieces of butter. Put meat back into shells that have been cleaned, and pour over it a little warm vinegar to which some mustard has been added. Alternatively, substitute oil for the butter, and brown the crab meat under the grill.

Poultry

Scottish Chicken

Wash and dry chicken and cut into quarters. Put into large saucepan with just enough water to cover and bring to a boil. Skim before putting in some whole mace and a little sprig of parsley. Cover and stew for about an hour. Chop half a handful of clean washed parsley and add. Beat 6 eggs, wait until liquid returns to a boil, and pour eggs over liquid. Put all in a deep hot dish (discarding mace and parsley) and serve.

Meat

Minced Collops
(coarsely chopped meat)

1 onion
drippings
1 pound chopped beef or
    rumpsteak
salt and pepper
pinch of nutmeg
stock

1 tablespoon mushroom
    ketchup
2 tablespoons bread crumbs or
    oatmeal
mashed potatoes
hard-boiled egg slices
toast

Fry finely chopped onion in a little drippings, then add minced meat, season with salt and pepper and a pinch of nutmeg, moisten with about 1 cup of stock or water and simmer for 1 to 1½ hours. Then add ketchup, bread crumbs (or oatmeal), mix all together and cook for 5 to 10 minutes. Put on a hot dish surrounded with a border of mashed potatoes. Garnish with slices of hard-boiled egg and small pieces of toast.

Haggis

1 sheep's paunch (including heart, liver)	1 or 2 onions, finely chopped
½ pound suet, minced	pepper and salt
1 cup oatmeal	milk

Clean and soak paunch in cold salted water for about 12 hours. Then turn inside out and set aside until needed. Put the pluck in cold water, bring to a boil, and simmer 1½ hours. Remove from water and cut off the pipes and gristle. Grate half of the liver (discard other half) and mince the heart. Mix in a bowl with finely chopped suet, browned oatmeal, onions, and season liberally with salt and pepper. Moisten with the water in which the pluck was boiled. Put mixture in the paunch, sew up the opening, and leave enough space for the oatmeal to swell. Put in a large saucepan of hot water with some milk added, and boil for 3 hours. Be ready to prick the haggis with a needle as soon as it begins to swell. Serve haggis plain, without any gravy or garnish. Scotsmen drink straight whisky with it.

Hotch-Potch

1½ to 2 pounds neck of mutton	salt and pepper
1 small cabbage or cauliflower	1 pint fresh peas and beans
2 small white turnips	1 teaspoon sugar
6 leeks	1 tablespoon parsley, chopped
6 carrots	

Cut meat into pieces. Prepare the vegetables and shred or dice them. Put meat and vegetables (except peas and beans) into a large saucepan with 12 cups water and seasoning. Simmer at least 1 hour. Add peas and beans and simmer until all vegetables are cooked. Check the seasoning and add sugar and chopped parsley. Take out the meat, which is eaten separately, and serve the soup in a bowl. Yield: 4 servings.

Inky-Pinky
(beef hash)

Trim the fat from a few slices of cold roast beef and cook in gravy, adding a sliced onion and a few sliced cooked carrots. Season with a little vinegar, salt, and pepper. Before serving, remove the onion, thicken sauce, and serve with fried bread.

Desserts, Bread

Marmalade

Split the skin of Seville oranges with a small, sharp knife, and cut in four without piercing the pulp of the orange. Remove the skin without breaking it, and cut into thin strips about ½ inch long. Carefully remove the pith and seeds, dividing oranges into 6 or 8 sections. Put them in an earthenware container and cover with just over 1 quart of cold water to each pound of fruit. Let stand for 24 hours. Then turn into a pan, bring to a boil, and simmer until reduced in half. Let mixture stand another 24 hours. Then weigh the fruit and liquid and add an equal weight of sugar. Put all in a preserving pan, bring to a boil, skim, and simmer until syrup stiffens when placed on a cold plate. Turn into pots and cover. Keep in a cool, dry place.

Shortbread Fingers

½ cup flour	¼ cup powdered sugar
¼ cup rice flour	¼ pound butter

Sift both flours and sugar together into a bowl. Add butter and mix until the consistency of shortcrust pastry. Roll out the dough on a floured board until ⅛-inch thick, prick all over with a fork, then cut into slices. Bake in greased baking pan in 425 degree oven until set, then reduce heat and bake slowly until crisp and lightly colored. Cool on tray a short time before serving. (Shortbread also may be pressed into a floured shortbread mold, turned out onto a greased baking tray, and baked in a 450 degree oven for 5 minutes. Then lower heat to allow shortbread to become crisp and golden brown.)

Bannocks

¾ cup flour	2 tablespoons butter
2 tablespoons baking powder	2 teaspoons sugar
½ teaspoon salt	milk
¼ cup oatmeal	

Sift flour, baking powder, and salt into a bowl and add oatmeal. Rub in the butter, add the sugar, and mix into a soft dough with a little milk. Roll out lightly to ½ inch thick. Using a plate, cut into round bannocks, then cut across into triangular pieces. Cook on a hot, lightly greased skillet for about 10 minutes, turning occasionally until browned.

Tea Scones

3 tablespoons butter	1 teaspoon sugar
2 cups flour	pinch of salt
½ teaspoon baking soda	milk
1 teaspoon cream of tartar	

Rub the butter into the flour. Add dry ingredients and mix with milk to a soft dough. Roll out ½ inch thick, cut into rounds, put onto a greased baking tray, and bake in 450 degree oven for 7 to 10 minutes.

6

The Latin Countries

France, Italy, Spain, Portugal

The Latin countries of Europe are among the best situated geographically for producing the foods and wines most of the world enjoys best. Surprisingly, almost without exception, each of the four countries, France, Italy, Spain, and Portugal, has its own distinct foods. Unlike the Scandinavians or the people of the British Isles, the people of the Latin countries seldom adopt each other's dishes, though they may adapt some of them.

Italy, developing its cooking from Greek, Roman, and Eastern culinary secrets of ancient times, for years led Europe as the gastronomical center. In the sixteenth century the court of Venice began producing dishes that world-travelers praised as they went from country to country.

Italian cooking is among the most varied in the world, chiefly because each of eighteen regional cooking areas produce their own specialties. Cheeses, fruits, and fish dishes are noteable, but Italy primarily is known today for its pastas: noodle or macaroni dishes made from fine wheat, garnished or stuffed with meats, vegetables, and topped with tomatoes, sauces, cheeses, and herbs. Meat, being expensive, is used sparingly. Pizza, which began as a pie for leftovers, has become a world-favorite food.

For all their love of good food, the Italians do not take dining as seriously as the French, who inherited the leadership in world gastronomy late in the eighteenth century. To a Frenchman, food is one of the great joys of life.

The cooking of France also is in great variety and shows definite regional influences. In the north of France, cooks make good use of butter. In the south, olive oil is used predominantly. The deft use of spices, herbs, and sauces is universal throughout France, often turning otherwise ordinary foods into culinary wonders.

Spanish food is rich, highly seasoned with garlic, onions, chili pepper, and Spanish paprika which is stronger than the paprika most American cooks use. Meats and fish are cooked primarily in oil, but the food is not oily or greasy.

Northern Spanish eat more heavily and heartily, while Andalusians in the south are content with less, as people are in warmer climes. Spanish cooks like to mix unusual foods and toss them into one interesting and delectable dish.

In Portugal, the food is zesty and exotic, generally different from Spanish cooking. Many unusual dishes came to Portugal from its colonies scattered all over the world, and they have been incorporated into the regional cooking of this beautiful land whose food beyond its borders is not only underrated but virtually unknown.

Not the least distinctive thing about the Latin countries is their wines. The vineyards of these four countries produce some of the world's best wines, so it is logical that wine is used extensively in the cooking and serving of food. Praise be.

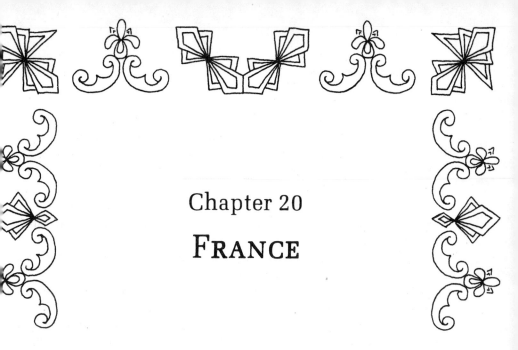

Chapter 20

FRANCE

In the morning, take a light French breakfast of *brioches* (sweet bread), butter, and coffee at your hotel on the Left Bank. Then cross the Seine to the Louvre and say good morning to Winged Victory and greet the Mona Lisa. Afterward a walk through the Tuileries Gardens past the Arc du Carrousel and up along the tree-shaded Champs Elysées' quaint shops and restaurants, and find yourself a sidewalk cafe. Sip a glass of wine at a good vantage point and watch as Frenchmen and (praise heaven!) Frenchwomen pass to and from the Arc de Triomphe or the Place de la Concorde.

In the afternoon, take lunch of salmon croquettes at a little side-street restaurant like the Colbert behind the Palais Royale gardens, then ride up to the top of the Eiffel Tower and look down over the magnificent city of Napoleon and Maurice Chevalier. Follow the Seine back to Notre Dame and then find yourself another sidewalk cafe at St. Germain Des Prés such as the Cafe de Flore, sip a glass of wine and watch the artists paint and the students argue.

In the evening, take dinner of *Boeuf à la Bourguignonne* (beef, Burgundy style) at Le Colisee on the Champs and watch the passing parade at their cosmopolitan . best. Then to Montmartre, to sit with artists and students this time on hard wooden benches at Lapin Agile for some French Bohemian atmosphere, brandied cherries, and folk singing. Or see the can-can girls at the Moulin Rouge or stripteasers at the Crazy

Horse Saloon. For medieval France, including dungeons, it's the Caveau des Oubliettes, and to spend an evening with young Parisians finding their own new style, it's Le Balajo. Afterward you can't do better than to hear the piano player at Harry's Bar and wait for dawn to come up.

Paris is not all there is to France, but almost. It's so easy to spend all of your time in the city of lovers that little time is left for anywhere else. Nearby the Ile de France has the palaces of Versailles and Fontainbleau, and antique villages with castles and woods full of stately poplars.

Normandy, an overnight drive from Paris, has Mont Saint Michel, a palace fortress begun in 709, which still stands impregnable as ever on a tiny island with a medieval village inside the stone walls. The Norman coast was, of course, the D-Day invasion beach for Allied forces in World War II. A fascinating diorama of the historic landing is on view in the town of Arromanches. Joan of Arc was burned at the stake in 1431 in Rouen, a medieval city full of beautiful churches and houses.

Winding hilly roads southeast of Paris lead to the famous wine country of Burgundy. To be in Dijon in September at wine festival time is like being in Germany's Rhineland in springtime, a delightful time of music and grapes. Lyon, another beautiful city, is rated by many Frenchmen as being gastronomically even greater than Paris.

In the Loire valley the kings of France had their summer palaces built out of Middle Ages fortresses. Provence, south in the Rhone valley, is rich with Roman history, and in beautiful Aix-en-Provence on the way to the Riviera, the artist Paul Cézanne's studio is open to view.

Cannes and Nice on the French Riviera have everything Monte Carlo has except perhaps Grace Kelly, and Monaco does not have Saint-Tropez. Visiting one of its sun-blessed beaches for the first time, friends and I were not sure our halting French read a sign correctly. It seemed to say "Bathing suits not permitted here." A quick look around confirmed that we did know our French.

The French Alps along the southeastern border has Chamonix, Grenoble, and other popular summer and winter resort areas all surrounded by ski slopes down which you expect to see Jean-Claude Killy breaking another record.

French cooking, of course, is legendary. No other country in the world conjures up so many images of gourmet dishes as France. Uniquely situated in varieties of climate that include cold winters and near-tropical summers, most everything good to eat or drink grows there and is properly taken advantage of by a people who love good food perhaps more than any other peoples. And also being situated next to Germany and Italy, the gastronomical wonders of those countries have been adapted over the ages.

French gourmet cooking originated in the provinces and was brought to Paris at the end of the eighteenth century to dazzle the court and win worldwide acclaim, eventually surpassing in favor the cuisine of Italy. The secret of French cooking lies in the expert use of seasonings and the talent to take even the least expensive cuts of meat or selection of vegetables and with the help of some herbs and sauces, turn them into dishes fit for a king's table. In a normal year's cooking, an American housewife, even one who has a full shelf of spices, may not use many of them more than a few times a year. A French housewife relies on her herbs and spices for every meal. Not to kill the taste of a meat or fish, but to enhance it.

Salads are one of the Frenchman's greatest joys, with a dressing prepared at the table. Soups are almost without number. Vegetables are lovingly prepared. An afternoon without bread and cheese, a fruit compote, and some wine is to a Frenchman an afternoon ill-spent.

Dinner invariably is begun with *hors d'oeuvres* that may include hearts of artichokes, anchovies, sardines, olives, eggs stuffed with fish or meat, pickled mushrooms. A fish course of scallops baked in the shell or fricassee of frogs' legs usually follows. A meat dish of perhaps a roast or duckling comes next, with potatoes served up in any of a variety of ways, with a tossed green salad. Uniquely flavored vegetables such as asparagus or string beans will be served next, followed by a cake or pastry, perhaps utilizing chestnuts which the French love and use abundantly. Wine and/or a liquor, *naturally!*

Appetizers

Champignons ou Cepes en Marinade
(marinated mushrooms)

Trim and wash ½ pound small button mushrooms. Cook for 5 minutes in salted boiling water, then drain and cool. Prepare the following marinade, which should be boiled for about 10 minutes:

½ cup vinegar	1 bay leaf
¼ cup olive oil	pinch of thyme
½ clove garlic, crushed	pinch of tarragon
pinch of marjoram	pinch of salt
2 peppercorns	1 teaspoon chopped parsley

Pour the boiling mixture over mushrooms in a deep bowl, cover, and set in a cool place to allow the mushrooms to marinate for several hours.

Fond d'Artichauts a L'Orientale
(oriental artichokes)

6 globe artichokes	salt and pepper
3 tablespoons olive oil	½ cup green peas, cooked
2 tablespoons butter	½ cup potatoes, cooked and
1 small onion	sliced
2 tender carrots	1 teaspoon chopped parsley
½ teaspoon sugar	and fennel
juice of half a lemon	

Strip stalk and leaves from each artichoke, keeping the heart. Mix oil with butter, add finely chopped onion and carrots, and cook for 3 minutes. Add artichoke hearts, sugar, lemon juice, a pinch of salt and pepper, and cover the saucepan and simmer slowly for 40 minutes. Add cooked peas and potatoes. Drain vegetables and chill before serving. When cold, sprinkle herbs on top.

Soups

Soupe à L'Oignon
(onion soup)

¼ cup butter
4 medium onions, sliced thin
4 cups meat stock or bouillon
1 teaspoon salt

⅛ teaspoon pepper
10 slices French bread
1 cup grated Parmesan cheese

Melt butter, add onions, and simmer slowly about 3 minutes until golden brown. Add stock, salt and pepper, and simmer about 20 minutes. Toast slices of French bread until very crisp. Place toasted bread in a large heated casserole or soup tureen and pour soup over it. Sprinkle grated Parmesan cheese on top. Yield: 4 servings.

Bouillabaisse
(fish stew)

½ cup olive oil
2 onions, sliced thin
2 tablespoons minced celery
2 cloves garlic, crushed
2 tomatoes, chopped
2 thin strips lemon peel
juice of 1 lemon
1 bay leaf
pinch of saffron

3 pieces fillet of sole
5 cups fish stock or boiling
   water
1 cup lobster meat, precooked
1 cup shrimp, cooked and
   shelled
1 pound scallops
toast
parsley

Heat olive oil and saute the onions, celery, and garlic. Add tomatoes, lemon peel, lemon juice, bay leaf, saffron, fillet of sole and fish stock and boil for 5 minutes. Add remaining fish and continue boiling for 5 minutes. (The secret is to boil the ingredients hard for a short time, blending the oil and water.) Strain the broth in soup plates in which are placed slices of toast. Garnish with the parsley. Arrange fish on a large plate and serve with the soup. Yield: 6 servings.

Pot-au-Feu
(pot on the fire)

2 pounds beef	1 pound shin bones
chicken leftovers or parts	2 large carrots
1 turnip	1 head of celery
1 tomato	1 leek
1 large onion stuck with cloves	bouquet garni
½ teaspoon salt	pepper

(This is a homemade stock used in many French dishes in place of commercial bouillon.) Prepare all ingredients and put them in 8 cups water and bring to a boil. Let boil while skimming off surface fat and residue until no more remains. Continue simmering about 5 hours. The meat and vegetables may be eaten, the stock saved for soups and meat and fish dishes.

Vichysoise Soup

4 leeks	4 cups chicken broth or bouil-
2 tablespoons butter	lon
1 minced onion	½ cup heavy cream
salt and pepper	chives or parsley
2 potatoes	

Wash leeks, cut white part finely and add to hot butter with onion and seasoning. Cover and cook slowly. Add stock and thinly cut potatoes, cook until vegetables are tender, then strain. Season to taste, stir in cream, and garnish with chives or parsley. Serve hot or cold. Yield: 4 servings.

Potage Julienne
(julienne soup)

2 carrots	½ teaspoon sugar
2 turnips	1 quart meat stock
2 onions or leeks	1 tablespoon butter
4 shredded lettuce leaves	pinch of basil, marjoram,
4 stalks celery	tarragon

Cut all vegetables into very thin strips (to *"Julienne,"* named after a French chef who originated the method). Cook vegetables and thin slices of onion in butter until browned. Add lettuce, sugar, and stock or bouillon and a few mixed soup herbs (basil, marjoram, and tarragon). Simmer slowly for 1 hour. While cooking, add 4 tablespoons green peas, a few asparagus tips, some shredded cabbage leaves, green beans, and any leftover scraps of vegetables. Yield: 4 servings.

Salads

Salade Parisienne
(Parisian salad)

boiled beef or veal
potatoes, cold cooked
onion
2 or 3 tomatoes
1 or 2 hard-boiled eggs

lettuce
French salad dressing (oil and
vinegar) (see French
dressings)
parsley

Cut meat into strips and place in salad bowl with sliced cold cooked potatoes and hard-boiled eggs, onion, tomatoes, and lettuce leaves. Add salad dressing, toss, and sprinkle with chopped parsley. Yield: 4 servings.

Salade Française
(French mixed salad)

lettuce or other greens
1 tablespoon wine vinegar
garlic or onion
1 tablespoon tarragon vinegar
1 teaspoon basil, chervil, or
thyme

¼ teaspoon salt
pinch of black pepper
¼ teaspoon dry mustard
4 tablespoons olive oil
hard boiled egg yolk

Use any lettuce or spinach leaves. Wash leaves thoroughly and drain in paper towels. Rub bowl with garlic or onion, but do not leave any in the bowl. Stir the vinegar into all the dry ingredients, then mix in the herbs, salt and pepper, then add the oil. Make the dressing just before serving and toss the salad at the table in a large bowl using wooden fork and spoon. (Finely minced fillets of anchovy may be added to the greens if desired.) Crush the hard-boiled yolk of an egg with a fork, put through a sieve, and add to the dressing. Yield: 2 servings.

Vegetables

Omelette aux Fines Herbes
(French omelettes)

6 eggs	2 tablespoons chopped parsley
3 pinches pepper	¼ cup butter
5 pinches salt	

Beat eggs in a bowl. Add pepper, salt, and parsley. Beat with a fork about 1 minute, thoroughly mixing egg whites and yolks. Do not overbeat. Melt butter in a pan and stir so it does not brown even slightly. When hot, pour in eggs. As they cook, stir them with a fork so they cook evenly. Shake and turn omelette pan occasionally. Fold the omelette to form an oval shape, shake over the heat, and serve on a hot dish. Yield: 3 servings.

Asperges au Gratin
(asparagus with cheese)

Place cooked asparagus in a buttered casserole. Sprinkle with grated Parmesan cheese, put a little butter on top, and bake in 325 degree oven until cheese is lightly browned.

Petits Pois à la Française
(green peas)

1 pound shelled green peas	⅛ cup sugar
½ cup water	4 tablespoons butter and
pinch of salt	2 tablespoons flour,
¼ cup small onions	blended together

Put all ingredients except blend of butter and flour into a casserole, cover, and cook in 350 degree oven for 30 minutes. Add butter and flour blend, shake casserole, and cook a few more minutes, then serve.

Potatoes

Pommes de Terre à la Boulangère
(potatoes and onions)

Wash and peel 1 pound of potatoes and cut in two lengthways, then cut into slices about ½ inch thick. Peel and slice a large onion. Grease a casserole dish, put a layer of potatoes on the bottom, season with salt and pepper, and add a layer of onions. Repeat, finishing with a layer of potatoes. Pour ½ pint of beef stock or bouillon over, place small pats of butter on top, and heat to boiling point, then cover and bake in 350 degree oven for 45 minutes to 1 hour. Yield: 4 servings.

Fish

Court-Bouillon de Poisson
(short-boiled fish)

2 tablespoons butter
⅓ cup diced celery
⅓ cup diced carrots
2 sprigs parsley, chopped
⅓ cup minced onions
6 peppercorns
½ bay leaf

2 tablespoons lime or lemon
    juice
1 tablespoon salt
2 cloves
8 cups water
3 pounds sole, perch, or
    haddock

Melt butter, add celery, carrots, parsley, and onions. Cook about 5 minutes. Add remaining ingredients except fish and let come to a boil. Add fish which has been cleaned and cut into ¼-pound pieces, and boil another 5 minutes. Reduce to simmer and cook until tender (about 6 minutes to the pound). When fish is cooked, put on a hot platter and serve with your favorite fish sauce. Strain liquid and save to use as fish stock. Yield: 4 servings.

Anguille en Matelote
(eels)

2 pounds eels	1 cup red wine
¾ cup onions, sliced	½ cup fish stock or hot water
2 cloves	5 tablespoons butter
1 bay leaf	12 mushrooms, sliced
½ clove garlic	12 small white onions
1 teaspoon parsley, minced	12 shrimp, cooked and shelled
dash of mace	4 tablespoons flour
salt and pepper	

Have eels skinned and cut into 3-inch pieces, then wash thoroughly. Place in a large pot and add sliced onions, cloves, bay leaf, garlic, parsley, mace, salt and pepper. Add wine, fish stock or water, and cover pot. Bring to a boil and cook 15 minutes. While fish is cooking, melt 2 tablespoons butter and saute the mushrooms and small onions. Add shrimp and cook for 10 minutes. When fish is tender, keep warm on a hot platter while making the sauce. Strain the liquid in which fish was cooked, melt remaining 3 tablespoons butter, add flour, and blend. Stir in the fish liquid and cook until mixture thickens, stirring constantly. Add sauted mushrooms, onions, and shrimp. Pour sauce over fish and serve hot. Yield: 4 servings.

Nymphes de Grenouilles en Fricassèe
(fricassee of frogs legs)

6 pairs large frogs legs with backs	2 whole cloves
2 tablespoons butter	½ teaspoon salt
1 cup mushrooms, chopped	dash of pepper
2 tablespoons chives, chopped	2½ tablespoons flour
1 small clove garlic, minced	½ cup dry white wine
1 tablespoon parsley, chopped	2 egg yolks
	½ cup cream

Remove skins from frog legs and backs and scald. Melt butter in a heavy frying pan, allow frog legs to heat in the pan. Add mushrooms, chives, garlic, parsley, cloves, and saute. Add 1 cup boiling water, salt and pepper, and cook covered until frog legs are almost tender. Mix flour with dry white wine and stir to make a smooth paste. Add to frog legs and, when tender, thicken gravy with egg yolks beaten with the cream. Yield: 4 to 6 servings.

Poultry

Canard aux Oranges
(duck with oranges)

1 4-pound duck	juice of 2 oranges
salt and pepper	½ cup Grand Marnier
¼ cup sugar	grated rind of 1 orange
1 tablespoon wine vinegar	

Sprinkle duck lightly with salt and pepper and roast for 1 hour. Ten minutes before duck is done, make the following sauce. In a saucepan, boil sugar and vinegar until it becomes thick. Add orange juice, Grand Marnier, and grated rind. Stir gently, then pour in the duck gravy, boil once, and pour over the duck. Yield: 4 servings.

Poulet à la Marengo
(chicken Marengo)

1 3-pound chicken	4 tomatoes
3 tablespoons oil	salt and pepper
10 small white onions	2 tablespoons flour
10 mushrooms	½ cup white wine
1 clove garlic	½ cup veal or chicken stock or
2 tablespoons butter	chicken bouillon

Clean chicken and cut into serving portions. Heat oil and brown the chicken on all sides. Place in a casserole. Saute onions, mushrooms, and clove of garlic in butter in a frying pan about 5 minutes. Add to cooked chicken in casserole. Peel tomatoes and cut into quarters and add to chicken. Season with salt and pepper. Cover casserole and bake in 350 degree oven about 1½ hours until tender. Remove chicken to a hot platter and keep warm while making sauce. To liquid in the casserole, stir in flour which has been mixed with a little cold water, and blend. Add wine and stock or bouillon and cook until mixture thickens. Pour over chicken and serve. Yield: 4 servings.

Meats

Boeuf à la Mode
(pot roast)

½ pound salt pork
4 pounds round or rump steak
salt and pepper
flour
6 slices bacon, minced
12 small white onions

1 bay leaf
2 cups white wine
⅓ cup celery, diced
⅓ cup carrots, diced
1 sprig parsley, minced
2 cups meat stock

Cut salt pork into strips ¼ inch wide and 4 inches long and lard the beef, making cuts run in the same direction as the grain. Season with salt and pepper and dredge well with flour. Brown the beef in the minced bacon. Add remaining ingredients, cover pot and cook slowly about 4 hours, not allowing liquid to boil. Remove to a hot platter. Skim fat from the sauce and serve with the roast. Yield: 6 servings.

Tendrons de Veau Bourgeoise
(breast of veal bourgeoise)

1½ pounds boned breast of
　　veal
flour
salt and pepper

2 tablespoons butter
6 carrots
1½ cups tomato sauce
1 onion, sliced thin

Cut veal into medium-sized pieces, dredge with flour, and sprinkle with salt and pepper. Saute in butter until well browned. Cut carrots into quarters. Pour tomato sauce into a casserole and put in the carrots, onion, and meat. Cover and cook in 350 degree oven for about 45 minutes until done. Yield: 4 servings.

Boeuf à la Bourguignonne
(beef, Burgundy style)

3 pounds chuck
½ cup flour
2 teaspoons salt
⅓ teaspoon pepper
3 tablespoons olive oil
6 tablespoons butter
¼ cup warm cognac
3 slices bacon, diced
2 cups diced onions

¾ cup grated carrots
2 cloves garlic, minced
3 cups dry red wine
2 tablespoons minced parsley
1 bay leaf
½ teaspoon thyme
12 small white onions
1 teaspoon sugar
12 mushroom caps

Cut beef into 2-inch cubes and sprinkle with flour, salt, and pepper. Heat olive oil and 3 tablespoons butter in a frying pan. Brown meat well on all sides, then put in a casserole or Dutch oven, pour warm cognac over, and set it afire. Add bacon, onions, carrots, and garlic. Cook over medium heat until vegetables brown. Add to meat with the wine, parsley, bay leaf, and thyme. Cover and bake in 350 degree oven for 2 hours. While meat is cooking, prepare the onions and mushrooms. Melt remaining butter in a pan, add onions and sugar and brown lightly. Remove onions and saute mushrooms for 5 minutes. Add onions and mushrooms to the meat after it has been baking for 1½ hours and check the seasoning. Yield: 6 servings.

Porc à la Boulangère
(pork à la Boulangère)

small pork roast or thick pork
    chops
salt and peper

1 onion
flour
8 potatoes

Saute finely chopped onion in fat trimmed from the meat. Dredge the pork with flour, and season with salt and pepper. Brown quickly in hot drippings or in a very hot oven so the juices are not lost. Peel potatoes and cut them in half if using pork chops, otherwise leave whole. Roll them in pan to coat with fat. Cook in a 400 degree oven about 45 minutes until meat and potatoes are done.

Saucisses au Vin Blanc
(sausages in white wine)

1 pound sausages	1 tablespoon flour
1½ cups white wine	1 cup stock
salt and pepper	2 egg yolks
1 tablespoon butter	1 tablespoon chopped parsley

Put sausages in a frying pan with wine and 2 pinches of pepper, cover and simmer about 8 minutes. Meanwhile make a sauce with the butter, flour, and stock. Cool slightly, then stir in egg yolks. Take sausages from pan, drain, and keep them hot. Add sauce to the wine in the frying pan, reheat without boiling. Stir in chopped parsley, season, and pour over sausages.

Navarin de Mouton
(mutton stew)

3 to 4 tablespoons butter	2½ teaspoons salt
3 pounds shoulder or neck of mutton	¼ teaspoon pepper
	6 to 7 cups water
¼ cup flour	6 to 8 medium turnips
bundle of mixed herbs	3 large carrots
(parsley, celery leaves,	12 small white onions
thyme, leek, mint)	1 or 2 large potatoes
6 whole black peppercorns	1 clove garlic

Heat butter in deep skillet and brown meat on all sides. (Meat should be on the lean side, boned, and cut in 2½-inch pieces.) Pour off two-thirds of the frying fat and retain for vegetables. Remove meat and place in covered pot or casserole. Brown flour in fat in the skillet, and stir into a paste with ½ cup cold water. Cook until smooth. Pour this over the meat, add herbs and all seasonings except the garlic. Pour water over the meat to cover it completely. Cover the casserole and simmer for 1 hour. Dice all vegetables and brown on all sides in the remaining fat. After mutton has cooked for 2 hours, add the browned turnips and carrots. Add onions 10 minutes later. Cover again and simmer 20 more minutes. Peel potatoes cut into slices ⅓-inch thick, dry on paper towels, and put on top of the other ingredients. Add garlic, cover, and cook slowly for 25 to 30 minutes. Do not stir the mixture after the vegetables are added. Skim fat from the stew before serving. Yield: 6 servings.

Sauces, Dressings

French Dressing

3 tablespoons olive oil
1 tablespoon wine vinegar

½ teaspoon salt
¼ teaspoon pepper

Mix all ingredients together. As variation, add a pinch of sugar and ¼ teaspoon prepared mustard.

Hollandaise Sauce

4 tablespoons butter
3 egg yolks

1 tablespoon wine vinegar
salt and pepper

Melt butter in a double boiler over hot water. Mix egg yolks, vinegar, salt and pepper, and add to the melted butter. Stir briskly until sauce is smooth and thick, but be careful not to let the sauce boil. Taste and add more seasoning if needed.

Bearnaise Sauce

2 shallots
3 stalks chervil
1 sprig tarragon
2 tablespoons dry white wine

1 tablespoon wine vinegar
2 egg yolks
4 tablespoons butter
salt and pepper

Chop shallots and herbs finely. Put wine and vinegar in a saucepan, add chopped shallots and herbs, and simmer until the wine is reduced by two-thirds. Strain and cool. Put egg yolks in a pan over hot but not boiling water, add 1 teaspoon cold water and herbs and wine mixture. Whip with an egg whisk, gently but constantly, adding a little of the butter piece by piece, until sauce is thick and creamy. Season to taste with salt and pepper.

Desserts, Bread

Crêpes Suzette
(French pancakes)

1 cup sweet butter	1½ cups milk
2 tablespoons powdered sugar	2 eggs, separated
grated rind of 1 orange and	1 tablespoon granulated sugar
1 lemon	½ cup orange juice
1 teaspoon vanilla	⅓ cup Cointreau
¼ cup flour	½ cup brandy
¼ teaspoon salt	

Cream the butter until it is very soft. Add powdered sugar, orange rind, lemon rind, and vanilla. Beat until well blended. Place in refrigerator until needed. Make pancakes in the following manner. Sift flour and salt into a bowl. Add 1 cup of milk and beat until mixture is smooth. Add egg yolks and beat thoroughly, then add rest of the milk and, when smooth, fold in the stiffly beaten egg whites.

Use very small pans (3 or 4), slightly greased. Pancakes should be only 4 or 5 inches in diameter. Use only about 2 teaspoons of batter per pancake. Lift the pan, pour in batter, tilting and turning from side to side so batter is spread evenly in a thin coating on the bottom of the pan, and place on the fire. Do the same to the other pans. Now the first pancake should be ready to turn. When baked on other side, remove to a large platter and keep in a warm oven until all pancakes are baked.

Just before serving, make the sauce in a chafing dish. Light the candle or lamp under the dish, place the flavored butter in the dish and melt it. When golden brown, slowly add orange juice and cook until liquid is reduced by one-half. Add Cointreau. When heated, place pancakes in the hot sauce one at a time. Heat first one side, then the other. Fold in half and place on outer edge of the pan until all pancakes are heated. Sprinkle granulated sugar over the pancakes and pour brandy over them. When brandy is hot, light it and serve pancakes in the burning sauce.

Compote de Poires
(compote of pears)

6 medium pears
2 cups sugar

1 stick cinnamon
1 cup wine

Peel the pears, leaving them whole. Cover with cold water. In a saucepan combine sugar and 1 cup of water and bring to a boil. Cook about 8 minutes. Add the cinnamon. Drain the pears and place in the sugar syrup, cover and cook gently until pears are tender but not mushy. Remove from syrup and place in a large bowl. Add wine to the syrup and cook until mixture thickens slightly. Pour over the pears and chill before serving.

Pommes au Four
(baked apples)

Core 6 apples and place in a buttered baking dish. Add ¼ cup of water. Mix ⅓ cup sugar with ¼ teaspoon cinnamon and fill centers of apples with mixture. Add 1 teaspoon butter to each hole. Bake until tender and serve each apple on a slice of cinnamon toast. Yield: 6 servings.

Brioche
(sweet bread)

1 cup milk, scalded
⅔ cup butter
2 teaspoons salt
½ cup sugar
2 yeast cakes

¼ cup lukewarm water
4 eggs, well beaten
4½ cups all-purpose flour
melted butter

Scald the milk and add the butter, salt, and sugar, stirring until butter dissolves. Cool. Dissolve yeast in lukewarm water and add the beaten eggs. Combine with the first mixture. Sift flour before measuring and then add to the mixture, beating the dough well. Cover with a cloth and let rise in a warm place for about 6 hours. Fill well-greased muffin pans about one-third full with dough.

Brush the tops with melted butter and let rise for 30 minutes. Bake in 425 degree oven for 20 minutes.

Croquants
(gingerbread cookies)

½ cup sugar
½ cup butter
2 egg yolks, well beaten
½ cup honey

2 tablespoons orange juice
½ teaspoon orange extract
3¼ cups flour
1½ teaspoons ginger

Cream the sugar and butter until well blended. Add eggs and honey and mix; stir in orange juice and extract. Sift the flour and ginger together and add slowly, mixing well after each addition. Chill dough for a few hours. Roll out thin and cut in fancy shapes. Bake on a butter cookie sheet in a 350 degree oven for 15 minutes.

Oeufs à la Neige
(snow custard)

1 quart milk
½ cup sugar

6 egg whites
6 egg yolks

Heat milk in a saucepan with the sugar. Beat the egg whites until very stiff. When milk begins to boil, put in beaten whites, a little at a time, turning so each piece may be cooked on both sides. Remove egg whites. Make a custard by adding the milk to the egg yolks, slightly beaten, and cook over water until it thickens. Add flavoring, strain, and pour into a deep dish. Place pieces of egg white on top and let the dessert cool before serving.

Croissants

½ ounce yeast
½–1 cup warm milk
pinch of salt
1¼ cups flour

1 tablespoon sugar
¾ cup butter
egg

Blend yeast with a little cold water and mix all the ingredients except the butter and egg, adding enough liquid to make a soft, rubbery dough. Put in a warm place to rise almost an hour. When it has doubled its bulk, put on a floured baking board and cool slightly. Soften the butter by beating with your hand, place it on the dough, then fold over the ends of the dough to cover it. Roll and fold as for a flaky pastry, putting it in a warm place to rest after it has been rolled twice. Then, after rolling and folding five times in all, roll out thinly, cut into wide strips, and then into large triangles and roll each into a crescent form. Place on an ungreased tray and put in a warm place for about 20 minutes. Brush over with egg and bake in 475 degree oven for about 10 minutes.

Pêches Melba
(peaches Melba)

3 peaches
1 cup sugar
vanilla ice cream

raspberry sauce (see below)
flaked almonds

Peel the peaches. Put sugar and 2 cups water in a pan and boil for 5 minutes. Add whole peaches, cover, and cook slowly for 10 minutes. Remove from heat and let stand about 30 minutes so peaches absorb syrup. Then remove peaches from syrup and cool in the refrigerator. Put some ice cream on the bottom of three small glass dishes and put a whole peach on top of each. Pour raspberry sauce over, and decorate with flaked almonds.

Sauce: Combine 3 tablespoons raspberry puree, jelly, or jam, 3 tablespoons powdered sugar, and 1 tablespoon Cointreau. Yield: 3 servings.

Mousse au Chocolat
(chocolate mousse)

4 1-ounce squares of unsweet-
ened chocolate
¾ cup sugar

5 egg yolks
1 tablespoon brandy
5 egg whites

Melt chocolate over hot water in top of a double boiler. Add sugar and ¼ cup water and stir until sugar dissolves. Beat egg yolks and gradually beat in the chocolate mixture, stirring constantly. Stir in the brandy. Cool. Beat egg whites until stiff. Fold into chocolate mixture. Pour into 6 or 8 individual molds and chill in refrigerator about 12 hours. Yield: 6 to 8 servings.

Chapter 21

ITALY

Perhaps nowhere else in Europe does the scenery, culture, and mood of its cities and regions change as much as it does in Italy. Its major cities, Rome, Venice, and Florence, are individual jewels in a crown of historic and artistic splendor.

Rome, The Eternal City, though crowded, hectic, and modern is also serene and ancient. Modern industry burgeons beside landmarks of Roman times so that just walking up a street, you are never quite sure of what century you're living in. To think that the sandals of Roman legions once trod the Appian Way is to never again think of ancient history as being a dead thing.

Venice and its canals and gondolas, with a full moon rising over the Lido, its rays catching the gold of the Piazza San Marco and St. Mark's Basilica, is among the unforgettable sights of Europe.

Florence, to me, is the most beautiful city in the world. Here Giotto built his Campanile, called the most beautiful bell tower in the world. Ghiberti sculpted his golden "Gate of Paradise" to adorn the Baptistery of San Giovanni. The Duomo is a Tuscan Gothic masterpiece, largest cathedral after St. Peter's in Rome. Michelangelo's *David*, Ghirlandaio's *The Last Supper*, Fra Angelico's *The Annunciation*, the bas reliefs of the della Robbias, masterpieces of the Uffizi Palace, and countless art objects and architecture from the fourteenth to seventeenth centuries compete with the sheer beauty of the city itself.

Add the northern lake region, Siena, Verona, Milan, Naples, Salerno and the gorgeous Amalfi Drive, and Italy becomes a masterpiece of its own.

One day in Rome, a friend and I decided we couldn't leave Italy without seeing Capri, that tiny island out in the blue Mediterranean off Naples. But we had limited funds and only the next day for it. American tour officials said it couldn't be done: Rome to Capri and back again in one day. So we turned to Italian travel officials who also said it couldn't be done, but they would try.

They arranged a one-day trip to begin the next morning. We would go by train from Rome to Naples, be met by a bus to take us to the wharf, then board a boat which would take us to Sorrento and finally to Capri. We would join a tour and spend the entire day on the island, then in late afternoon reverse our transportation arrangements and be back in Rome that night.

But the officials warned us that even if we made all the connections, it would be of no use. It had been raining all over Italy for three days and was expected to keep raining. Capri would be nothing in the rain.

We chanced the weather and started out next morning. Halfway to Naples we looked out the window and saw the rain stop and the clouds part, making way for a sun that stayed out all day. We made all the connections without incident, had a magnificent day on Capri, and only upon returning to Naples and trying to catch our return train to Rome did we run into a problem. The bus driver from the wharf accidentally took us to the wrong station, with only three minutes to catch our train to Rome.

About to throw up our hands and admit defeat, a Neapolitan boy in scuffed clothes and his face smudged with dirt, asked if he could help. We explained in English and he understood and waved for us to follow him. He ran on the double and we followed on a zig-zag race through the station and into another which adjoined. There we found our train about to pull away. We emptied our pockets of what *lire* we had, gave it to the boy, and jumped aboard. When we got back to Rome that evening and had lasagna and wine at Angelino's, we toasted Italy's acceptance of our challenge and the urchin who saw it to successful completion.

Italians have been accepting challenges since the days of the Roman Empire. At the crossroads of Europe, with their own and foreign legions making it a battleground, and in more recent years floods that threaten to drown it, Italy has emerged as one of the most prosperous and forward-minded countries.

The Italians are a diverse people of many moods, as might be expected in a country of such diverse climate and economic condition. Also diverse is the food of Italy, adapting to the same externals. In Milan and elsewhere in the north, a thick vegetable soup such as minestrone satisfies on a cold winter day. In Venice, on the Adriatic Sea, fish is a favorite food, especially *scampi*, a small shrimp-like crustacean. In Rome, housewives specialize in *fritto misto*, a fried mixture of chicken, cheese, green peppers, cauliflower, and mushrooms. Sicilians blessed with both rich soil and the Mediterranean Sea enjoy swordfish, sardines, eggplant, and nuts and olives in great abundance. In Sardinia, *gnocchi* (dumplings) and *polenta*, a cornmeal dish, are favorites. Neapolitans love *veal scaloppine*. All throughout Italy the pasta dishes, chicken, cheeses, and fresh fruits are served in tantalizing variety. Wine is drunk by practically all ages at all times.

Ravioli, spaghetti, macaroni, zucchini, cannelloni, veal parmigiana, lasagna, zabaglione, pizza, we who are about to eat salute you.

Appetizers

Antipasto
(foods before a meal)

Arrange layers of canned fish, cold meat, raw vegetables, stuffed eggs, olives, and cheese on a round or oblong platter from the inside to the outer rim. Among favorite ingredients are anchovies, sardines, tuna fish, salami, raw green peppers, pimentoes, pickled mushrooms, olives, tomatoes, radishes, spring onions, and Mozzarella and Ricotta cheese.

Bruciate Briachi
(burnt chestnuts)

Grill or bake chestnuts. Peel them and place them on a hot silver dish, and sprinkle them with sugar. Then pour hot rum over the chestnuts and set afire.

Bignè Caldi al Formaggio
(hot cheese puffs)

¼ cup butter
1 cup flour, sifted
3 eggs
⅓ cup grated Parmesan cheese

½ teaspoon salt
⅛ teaspoon pepper
cheese filling

Melt butter in 1 cup water and bring to a boil. Remove from heat, add flour all at once and beat. Beat until dough is glossy and shapes into a ball. Beat in eggs one at a time. Then beat in cheese, salt, and pepper. Shape into balls onto an ungreased baking sheet, leaving 2 inches between puffs. Bake in preheated 425 degree oven for 15 minutes. Reduce heat to 350 degrees and bake another 20 minutes. Cut a slit into each puff and fill with a little cheese filling (see below). Before serving, put filled puffs into a 425 degree oven for 2 to 3 minutes. Serve hot.

Cheese Filling

¼ cup butter
½ cup flour
½ teaspoon salt
¼ teaspoon pepper

¾ cup milk
½ cup grated Parmesan cheese
1 egg yolk

Melt butter, then remove from heat. Stir in flour and seasonings. Stir in milk until well blended and smooth. Cook over low heat, stirring constantly, until thick but smooth. Beat in cheese and egg yolk. Cook until mixture is blended and Parmesan cheese has melted.

Soups

Minestrone

¼ pound bacon, chopped
¼ pound ham, chopped
¼ pound Italian sausage, chopped
2 onions, chopped
2 tomatoes, chopped
½ cup rice

½ cup dried beans
1 stalk celery, diced
6 cups meat stock
¼ head cabbage, shredded
1 cup mixed green vegetables
salt and pepper
grated Parmesan cheese

Saute bacon, ham, sausage, and onions together until lightly browned. Add tomatoes, rice, beans (which have been soaked in cold water for several hours), celery, and stock. Simmer until beans are tender, skimming off the fat several times. Add shredded cabbage and mixed green vegetables such as lima beans, peas, spinach, string beans, and asparagus. Simmer until soup is thick and vegetables are soft. Season with salt and pepper. To serve, sprinkle with grated cheese. Yield: 4 to 6 servings.

Salads

Melanzane
(eggplant salad)

1 large eggplant
¼ cup dry white wine
¼ cup wine vinegar
1 teaspoon salt
½ teaspoon pepper
1 small onion, minced

1 garlic clove, minced
1 teaspoon dried basil
2 bay leaves
¾ cup olive oil
½ cup minced parsley
tomato wedges

Cut unpeeled eggplant into 1-inch cubes. Cook in boiling water, enough to cover, for 5 to 8 minutes until eggplant is soft but still retains its shape. Drain on paper towels. Combine wine, vinegar, salt, pepper, onion, garlic, basil, and bay leaves. Pour over eggplant cubes. (Do not use an aluminum container.) Toss well.

Marinate overnight or at least 8 hours. Before serving, toss with olive oil and parsley, pour off excess liquid. Serve with tomato wedges. Yield: 4 servings.

Il Cappon Magro
(mixed vegetable salad)

Rub some unsweetened biscuits with a little garlic and place the following cooked vegetables on top, building into a pyramid: string beans, pieces of carrots, potatoes, celery, cubed beets, and clusters of cooked cauliflower. Dress with oil, vinegar, and salt. Garnish with pieces of cooked fish and lobster. To top it off, stick olives, anchovies, and hard-boiled eggs on toothpicks into the salad.

Vegetables

Zucchini

2 tablespoons butter
½ cup sliced onion
1 tablespoon dry Italian salad
    dressing mix

1½ pounds zucchini, sliced
1 tablespoon grated Parmesan
    cheese

Melt butter in a skillet. Add onion and cook over moderate heat until tender. Stir in ½ cup water and salad mix. Add zucchini. Cover and cook for 5 to 8 minutes, stirring constantly, until tender. Sprinkle with grated Parmesan cheese. Yield: 4 servings.

Florentine Spinach

4 tablespoons flour
4 tablespoons butter, melted
1¾ cups milk
salt and pepper

3 eggs
3 cups cooked and chopped
    spinach

Blend flour and melted butter and slowly add milk, stirring constantly. Season with salt and pepper. Beat eggs lightly and add to white sauce, then add spinach. Pour all into a buttered mold, cover and bake in a pan of hot water in a 350 degree oven about 1 hour. Yield: 4 servings.

Broccoli alla Florentina

1 pound broccoli
5 or 6 tablespoons of oil

3 or 4 cloves of garlic
salt and pepper

Cook broccoli in boiling salted water. When tender, drain thoroughly, and chop coarsely. Heat the oil in a skillet, and add cloves of garlic. When garlic starts to brown, add broccoli. Season with salt and pepper. Cook 20 to 30 minutes, stirring occasionally.

Pastas, Rice, Dumplings

Maccheroni al Forno
(baked macaroni)

½ pound large macaroni
butter
oil

1 pound large tomatoes
salt and pepper
Parmesan cheese

Boil macaroni in a large saucepan of salted water until tender. Drain in a colander, then transfer into a casserole dish, and add a little butter and oil and the sliced tomatoes. Season well with salt and pepper and bake in 350 degree oven for 20 to 30 minutes. Sprinkle with grated Parmesan cheese. Yield: 4 servings.

Risotto alla Milanese

1 cup rice
¼ cup butter
1 small onion, minced
4 cups chicken broth or bouillon

½ cup Marsala wine
salt and pepper
½ teaspoon saffron
1 cup grated Parmesan cheese

Wash rice several times. Drain and dry with a towel. Melt half of the butter in a deep skillet and saute onion until golden brown. Add rice and cook for 10 minutes, stirring constantly. Add half of the broth or bouillon, which has been brought to the boiling point and wine. Cook over low fire and stir constantly. As rice cooks, add more broth, a little at a time, so rice does not become too moist or too dry. When rice is almost tender, season with salt and pepper and add remaining butter and the saffron which has been dissolved in some of the broth. Before serving, sprinkle with Parmesan cheese. Yield: 4 servings.

Fettuccine Verdi con le Erbe
(green noodles with basil)

1 pound green noodles
1 cup butter cut into small
    pieces
3 tablespoons shredded basil
    leaves

1 or 2 garlic cloves, crushed
1 teaspoon salt
1 teaspoon pepper
½ cup sour cream, heated
1 cup grated Parmesan cheese

Cook noodles until tender. Drain and put into a hot serving dish. Toss remaining ingredients except cheese onto noodles until they are covered. Serve on hot plates. Garnish with Parmesan cheese. Yield: 4 servings.

Polenta
(cornmeal dish)

For polenta:
1¼ teaspoons salt
1 cup cornmeal, white or
    yellow

For filling:
2 tablespoons bread crumbs

3 tablespoons butter
1 cup (¼ pound) fresh
    mushrooms, sliced
2½ tablespoons Parmesan
    cheese
6 tablespoons cream
¼ teaspoon salt

Gradually add cornmeal to 1 quart boiling salted water, stirring constantly. When thick, place pot in a pan of hot water, or use a double boiler. Cover and cook about 2 hours over boiling water, then let it set overnight. Next day, pour it into a baking dish. Slice the *polenta* loaf across into 3 layers. Butter the baking dish and sprinkle with bread crumbs. Lay the top slice into the bottom of the dish, dot with butter, add one-half of the mushrooms. Moisten with cream and sprinkle with some of the grated Parmesan cheese. Lay the second slice of *polenta* on top. Repeat the same procedure with the butter, mushrooms, cream, and cheese. Put the last slice of *polenta* on top and dot with butter. Cover and bake 1½ hours in 350 degree oven. Serve as a main dish or with meat or fish. Yield: 4 servings.

Gnocchi
(dumplings)

1½ cups milk
1 cup Farina or Cream of Wheat
½ cup butter

2 cups grated Parmesan cheese
3 eggs
1½ teaspoons salt

Bring milk and 1½ cups water to a boil. Gradually stir in farina and salt, being careful to avoid lumping. Cook over medium heat until thick. Remove from heat and beat in ¼ cup of the butter, ½ cup cheese, and the eggs. Mix well. Spread about ¼-inch thick on a shallow platter or cookie sheet. Cool. Cut into circles with rim of a glass or a cookie cutter. Arrange in a buttered baking dish in overlapping layers. Sprinkle each layer with remaining cheese and butter. Bake in preheated 350 degree oven about 30 minutes until golden and crisp. Yield: 4 servings.

Pizza

1 cup flour
salt
½ ounce yeast
4 tomatoes
Mozzarella cheese
Pepperoni or other Italian sausage

6 anchovy fillets
Optional: black or green olives, sauted onions, chopped mushrooms
oregano
basil
1 tablespoon olive oil

Put the flour in a bowl and add a pinch of salt. In a separate bowl, mix the yeast and a little warm water. Put yeast mixture into the flour and mix well. Add enough warm water (about a cup) to make a stiff dough. Knead it thoroughly until dough becomes elastic. Put in a warm place, cover with a cloth, and allow it to double its bulk. Roll out dough on a floured board to ¼-inch thickness.

While dough is rising, prepare tomatoes, cheese, anchovies, and meats and optional ingredients. Peel the tomatoes and chop them into small pieces. Cut cheese and meat into thin slices, and halve the anchovies.

Spread pizza dough on a baking sheet, cover with a layer of cheese to keep the pizza from becoming soggy, then cover it with the tomatoes and arrange meat and anchovies on top. Sprinkle with oregano and basil. Pour a little olive oil over it and a little onto the baking sheet. Bake in a preheated 400 to 450 degree oven for 25 minutes. Add more cheese on top and bake for another 5 minutes.

Fish

Trote in Bianco
(trout in white wine)

1 4½-pound trout	2 cups water
2 cups dry white wine	1 teaspoon salt
2 peppercorns	1 bay leaf
1 small onion, sliced	½ small carrot
1 small piece celery	1 sprig parsley
2 slices lemon	¼ cup olive oil

Clean trout and set aside. Combine all ingredients except trout. Simmer in a skillet, covered, about 30 minutes. Strain. Bring liquid to a gentle boil and place the trout in it. Simmer, covered, over a very low heat, without allowing it to boil, for from 10 to 15 minutes. Remove fish to a hot platter. Serve with a green sauce (see Sauces, this section). Yield: 4 servings.

Pesce Fritto
(deep-fried fish fillets)

Italians fry their fish in olive oil rather than butter or shortening.
The oil adds a distinctive flavor and produces a crisper fish.

4 medium-sized fish fillets	salt
½ cup flour	lemon slices
1 cup olive oil	parsley

Dredge fish in flour. Fry in hot olive oil for about 8 minutes on
both sides. Drain on paper towels. Sprinkle with salt and serve
garnished with lemon wedges and parsley. Yield: 4 servings.

Poultry

Pollo Risotto
(chicken and rice)

1 2-pound boiling chicken	basil
2 onions, sliced	salt and pepper
¼ pound butter	1 glass white wine
1 piece celery, chopped	1 cup rice
¼ pound mushrooms	olive oil
3 tomatoes	2 cups chicken stock or bouil-
1 green pepper, chopped	lon
1 thick slice ham	¼ pound Parmesan cheese,
2 cloves garlic	grated
thyme	

Skin and bone the chicken and slice it before cooking. Fry a
sliced onion in 4 tablespoons melted butter until golden. Add
chopped vegetables, chicken, ham, and garlic, and fry together
for 2 or 3 minutes. Add thyme and basil, season with salt and
pepper. Add wine, cover with water, and cook slowly, covered,
for 2 hours.

Cook rice for risotto as follows:
Use Italian or Patna rice. Fry a sliced onion gently in olive oil
until soft and tender. Pour in the rice. Stir rice about in the oil
until each grain is saturated. Gradually add hot chicken stock or

bouillon, about ½ cup at a time. Continue adding stock until rice is cooked, about 30 minutes.

Just before serving the chicken risotto, put the rice in with the chicken and sauce prepared above and stir in the grated Parmesan cheese and 2 tablespoons butter. Yield: 4 servings.

Pollo
(chicken)

¼ cup flour	½ teaspoon salt
1 young spring chicken, jointed	¼ teaspoon pepper
	1 bay leaf
2 tablespoons lemon juice	grated Parmesan cheese
¼ cup olive oil	4 tablespoons butter

Lightly flour the pieces of chicken. Mix lemon juice, olive oil, salt, pepper, and bay leaf. Beat thoroughly and pour over the chicken. Let stand about 1 hour, then drain off the liquid. Roll chicken in Parmesan cheese and fry in butter. Yield: 4 servings.

Meats

Forcemeat Balls

½ pound minced veal	eggs
1 pound minced ham	1 cup flour
parsley	butter
basil	3 onions, chopped
thyme	2 sticks celery, chopped
cinnamon	2 carrots, chopped
salt and pepper	

Mix veal and ham with the finely chopped herbs, cinnamon, salt, and pepper. Bind mixture with egg. Shape into balls. Roll in flour. Melt butter and brown vegetables in it. Add 1 cup of water, season with salt and pepper, and bring to a boil. Cook the meatballs in this sauce for 45 minutes. To serve, arrange meatballs on a dish and pour sauce over them. Yield: 4 servings.

Fritto Misto
(mixed grill)

8 chicken livers, chopped	egg
4 small lamb chops, boned	salt and pepper
8 forcemeat balls (see above)	basil
bread crumbs	oil for frying

Cut all meat into very small pieces, dip in fine breadcrumbs, coat with egg, season with salt, pepper, and basil. Fry quickly in a skillet of smoking hot olive oil. Yield: 6 servings.

Mostaccioli

1 tablespoon butter	2 cups canned tomatoes
1 pound ground round steak	¼ pound mushrooms
1 large chopped onion	¼ cup olive oil
1 clove garlic cut in halves	½ pound mostaccioli noodles
¾ teaspoon salt	grated Parmesan cheese
⅛ teaspoon pepper	freshly grated black pepper

Melt one tablespoon butter in a deep skillet. Brown in it the round steak, chopped onion, and garlic halves. Cover with boiling water. Add ¾ teaspoon salt and ⅛ teaspoon pepper. Simmer covered until almost dry. Take out the garlic. Add canned tomatoes. Cook, simmering and stirring frequently, until sauce is thick, about 1 to 1½ hours. Add mushrooms when sauce is partly done. When sauce is almost done, add ¼ cup olive oil. Cook until tender ½ pound mostaccioli noodles. Serve mostaccioli on a hot platter, first with a layer of the noodles, then the sauce, then sprinkle generously with grated Parmesan cheese and freshly grated black pepper. Repeat layers until all ingredients are used. Yield: 4 servings.

Ravioli
(filled dough or noodles with meat or cheese)

1½ cups flour	⅛ teaspoon salt
1 egg, slightly beaten	

Sift flour in a bowl, make a well in the center, and drop in the egg, salt, and 1 tablespoon cold water. Mix with a fork and then knead for 20 minutes. Chill dough for 30 minutes. Roll out very thin on a floured board and cut into rounds about 3 inches in diameter. On each circle of dough place 1 teaspoon of one of the fillings below. Fold dough in half and press edges together and boil in salted water about 12 minutes. Remove from liquid and serve with tomato sauce and grated Parmesan cheese.

Meat Filling

1 cup cooked chicken or veal
1 egg, beaten
1 tablespoon butter
salt and pepper

1 tablespoon grated Parmesan
   cheese
½ teaspoon minced parsley
¼ teaspoon grated lemon peel

Put meat or chicken through a food chopper. Add beaten egg and butter and mix well. Stir in remaining ingredients and mix until well blended.

Cheese Filling

1 cup cooked spinach
½ cup cottage cheese
1 tablespoon grated Parmesan
   cheese

1 egg, well-beaten
salt and pepper
1 tablespoon bread crumbs

Mince spinach and drain thoroughly so it is very dry. Combine with remaining ingredients and mix well.

Spaghetti alla Napolitana
(spaghetti, Naples style)

2 tablespoons olive oil
1 onion, minced
1 clove garlic, minced
¼ cup minced ham
3 slices Italian sausage,
   chopped fine
6 mushrooms, chopped

1 cup meat stock or beef
   bouillon
1 cup tomato juice
salt and pepper
cooked spaghetti
grated Parmesan cheese

Heat olive oil and cook onion and garlic until golden brown. Add meats and mushrooms and cook about 5 minutes. Stir in meat stock or beef bouillon and tomato juice. Add salt and pepper to taste. Cover and cook slowly until mixture is thoroughly blended. Cook spaghetti for 18 to 20 minutes in rapidly boiling salted water. Drain and serve with sauce and topped with grated Parmesan cheese. Yield: 4 servings.

Veal Scaloppine

1¼ pound boned veal shoulder
¼ cup flour
salt and pepper
¼ cup salad oil
¼ cup minced onion

1 small can whole mushrooms, drained
1 cup tomato juice
½ teaspoon sugar

Preheat oven to 350 degrees. Cut veal into 1¼-inch cubes and roll in flour combined with ¼ teaspoon salt and a dash of pepper. Heat salad oil in a skillet and saute minced onion until tender, then remove onion to a greased 1-quart casserole. In the remaining oil, saute the veal until it is brown on all sides. Arrange veal in the casserole with the mushrooms, tomato juice, sugar, ¾ teaspoon salt, and a dash of pepper. Bake uncovered for 1¼ hours until tender. Yield: 2 servings.

Veal Parmigiana

2 eggs, beaten
salt and pepper
1 pound veal cutlets
1 cup fine dry bread crumbs
½ cup grated Parmesan cheese

½ cup olive oil
2 cups canned Italian tomatoes
½ pound Mozzarella cheese, sliced

Combine eggs and a little salt and pepper. Dip cutlets into beaten eggs and shake off excess moisture. Combine bread crumbs and Parmesan cheese. Coat cutlets on all sides with the mixture and shake off excess. Heat olive oil in a skillet. Brown cutlets in it on both sides, about 5 to 8 minutes depending on size and thickness of cutlets. Place cutlets in a greased shallow baking dish. Top with canned tomatoes and cover with Mozzarella slices. Bake in preheated 350 degree oven about 10 to 15 minutes until mozzarella is melted and golden. Yield: 2 servings.

Il Fegato alla Veneziana
(liver, Venice style)

Fry small, thin slices of calves' liver in a mixture of butter and olive oil with a little chopped onion and parsley and season with salt and pepper.

Lasagna

¼ cup minced onion
1 tablespoon salad oil
½ pound minced chuck steak
1 garlic clove, sliced
¾ teaspoon salt
⅛ teaspoon pepper
½ teaspoon oregano
2 tablespoons chopped parsley

1 can tomatoes
1 8-ounce can tomato sauce
¼ cup grated Parmesan cheese
¼ pound lasagna noodles
½ pound Mozzarella cheese,
    thinly sliced
½ pound ricotta or cottage
    cheese

Prepare the meat either the day before or early on the day of serving. Begin by sauteing the onion in hot oil in a skillet. Add the meat and cook until the redness disappears. Mash the garlic with the salt and add to the meat with the pepper, oregano, parsley, tomatoes, tomato sauce, and 1 tablespoon grated Parmesan cheese. Simmer covered for 30 minutes, then cool and refrigerate overnight or for about six hours. About 45 minutes before serving, preheat oven to 350 degrees and cook lasagna noodles as directed on the package. Drain, then cover with cold water. Put one-third of the meat sauce in a baking dish, add a layer of drained lasagna placed lengthwise, then a layer of Mozzarella, a layer of ricotta or cottage cheese, and 1 tablespoon Parmesan. Repeat, ending with the last of the sauce and Parmesan. Bake for 30 minutes. Yield: 3 servings.

Sauces

Ragù alla Bolognese
(Meat sauce, Bologna style)

¼ pound bacon, minced
1 tablespoon butter
1 medium onion, minced
1 carrot, minced
¼ stalk celery, minced
½ pound lean beef, ground twice
¼ pound chicken livers, minced

1 cup dry white wine
1 cup beef bouillon
2 tablespoons tomato paste
salt and pepper
⅛ teaspoon ground nutmeg
2 teaspoons grated lemon rind
2 cloves
1 cup sour cream

Mince bacon, butter, onion, carrot, and celery together on a cutting board, until they are of a paste consistency. In a heavy saucepan, cook the mixture over a low heat until slightly browned. Add beef and brown evenly. Add chicken livers and cook for 2 minutes. Combine wine, bouillon, and tomato paste and blend well. Add to meat mixture. Season to taste with salt and pepper. Stir in nutmeg, grated lemon rind, and add the cloves. Simmer covered over low heat for 45 minutes, stirring occasionally. Before serving, heat sour cream but do not allow it to boil. Stir hot cream into the meat sauce. Serve over spaghetti or noodles.

Salsa Verde
(green sauce)

2 tablespoons dried capers
1 minced garlic clove
1 tablespoon minced onion
1 anchovy, chopped
2 cups parsley heads

1 teaspoon dried basil
¾ cup olive oil
juice of 2 lemons
1 teaspoon salt
¼ teaspoon pepper

Combine capers, garlic, onion, and anchovy, all chopped. Mince together parsley and basil and combine with caper mixture. Add oil, lemon juice, salt and pepper. Put in blender and make a puree. (Used on meats, fish, and vegetables.)

Desserts, Pastries

Dolce Ravioli
(sweet pastries)

1¾ cups pastry flour
3 tablespoons shortening
½ pound cottage cheese
2 tablespoons sugar
1 egg white

2 egg yolks
½ teaspoon vanilla
fat for frying
powdered sugar

Mix flour and shortening together with enough cold water to form a stiff dough. Roll out very thin on a lightly floured board. Combine remaining ingredients and use as a filling for the pastry. Cut dough into 3-inch squares. Place 1 teaspoon of the filling on a square of pastry and cover with another square. Seal edges by pressing them together with the tines of a fork dipped in flour. Repeat until all squares have been filled. Fry in deep hot fat until golden brown. Sprinkle with powdered sugar.

Marsala Sabayon (Zabaglione)
(dessert or cake filling)

½ cup Marsala wine or white
    sauterne

⅓ cup sugar
3 egg yolks

Beat wine, sugar, and egg yolks together and place in the top of a double boiler over boiling water. Beat with egg beater about 5 minutes until stiff enough to form peaks. Serve as a custard or use as a sauce or dressing for cakes or other desserts.

Cavallucci di Siena
(Siena nut cakes)

1 cup sugar
¼ pound shelled walnuts
⅓ cup candied orange peel
pinch of mixed spices

½ teaspoon anise seed
grated nutmeg
2 cups flour

Put sugar in a saucepan with a little water until it is cooked into a threadlike consistency. Immediately add nuts, finely chopped, candied peel, and the flavoring. Mix thoroughly and pour mixture on a well-floured board. Mould into little cakes about the size of an egg, about 1½ inches long. Sprinkle with flour and bake in 350 degree oven until golden brown.

Castagne
(chestnuts with whipped cream)

2 cups (1 pound) raw chestnuts ¾ cup whipped cream
⅛ teaspoon salt 1 teaspoon vanilla
6 tablespoons powdered sugar

Cook chestnuts in enough water to cover for 15 to 20 minutes. Drain, peel, and skin the nuts. Put parboiled chestnuts in a pot with 1½ cups water, add salt, cover and cook until soft. Mash until smooth. Add sugar. Save ⅓ cup whipped cream to garnish. Use remaining cream and stir into chestnut mixture. Add vanilla. Pour into dish and refrigerate for at least 6 hours. Serve in a glass dish and garnish with remaining whipped cream.

Segreto della Dama
(lady's secret)

¼ pound vanilla wafers 6 tablespoons butter
1 egg yolk ¼ cup roasted hazelnuts,
1 egg coarsely chopped
1 cup powdered sugar ½ cup sweet cream, whipped
⅓ cup cocoa wafers to decorate

Crumble wafers without making them too fine. Place eggs and sugar in a bowl and beat until smooth. Add cocoa and mix well, then add melted butter and stir in the nuts and crumbled wafers. Grease a baking tin, line with waxed paper, put mixture in, and refrigerate for 2 hours. To serve, unmold and remove paper. Decorate with the cream and wafers.

Chapter 22

SPAIN

There are many Spains, then and now; all of them fascinating. There is the Spain of prehistory, when unknown hunters painted wild stag and ibex on the walls of paleolithic caverns that still exist. And the Spain of the Greek traders whose ships plied the Mediterranean and penetrated the Iberian peninsula in the seventh century B.C.

There is the Spain of Carthage, of Julius Caesar, the Vandals, the Visigoths of Aquitaine, and the Moors. And the Spain of Christian kings whose court intrigues rival the best (or worst) of that sort of thing. There is the Spain of the Inquisition in the fifteenth century which routed suspected traitors and heretics in one of history's most infamous chapters, while shortly after, Spaniards explored and settled America, Mexico, and most of Central and South America.

Meanwhile, back at home, Joanna the Mad and her husband Philip the Handsome had their turns on the Spanish throne, followed by Frenchmen in the court as Napoleon stormed across Europe. And while America was fighting the British in the War of 1812, Spain was winning its independence, then found itself plunged into war with us over its possessions of Cuba and Puerto Rico.

Spain sat out World War I, having its own troubles establishing its political identity, a situation which worsened until the monarchy fell in 1930 and both internal and external power struggles between Communists, Fascists, and Socialists culminated in Spain's Civil War. The three-year battle provided a romantic background for some novelists, but it took a million Spanish lives and virtually destroyed what was left of a nation once one of the most powerful in Europe. Spain had been most brutally used as a testing ground for a greater war in which it declared its neutrality but left little doubt of its pro-Axis sympathies, regarding Communism as the greater enemy.

Under one of Europe's most controversial leaders, General Francisco Franco, who has led Spain since 1939, the country has gradually been reborn. Though still far from prosperous, Spain enjoys the second largest tourism trade in Europe, after Italy. What attracts hundreds of thousands to Spain each year is a nation blessed by the sun, with a mysterious and romantic culture, and a proud and agonizingly religious people whose sights, music, folklore, and food are among the most attractive and inspired anywhere.

Madrid, the capital, typifies reborn Spain, a most pleasing city in which modern architecture preserves the grace of old Spain. In the Prado Museum are the masterpieces of El Greco, Velazquez, Murillo, and Goya as well as those of Italian and Flemish giants. But for an equally exciting contemporary experience, sit on the terrace of one of the cafes on the Castellana and, beneath fragrant acacia trees, enjoy an Andalusian salad, Spanish omelet, or Castillian veal, and watch the lovely senoritas stroll by with black lace *mantillas* covering their shoulders. Then drive to nearby El Escorial and visit the monastery with the tombs of Spain's kings and queens. Not far from Escorial is The Valley of the Fallen, where lie the Spanish dead of both sides in the Civil War. North and west of Madrid are the picture-postcard towns and countryside of old Castile.

In Toledo, Moorish Spain stands next to Christian Spain, and besides El Greco's charming house and garden there is the splendor of the thirteenth century cathedral that is one of Europe's most beautiful.

On the nine days of July between the 6th and 15th when the bulls are run in Pamplona, you will look for and probably find sidewalk cafe tables with Hemingway characters out of *The Sun Also Rises*. You can watch from safe balconies as the darkly handsome, slim young men of Navarra run ahead of the charging bulls who are allowed to use the streets and sidewalks on their rampaging way to the *corrida*. Or you can throw caution to the wind and run along with them.

Hannibal and his elephants came through Barcelona enroute to Rome. The city, which dates to 230 B.C., has seen and preserved most of the history of its country and is one of its most beautiful with palaces, churches, monasteries, museums, and with the magnificent blue Mediterranean at its doorstep.

The beaches of the Costa Brava rival the sixteen Balearic Islands for places to enjoy splendor in the sun. Majorca is particularly lovely with its recreated old Spanish village at Son Dureta containing mosques, towers, chapels, and Moorish homes.

The Spain of old and the Spain of most of our imagination comes alive perhaps best in Andalusia, with its capital, Seville. Here is the Spain of Carmen; of the Alcazar, incredibly ornate palace fortress of Arab princes; Santa Cruz' pastel houses and gardens; gypsies singing and dancing. During Holy Week before Easter, there is the paradoxical panoply of barefoot penitents carrying huge wooden crucifixes while on the balconies of hotels the less serious celebrate by shooting off fireworks.

Granada has the Alhambra, and even Arabia is hard put to equal the majesty of the ornate Arabian Nights palace.

The food of Spain is as varied as the country's history and culture. Various regions have their own specialties, but there are common denominators. Rice, beans, peppers, tomatoes, pimiento, olive oil, spices, oranges, garlic sausages, chicken, and fish are all staples. Bread, pastries, cakes, and fresh fruits are plentiful. Spain is Europe's third largest producer of wine, the most famous being sherry which is a popular apéritif and also is widely used in cooking. For a nation constantly beset by foreign interlopers, Spain has retained its spicy and most exciting culinary identity.

Spanish cooking has been likened to bullfights, Flamenco dancing, and the paintings of Goya: it is vivid, highly colored, full of the vigor of life, not a little mysterious, and always exciting.

Appetizers

Huevos Rellenos
(stuffed eggs)

6 hard-boiled eggs
1 small can tuna fish
2 tablespoons butter
1 tablespoon tomato sauce
salt and pepper

garlic salt
1 tablespoon finely grated
onion
mayonnaise
1 tin of pimiento

Cut hard-boiled eggs in half lengthwise and remove the yolks. Mix tuna, butter, and tomato sauce and make a puree. Season with salt and pepper and fill the egg whites with the mixture. Add garlic salt and grated onion to the mayonnaise and cover the eggs with it. Sieve the egg yolks and sprinkle a little on top of the mayonnaise. Garnish with strips of pimiento. Yield: 6 servings.

Soups

Gazpacho
(cold vegetable soup)

5 medium tomatoes
2 medium cucumbers
1 large onion
1 medium green pepper
4 cups French or Italian bread
   crumbs

2 teaspoons garlic
¼ cup red wine vinegar
4 teaspoons salt
4 tablespoons olive oil
1 tablespoon tomato paste

Peel and coarsely chop the tomatoes, cucumbers, and onion. Remove seeds and ribs, and coarsely chop green pepper. Trim crusts from dry French or Italian bread and coarsely crumble the bread. Finely chop the garlic. In a deep bowl, combine the vegetables, garlic, and bread. Mix together thoroughly, then stir in 4 cups water, vinegar, and salt. Ladle the mixture 2 cups at a time into a blender and blend at high speed for 1 minute until it is a smooth puree. Pour into a bowl and beat in olive oil and tomato paste with a wire whisk. Cover the bowl with plastic or foil and refrigerate at least 2 hours until chilled. Before serving, whisk or stir the soup lightly and ladle into a large chilled bowl or individual soup bowls. Garnish with a cup of bread cubes, ½ cup finely chopped onions, ½ cup peeled and finely chopped cucumbers, and ½ cup finely chopped green peppers. Yield: 4 servings.

Sopa de Pescado à la Mallorquina
(Majorcan fish soup)

2 onions	oil
1 clove garlic	¾ cup rice
3 tomatoes	milk
2 pounds haddock	salt
parsley	

Chop 1 onion, the garlic, and 1 tomato and put them in water with the fresh haddock. Bring to a boil and simmer 10 minutes. Remove fish, skin and bone it, and set it aside. In a skillet, fry a sliced onion, the remaining 2 tomatoes, skinned and peeled, and the parsley, minced, in oil. Add fish bones and the broth in which the fish was cooked. Simmer 20 minutes, adding more water if necessary. Strain the fish stock. Return stock to the pan, bring to a boil, and add the rice. Cook rapidly for 15 minutes. Just before it is done, return the fish, broken into pieces, and reheat. Add a little milk, season with salt, and serve. Majorcans top the soup with thin slices of bread. Yield: 4 servings.

Salad

Ensalada Valenciana
(salad Valenciana)

Place a slice of toast that has been rubbed with garlic in a salad bowl. Over it place lettuce, sliced oranges, and pimientos. Make a dressing of the yolks of 2 hard-boiled eggs, pounded in a mortar, adding 3 tablespoons of oil, 1 teaspoon vinegar, 1 tablespoon lemon juice, salt, and pepper.

Ensalada de Pimientos y Tomate
(pimiento and tomato salad)

Cut some uncooked red or green pimientos in strips and mix with sliced tomatoes. Make a dressing of oil, vinegar, salt and pepper, and a little pounded garlic.

Vegetables

Huevos en Ajillo
(eggs in onion sauce)

2 tablespoons olive oil	6 eggs
3 medium onions, sliced	salt and pepper
1 sweet pepper, sliced	parsley

Heat olive oil in a skillet and brown onions and sweet pepper slowly until tender. Break eggs into a bowl and beat slightly, then add seasoning and pour over the onions. Stir mixture until eggs are cooked. Remove to a hot platter and garnish with parsley. Yield: 4 servings.

Berengenas Rellenas
(stuffed eggplant)

1 eggplant	2 tomatoes, skinned
1 onion, finely chopped	salt and pepper
2 cups cooked chicken, chopped	oil

Cut eggplant in half lengthwise, put in boiling water and cook for 10 to 12 minutes. Remove from water and scoop out the pulp without breaking the skin. Lightly brown the onion, chicken, tomatoes, and some of the eggplant pulp seasoned with salt and pepper in hot oil. After cooking mixture slightly and mixing it together, use to stuff the eggplant shells. Put in a baking pan in 350 degree oven and bake for 15 minutes. Garnish with chopped parsley. Yield: 2 servings.

Tortilla a la Española
(Spanish omelette)

½ pound spinach
1 small onion
2 or 3 slices ham
¼ pound mushrooms
parsley
butter

2 or 3 tomatoes
1 clove garlic
8 eggs
1 cup tomato sauce
Spanish sauce

Cook spinach with a little minced onion in water. Drain and chop up. Prepare a mince of ham with a few mushrooms and a generous amount of parsley. Saute in butter and keep warm. Peel, seed, and chop up the tomatoes, crush the garlic, and saute together in another pan. Next, make an omelette with 4 eggs and the spinach mixture. Make another omelette of the rest of the eggs and the tomato mixture. Serve with the spinach omelette covered with the mince and topped by the second omelette. Serve with a Spanish sauce (see below, under sauces). Yield: 4 to 6 servings.

Potatoes, Rice

Tarta de Patatas
(potato tart)

1½ pounds potatoes
2 tablespoons flour
butter

salt and pepper
4 slices bacon
4 tablespoons cream

Boil potatoes in the jackets. When tender, peel and sieve or mash into a bowl. Mix in flour and butter to taste, season with salt and pepper. Mixture should be pastry-firm. Flour the baking dish in which the tart is to be baked. Spread a thin layer of the potato mixture over the dish about ½ inch thick and prick it with the tines of a fork. Cover with strips of bacon and add the cream. Bake in a 400 degree oven for 15 minutes and serve hot. Yield: 4 servings.

Arroz con Jerez
(rice with sherry)

1 onion
oil
2 cups rice
1½ cups sherry

2 cups beef stock or bouillon
1 tablespoon butter
salt

Slice the onion and saute in oil. Add rice and stir for 2 minutes. Pour in the sherry. Stir until sherry is absorbed, then add the boiling stock or bouillon. Cover and cook in 350 degree oven for 20 minutes. Add butter and season with salt before serving.

Fish

Cod Byscayenne

2 tablespoons olive oil
6 shallots, chopped
2 cloves garlic, chopped
2 pounds cod, shredded
2 medium raw potatoes, sliced

2 tomatoes, sliced thin
1 green pepper, chopped fine
salt and pepper
1 cup water

Heat the olive oil and saute shallots and garlic about 5 minutes. Do not allow to brown. Add cod and mix thoroughly. Place ½ of mixture on bottom of a buttered casserole, cover with sliced potatoes and tomatoes, then with the green pepper. Put rest of cod mixture on top. Season with salt and pepper, add water, and bake covered in 350 degree oven for 1 hour. Yield: 4 servings.

Truchias Obscuras
(smothered brook trout)

6 brook trout
salt
4 tablespoons butter, melted
½ cup bread crumbs
¼ teaspoon nutmeg

¼ teaspoon saffron
¼ teaspoon pepper
¼ teaspoon thyme
1 teaspoon minced parsley
½ cup dry white wine

Clean and dry the fish, then season well with salt. Grease the sides and bottom of a large roasting pan with the melted butter.

Combine bread crumbs with the seasonings and parsley and mix. Spread half of this mixture on the bottom of the pan. Place fish on the crumbs and add the wine. Do not place fish one on top the other. Sprinkle top of fish with remaining crumbs. Bake in 350 degree oven for 20 minutes, basting frequently. Yield: 6 servings.

Arenques a la Española
(Spanish herrings)

8 herrings	2 eggs, separated
2 cups milk	1 tablespoon olive oil
salt and pepper	2 tablespoons butter
⅛ cup flour	

Clean herrings and split them open. Remove head and backbone. Marinate them 2 or 3 hours in a mixture of 1 cup milk, salt and pepper. Warm remaining cup of milk and stir into the flour. Beat yolks of egg and add to milk with oil. Season with salt. Mixture should be of the consistency of thick cream. Before using mixture, whisk the whites of egg and fold in. Dip each fish in the mixture, completely covering each. Fry in hot oil or butter.

Poultry

Arroz con Pollo
(rice with chicken)

1 3-pound chicken	1 teaspoon paprika
¼ cup olive oil	2 bay leaves
1 clove garlic, crushed	1 cup tomatoes
3 onions, chopped fine	pinch of saffron
2 green peppers, chopped fine	2 cups rice
1½ teaspoons salt	3 pimientos, cut fine
½ teaspoon pepper	

Cut chicken into eating portions. Heat oil in a large skillet and brown the chicken. Add garlic, onions, and green peppers. Cook about 5 minutes. Add salt, pepper, paprika, bay leaves, and tomatoes. Cook about 15 minutes. Add 6 cups boiling water and pinch of saffron. Wash and drain rice and add to chicken. Cover and boil slowly about 1 hour, stirring occasionally. Add pimientos during last 15 minutes of cooking. Yield: 4 servings.

Stewed Chicken à l'Espagnol

1 5-pound chicken
salt and pepper
flour
¼ cup butter
2 medium onions, sliced
1 cup green olives, pitted and
    chopped

1 green pepper, finely chopped
2 cups canned tomatoes
1 teaspoon sugar
2 cups canned peas
1 cup canned mushrooms,
    sliced
1 teaspoon salt

Clean and cut chicken into serving pieces. Season well with salt and pepper and dredge with flour. Melt butter in large skillet and when hot, brown chicken well. Remove chicken and add sliced onions, olives, green pepper, canned tomatoes, and sugar. Cook for 10 minutes. Place chicken in skillet and add liquid from canned peas and mushrooms with enough water to cover. Simmer covered for 1½ hours until tender. Add peas and mushrooms, 1 teaspoon salt, and for each cup of liquid used, mix 1 tablespoon flour with a little cold water until smooth and stir into hot stew and continue stirring until mixture boils. Cover and cook for 20 minutes. Yield: 5 servings.

Meats

Guisado
(Spanish beef stew)

3 small onions, chopped
1 clove garlic
2 tablespoons minced parsley
¼ cup olive oil
2 pounds bottom round of beef
2 teaspoons salt

⅛ teaspoon pepper
3 green peppers, cut in strips
6 raw potatoes, cubed
1 large can tomatoes
flour

Saute chopped onions, garlic, and parsley in olive oil in a deep skillet until onions are golden brown. Remove garlic. Cut meat into 1-inch cubes and brown in the hot oil. Add salt and pepper, green peppers, and 4 cups boiling water to cover the meat. Cover and simmer about 1 hour, then add potatoes and continue cooking for 1 hour or longer until meat is tender. After 45 minutes, add tomatoes. For each cup of water, measure 1 tablespoon flour and mix with cold water to a smooth paste. Add to the hot stew, stirring constantly until mixture boils. Cook for 10 minutes. Yield: 4 servings.

Castillian Veal

1 small leg of veal	¾ cup sherry
3 strips of bacon	12 small white onions, peeled
1 carrot, slivered	½ cup pitted olives
½ cup olive oil	1 bay leaf
1 tablespoon flour	sprig of thyme

Lard the veal with bacon strips and carrot slivers, place in a roasting pan with the oil, and cook until browned. Add flour, sherry, and 2 tablespoons water to the roasting pan. Cover and cook for 2 hours in 350 degree oven. After the first hour, add peeled onions, olives, bay leaf, and thyme. To serve, cut meat in slices and arrange on a hot platter garnished with onions and olives. Yield: 4 servings.

Pimientos Rellenos
(stuffed peppers)

4 ounces hazelnuts	salt and pepper
slice each of ham and lean pork	2 eggs
	bread crumbs
5 red peppers	saffron
3 tomatoes	2 egg yolks
2 courgettes (optional)	1 teaspoon vinegar
1 slice fat bacon	parsley
butter	

Roast the hazelnuts, then crush them and reserve 2 tablespoonfuls. Mince together the ham, lean pork, 1 pepper, tomatoes, courgettes (if you can find them), and fat bacon. Remove tops from remaining peppers and scrape out seeds. Saute the minced mixture in butter and seasoning. Add the hazelnuts (still reserving 2 tablespoonfuls). Fill peppers with the mixture. Beat eggs and mix with fine bread crumbs. Heat butter in a casserole, fill peppers with bread crumb mixture, and arrange peppers, filling spaces between them with the reserved nuts and some bread crumbs seasoned with a little saffron. Add a little water and simmer until peppers are tender. Make sauce by beating egg yolks with vinegar. Chop parsley finely, and add to egg yolks. Serve sauce separately. Yield: 4 servings.

Chuletas de Cerdo
(pork chops)

4 pork chops	parsley
oil	lemon peel
thyme	salt
2 cloves garlic	

Marinate pork chops for 24 hours in oil, thyme, whole garlic, parsley, and lemon peel, then sprinkle with salt. Turn chops over occasionally to marinate on both sides. About 15 minutes before serving, remove chops and drain, then dry on a towel. Grill on a hot grill. Serve with a favorite sauce (see below). Yield: 4 servings.

Sauces

Salsa Picante
(piquante sauce)

2 shallots	4 tablespoons butter
3 tablespoons vinegar	1 tablespoon flour
salt and pepper	1 cup beef stock or bouillon
parsley	3 gherkins

Mince shallots and put in saucepan with vinegar, salt, pepper, parsley, and a little butter. In a separate pan, make sauce with the flour, remaining butter, and all but ¼ cup of the stock. When this mixture comes to a boil, add vinegar mixture and remaining ¼ cup of the stock. Boil again. Before serving, slice the gherkins and add them to the sauce. Season to taste and serve.

Salsa Española
(classic Spanish sauce for meat or fish)

4 tablespoons butter
1 onion
3 tablespoons flour
1 clove garlic
1 carrot

trimmings of raw veal or ham
6 cups of beef bouillon or stock
salt and pepper
bouquet garni

Melt butter in a skillet and let it brown. Add finely minced onion and saute until brown. Add flour and stir for a minute or two. Brown but do not burn the mixture. Add a clove of garlic, whole, and the carrot sliced. Put meat in and keep stirring. Moisten with stock. Simmer, add seasoning of salt and pepper and bouquet garni. When all has dissolved into a rich brown gravy, add remaining stock and simmer for 2 to 3 hours. Skim and strain through a fine sieve, then keep in a cool place. The sauce should be like a thick cream.

Desserts, pastries

Roscoqs de Jeringas
(almond twists)

2 cups almonds
3 tablespoons grated lemon
rind

3 tablespoons granulated sugar
3 egg whites

Grind almonds until they are very fine. Add grated lemon rind and sugar and mix well. Beat egg whites until stiff but not dry and fold into almond mixture. Place mixture in a pastry bag and form small twists on a buttered baking sheet. Bake in 350 degree oven until golden brown.

Bizcochos de Madrid
(Madrid biscuits)

½ cup butter, melted
1 tablespoon grated orange
   rind
2 tablespoons brandy

7 egg yolks
3 cups flour
pinch of salt
1 teaspoon baking powder

Combine butter, orange rind, brandy, and six of the egg yolks and beat for 12 minutes. Sift together flour, salt, and baking powder and add a little at a time, beating after each addition. Shape small pieces of dough into twists and place on a well-buttered cookie sheet. Beat remaining egg yolk and brush tops of the twists. Bake in 400 degree oven about 20 minutes.

Bizcocho de Patates Domenech
(Spanish cake)

4 egg whites
2 egg yolks
1¾ cups sugar
grated rind of 1 lemon

1 cup potato flour mixed with
   6 tablespoons regular flour
shredded almonds

Break eggs into a saucepan, pour in sugar, and place pan over very low flame. Beat thoroughly with an egg whisk until very light and fluffy. When nearly doubled in volume, slowly stir in grated lemon rind and the combined flours. Beat 10 more minutes, then pour into a well-greased mold containing shredded almonds. Bake at 350 degrees until lightly browned.

Churros
(puffy crullers)

3 tablespoons butter
⅛ teaspoon salt
1 cup flour
2 large eggs
1 teaspoon rum

1½ tablespoons sugar
pinch of mace
oil for frying
powdered sugar

Mix butter, salt, and ⅔ cup water and bring to a boil. Take off heat and stir in flour, making a smooth paste. Return pan to very low heat and stir until paste does not stick to pot or to a wooden spoon. Set the paste aside. Beat each egg individually and add them one at a time, stirring vigorously and smoothing out the paste. Add rum, sugar, and mace. Chill paste in the refrigerator. When firm, put into a pastry bag. Heat the oil. On a piece of stiff, oiled paper, press the crullers into 8-inch length and ¾-inch width. Slip them from the paper into the hot oil, allowing them to become golden brown on both sides. Place a sheet of absorbent paper on a baking sheet in a warm oven. Drain crullers on the paper and sprinkle with powdered sugar. Yield: 8 to 10 large crullers.

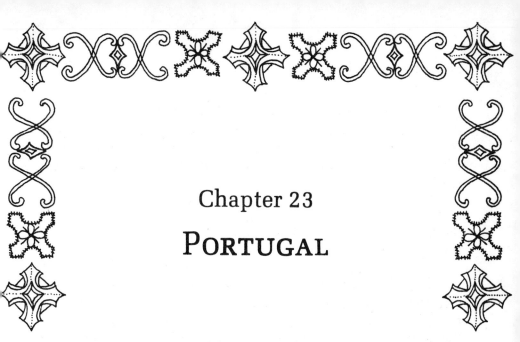

Chapter 23

PORTUGAL

Even though it is close to Spain, one of Europe's most popular tourist meccas, Portugal remains virtually undiscovered, a paradox because Portuguese explorers in the fifteenth century discovered so much of the western world.

Portugal is one of Europe's best surprises. It is a most beautiful country with a rich history and culture and some of the friendliest and happiest people. Yet underneath their gay exterior the Portuguese are a melancholy people. To understand this sad part of their character you must listen to their national song, the fado, which in Portuguese means "fate." And fate to the Portuguese always has an unhappy ending.

Perhaps this deep-rooted sadness comes from the nation's faded glory. Once one of the richest nations on earth, when its explorations to America, India, Brazil, China, and Japan brought home vast treasures, a century later Portugal fell into the hands of Spain. After regaining its independence in the seventeenth century, Portugal continued to decline. The monarchy was abolished in 1910. Portugal's losses as a result of World War I brought the country near to bankruptcy.

Portugal remained virtually isolated from the rest of Europe under the long regime of Prime Minister Antonio Salazar, a professor of political economy who vainly sought to improve Portugal's condition by a policy of isolationism. Since Salazar became ill in 1968 and was replaced, the new regime has gradually opened up Portugal to western affairs, and the future of this fascinating country appears to be much improved. However, a colonial war in Angola, a Portuguese province in West Africa, is draining both the economy and the national spirit.

Earlier Portuguese history parallels that of Spain, chronicling invasions by the Romans, Vandals, and the Moors. Evidences of the invaders' cultures are apparent as well throughout Portugal.

Lisbon, Portugal's major city, is a handsome blend of old and new, stretching out proudly beneath the outstretched arms of Christ the King, a 732-foot statue on the banks of the Tagus river facing the city. The monument was erected in 1959 in thankfulness for being spared in World War II, in which Portugal remained neutral. It also is evidence of how openly the Portuguese practice their Roman Catholic religion. Remember this is the country of Fatima, a village atop a mountain range 107 miles from Lisbon where in 1917, according to the legend of the miracle, the Virgin Mary appeared before three peasant children on repeated occasions. Pilgrims of all faiths revere the shrine and visit there each year.

Lisbon's tree-lined boulevards and modern hotels and office buildings are within only short walks of charming cobblestoned side streets with quaint old houses adorned by colored tiles. Street vendors and shopkeepers display a wide variety of fresh flowers, which the Portuguese seem to always have in great abundance. Ancient Portugal comes alive in the Alfama quarter where you will find dark-haired, dark-eyed girls carrying jugs to fountains, old men spinning stories to young boys as they repair fish nets together, and shopkeepers welcome you with genuine smiles to enjoy some fresh fruit and wine.

Just west of Lisbon lies Estoril, one of Europe's most beautiful resort areas with sand beaches and palm trees, casino, and pastel-colored villas. North of Lisbon are charming farm villages such as Obidos and countryside where peasants still ride donkeys and work the land by hand.

The Portugal of fishing lore is evident all along the coast but perhaps most appealing in Nazaré in the northwest, high above a 300-foot cliff where stands the Chapel of Our Lady of Nazaré, a fishermen's shrine. Portuguese women still huddle together anxiously, wrapped in their black shawls as they watch their men go down to the sea in ships. Local tradition forbids women widowed by the sea from remarrying.

Northern Portugal is most famous for its port wine, the Douro valley being the only place in the world where true port wine is made. And true port wine, you may be surprised to learn, is laced with brandy. When the grapes are harvested in autumn, the wine region's leading city, Oporto, and neighboring villages attract wine lovers from near and far.

Three hundred miles off the coast of Portugal, about an hour's flight by jet from Lisbon, lies the island of Madeira, even more beautiful and less spoiled than the mainland. In only thirty-five miles of length and fourteen miles of width, Madeira has mountains peaking at 6,000 feet, high cliffs overlooking magnificent rocky shores, verdant valleys rich in fruits and wildflowers, thick forests sloping to the sea, and some of the most spectacular coastline in the world.

Funchal, Madeira's capital, is a pastel paradise of villas and gardens built into the mountainside above the crescent bay, where the beaches are uncrowded and the days are one long *siesta*.

Portuguese food is logically related to the Spanish, but has its own distinctiveness, notably an even more abundant use of tomatoes and onions. The food is relatively simple, yet it will appeal as being zesty, exotic, and exceptionally fresh. Wine is used in preparing many of the foods. Portuguese cooks love to combine many ingredients, perhaps a result of the days when so many varieties of foods were brought home from their many colonies.

Fish caught in great variety and abundance naturally finds its way into the national food. Lobster, stuffed crab, mussels, small clams, *bacalhau* (salt cod), and even squid and octopus are favorites. In the north, a soup of potatoes, shredded cabbage, and sausage called *caldo verde* is traditional. All along the coast fish soups are popular.

When you're on Madeira, sitting on the veranda of the Clube de Turismo da Madeira, high on a cliff near the heart of Funchal, dining at poolside above the sea and having shrimp croquettes or

Portuguese steak with vintage port and dessert of walnut pudding or "sighs of a nun," a delicious lemon-flavored pastry, you certainly will sigh the sigh of a very contented traveler who is sure at last he has found the place like no other.

Soups

Canja com Arroz
(chicken rice soup)

1 cup rice
8 cups chicken stock or
   chicken bouillon
1 tablespoon olive oil
2 carrots, chopped fine
2 turnips, chopped fine
2 onions, chopped fine

2 tomatoes, chopped fine
6 sprigs parsley, chopped fine
2 cups cooked chicken cut in
   1½-inch pieces
salt and pepper
2 egg whites (optional)

Rinse rice in water 4 or 5 times. Bring stock or bouillon to a boil, pour rice in. Heat olive oil in a skillet. Fry vegetables until slightly browned, then add to the stock. Cook slowly, covered, until all ingredients are soft. Add tender chicken pieces and seasoning. Cook a few minutes longer. If soup is not thick enough, add egg whites slightly beaten, mixed with a little of the hot soup. Do not let soup boil again. Yield: 4 servings.

Caldo Verde
(green soup)

4 large potatoes, peeled and
   sliced
2 teaspoons salt
½ teaspoon pepper
6 tablespoons olive oil

1 pound spinach, kale, or
   lettuce cut into fine strips
4 ounces smoked garlic sausage

Cook potatoes in a covered pan in 8 cups boiling water with salt and pepper until tender. Remove and coarsely mash the potatoes and return to cooking water with olive oil. Bring to a boil, add greens, and boil uncovered for about 3 minutes until greens are tender but crisp. Season to taste. Serve with a few slices of sausage that have been simmered or slowly browned. Yield: 6 servings.

Salad

Salada Verde
(green salad)

crisp chilled leaf lettuce	white wine vinegar
watercress sprigs	coarse salt
olive oil	sweet onions (optional)

Cut leaf lettuce into fine julienne strips and place in a chilled salad bowl. Add watercress in a generous amount. Dress with olive oil, vinegar, and salt to taste. Thin rings of sweet raw onions may be added to the salad. Delicious with fish or meat dishes.

Vegetables

Cogumelos com Arroz
(mushrooms and rice)

10 ounces fresh button mush-rooms, sliced	⅔ cups rice
⅓ cup olive oil	¼ teaspoon salt
2 large onions, minced	3 tablespoons tomato puree
½ clove garlic, minced	2 tablespoons parsley, minced

Saute mushrooms in heated oil. Drain and put oil in a covered baking dish. Heat oil in the dish, saute the onions and garlic until golden. Add washed and dried rice and stir, allowing rice to get yellow. Cover all with water (to 1½ cups). Water must cover rice at least ½ inch. Add seasoning and tomato puree, parsley, and sauted mushrooms. Cover the baking dish tightly and bake in 375 degree oven until done, about 45 minutes. Yield: 4 servings.

Fish

Bacalhau à Gomes de Sà
(dried cod)

2 pounds dried cod	4 hard-boiled eggs
2 large onions	parsley
¼ cup olive oil	wine vinegar
1 large clove garlic, crushed	olive oil
3 large potatoes	black pepper
18 black olives	

Soak cod in cold water for 24 to 48 hours until it is very moist, changing the water several times, then drain. Simmer cod, covered, in enough water to cover it, for 15 minutes. Slice onions ¼ inch thick and saute in olive oil until golden, then stir in garlic. Peel potatoes and boil in salted water, then slice to ¼ inch thick. In a casserole, arrange a layer of half the potatoes, top with half the cod and half the onions, then repeat. Bake in 350 degree oven for 10 minutes until lightly browned. Garnish with olives and eggs either sliced or quartered, sprinkle with parsley. Add vinegar, oil, and pepper to taste.

Bacalhao Fresco à Portuguesa
(baked cod, Portuguese style)

1 medium eggplant, cut in 6 even slices	3 pounds fresh cod
¼ cup olive oil	1½ teaspoons salt
3 large onions, sliced	¼ teaspoon pepper
3 tablespoons salted capers	4 medium tomatoes, peeled and chopped
½ teaspoon cumin seeds, pounded	2 cloves, heads removed
1 cup rice, boiled	3 tablespoons lemon juice
	2 tablespoons butter

Saute eggplant in hot olive oil until it is a light yellow. Place in a baking dish. In the eggplant oil, saute the onions, separating them into rings. Allow them to become soft but not brown. Wash and soak salted capers in cold water for a few hours, then drain and chop. Mix capers and cumin into rice. Put a layer of onion rings over eggplant slices, then a layer of cooked rice. Clean cod, split lengthwise, remove bones, and rub with salt, pepper, and paprika. Put layer of fish on top of the rice, add tomatoes and cloves, pour ½ cup water over all to cover, sprinkle with lemon juice, and dot butter on top. Bake covered in 400 degree oven for 30 minutes. Uncover and bake another 10 to 15 minutes. Yield: 6 servings.

Croquettes de Camaroes
(shrimp croquettes)

2 tablespoons onion, sliced thin and then minced	¾ pound cooked shrimps
	1 teaspoon salt
2 small cloves garlic, minced	¼ teaspoon pepper
1 tablespoon butter	½ teaspoon paprika
4 teaspoons fennel leaves, chopped	2 eggs
	½ cup bread crumbs
2 slices stale white bread, diced	2 tablespoons flour
	fat for frying
3 tablespoons milk	

Saute onion and garlic in butter until golden brown. Remove from fire and add fennel leaves and diced bread. Heat milk and pour over bread. Let stand 5 to 10 minutes until bread is soft. Add shrimps with seasoning, eggs, bread crumbs, and flour to first mixture. Shape into rolls the size of a small sausage. Fry in deep fat until well browned, about 5 or 6 minutes. Yield: 8 croquettes.

Espinafre con Sardinhas
(spinach with sardines)

1 large tin sardines	2 tablespoons onion juice
2 cups cooked spinach, chopped	1 hard-boiled egg, chopped
	¼ teaspoon salt
½ cup bread crumbs	¼ teaspoon pepper
juice of ½ lemon	butter

Skin, bone, and chop the sardines. Mix with spinach, bread crumbs, lemon, and onion juice, some of the spinach liquid, the chopped egg white and half the chopped yolk. Season to taste. Put in a buttered baking dish, sprinkle remaining egg yolk on top and dot with butter. Bake for 15 minutes in 350 degree oven. Yield: 4 servings.

Poultry

Galinha Cerehada à Portuguesa
(Portuguese chicken)

1 chicken	3 tomatoes, chopped
olive oil	⅔ cup small cooked
butter	mushrooms
1 onion, chopped	salt and pepper
1 clove garlic	

Cut chicken into serving pieces and cook in a little oil and butter in skillet until golden. Add onion and garlic. When onion is slightly golden, add tomatoes and mushrooms. Season with salt and pepper. Simmer gently for 45 minutes. Serve chicken on a hot dish and pour the sauce and mushrooms on top. Garnish with small cooked tomatoes. Yield: 4 servings.

Arroz de Frango
(chicken and rice casserole)

2 onions, chopped	1 chicken, skinned and jointed
2 carrots, chopped	olive oil
chopped parsley	1 cup washed rice
salt and pepper	paprika or sausage

Place onions and carrots in a casserole, add some chopped parsley, salt and pepper, and jointed and skinned chicken pieces. Braise in olive oil until chicken is browned, then remove and sieve the gravy. Add 2 cupfuls water and 1 cup of rice in an ovenproof dish. Add chicken and cover with remaining rice. Top with paprika or spicy sausage. Brown in 350 degree oven and garnish with parsley. Yield: 4 servings.

Meat

Bife Portuguesa
(Portuguese steak)

4 ¾-inch thick filet mignons
2 cloves garlic, crushed
2 tablespoons wine vinegar
salt and pepper
3 tablespoons butter
3 tablespoons olive oil

1 bay leaf, crushed
2 cloves garlic, split
4 ounces ham, thinly sliced
chopped parsley
2 lemons cut into wedges

Rub meat with crushed garlic, vinegar, and salt and pepper to season. Heat butter and olive oil in skillet. Add bay leaf, split garlic, and steaks. Saute steaks quickly on each side, keeping center rare. Add ham and saute just until lightly brown, place on top of each steak. Sprinkle with parsley, garnish with lemon wedges, and pour pan juices over the steaks. Yield: 4 servings.

Lombo de Porco
(pork loin)

1 tablespoon shortening
1 tablespoon butter
2 pounds loin of pork
salt
2 onions, sliced
2 tomatoes, sliced

2 carrots, sliced
parsley
6 tablespoons white wine
salt and pepper
mixed cooked vegetables

Combine shortening and butter in saucepan. When melted, put in the loin of pork which has been well-rubbed with salt. Cook to a brown color, turning so both sides are browned. Add sliced onions, tomatoes, carrots, a little parsley, and white wine to moisten. Season highly with salt and pepper and simmer for 2 to 2½ hours until meat is tender. Place loin on a hot dish, strain sauce over it, and garnish with cooked vegetables (small potatoes, carrots, eggplant, pimentos) which have been fried in a little butter. Yield: 4 servings.

Lombo de Vitela a Portuguesa
(loin of veal)

loin of veal
white wine
1 clove garlic

salt and pepper
melted butter and lard

Place veal in a deep dish with white wine, garlic, and season with salt and pepper. Let it marinate several hours, turning several times. Remove garlic and half of the wine, brush the veal with melted butter and lard, and roast, basting often, with the sauce. Yield: 4 servings.

Desserts, pastries

Croquettes com Amendoas
(almond croquettes)

3 egg whites
¼ cup powdered sugar
½ cup port wine
⅛ teaspoon salt
1 teaspoon grated orange rind
¼ pound whole almonds,
    blanched and grated

6 bitter almonds
¼ cup cupcake crumbs
2 tablespoons powdered sugar
2 egg yolks
½ cup dried bread crumbs
oil for frying

Slightly beat the white of an egg with sugar, wine, salt, and orange rind. Fold almonds into egg mixture. Beat remaining egg whites and fold with cake crumbs into the almond mixture. Stir to a thick paste and shape into small, oblong croquettes or balls the size of a golf ball. Beat egg yolks with 2 teaspoons water. Dip croquettes into the egg-water mixture, then into the bread crumbs and dust lightly with powdered sugar. Fry in deep hot oil about 5 to 6 minutes until light brown and cooked. Drain on paper towels. Yield: 4 servings.

Pudim de Noses
(walnut pudding)

½ pound walnuts
cinnamon ·

5 eggs
1 cup sugar

Shell walnuts and pound in a mortar to a smooth paste with the cinnamon. Beat eggs and sugar together, add nuts, and mix and beat thoroughly. Pour mixture into buttered mold and cook in a saucepan of water that is constantly simmering. When set, remove from mold and let stand until cold.

Pudim de Macãs
(apple pudding)

8 large cooking apples
1½ cups sugar
1 cup seeded raisins
½ cup citron peel, finely
   chopped

½ cup seedless raisins
½ cup blanched and shredded
   pistachio nuts
juice of ¼ of a lemon

Core, peel, and slice five of the eight apples. Add sugar and enough water to cook them. Stew until apples are tender, then add dried fruit, peel, and nuts, stirring frequently. Core and peel remaining 3 apples and cut into thin rings. Sprinkle with lemon juice and put half of them in bottom of a buttered baking dish. Spread cooked apples over them, place remaining raw slices on top. Bake 30 minutes in 350 degree oven. Yield: 6 servings.

Suspiros de Freira
(sighs of a nun)

6 tablespoons butter
3¾ cups sugar
flour
3 eggs

icing sugar
2 or 3 pieces thinly cut lemon
   rind
powdered cinnamon

Mix butter, ¾ cup sugar, and 2 cups hot water in a saucepan and bring to a boil. Quickly stir in enough flour to hold dough together. When dough leaves the sides of the pan, take off the heat and beat in the eggs, one at a time. Roll out dough on slightly floured board to about ½ inch thickness and cut into small squares. Make a syrup with 3 cups sugar and 1½ cups hot water and lemon peel. Boil for 2 to 3 minutes and cook the pastry squares in it, a few at a time. Drain and serve on a hot plate. Dust with cinnamon and sugar.

Bolo de Principe
(prince's pudding)

5 eggs
1¼ cups sugar
grated semi-sweet chocolate

grated peel and juice of 1 lemon

Beat eggs and sugar until sugar is dissolved. Beat in lemon peel and juice. Pour pudding into a shallow baking dish in which pudding is about 1 inch deep. Set into a baking pan with hot water about ½ inch deep in the bottom. Bake at 325 degrees for 30 minutes or until set. Remove from water, and cool on a rack. Serve in individual dessert dishes. Sprinkle grated chocolate on top.

7

The Balkans

Greece, Albania, Bulgaria, Rumania, Yugoslavia

Some of the world's most noble history has come from the Balkans, an area today perhaps more troubled than it has ever been. Those who have fled political persecution or been exiled take with them a love of and faith in their old country that borders on fanaticism. To earn such loyalty, a nation must truly be dear and deserving. Especially in the case of Greece, the cradle of civilization, few dispute that this is so.

For centuries the Balkans have been the battleground for wars with the Turks. Never recovering sufficiently, they now are under Communist influence. Those who come to America from Greece and elsewhere in the Balkans bring with them a longing to return, but only if things can be as they were. When they can't, they carry their nation's banner in their heart and, as often, under their belt. The food, the drink, the music, the celebration of life comes with them no matter where they go or whether they ever will return.

As the northern Baltic states of Poland, Estonia, Latvia, and Lithuania are bound culturally and gastronomically to the Slavic races and to Russia, the southerly Balkan countries of Greece, Albania, Bulgaria, Rumania, and Yugoslavia are most strongly influenced by Turkey and other Near Eastern nations.

Though they have political differences, the Balkan states are more closely tied to each other in the matter of cooking. Because of wars and more subtle cultural invasions, the food of the Balkans also reflects Slavic and Germanic tastes. Festive dishes are, in addition, tied strongly to religious customs among native Roman Catholics, Greek Orthodox, and Mohammedans.

Substantial and highly-seasoned are the chief words for the foods of the Balkans. Garlic, peppers, herbs and spices, dried mushrooms, mutton, lamb, fowl, cheese, and great varieties of fresh fruits and vegetables are among the staples. The milk of goats, cows, and sheep provide cream and cheese which is used in many dishes. Balkan people believe sour milk and buttermilk greatly add to a long, healthy life.

Garlic and olive oil are more widely used in Greece and Bulgaria, while Rumanians prefer their dishes laced with dill and prepared in lard. Potatoes are not a staple as in the northern countries. Millet and other grain products are used instead.

Balkan cooks enjoy blending unusual combinations of foods, often adding fruits which American cooks would not consider. Adaptations of the popular peasant dishes of their neighbors are many, including Austrian and German dumplings, Hungarian goulash and strudel, Russian borsch, Turkish pilaf, Italian polenta, Slavic cabbage stuffed with meat and rice, and the universally popular European stew with meat or chicken and lots of fresh vegetables done up in sour cream.

Rich pastries and desserts with syrup, a Turkish and Syrian influence, are found in restaurants and homes alike, and wines and brandies are taken at most meals. *Ouzo,* a sweet, anise-flavored liqueur, is the national drink of Greece, and *slivovitz,* a dry, colorless, slightly bitter plum brandy of Serbo-Croatian origin, is popular throughout the Balkans and the Near East.

The Greeks make greater use of fish and olives, and their cooking is slightly less rich than their Balkan neighbors. Apricots, grapes, melons and other fruits and a profusion of nuts are used with meat, fish, and vegetable dishes. Lemon is squeezed over a great variety of foods.

When the sun dips into the sea and the lamps are lit, when the last of the lamb with okra and all of the crumbs of the spiced cake are gone, when the *ouzo* is poured and the men in the cafe begin to tune the eight strings of their bouzoukis and the impromptu dance begins, even if you are far away, you are home again in the Balkans.

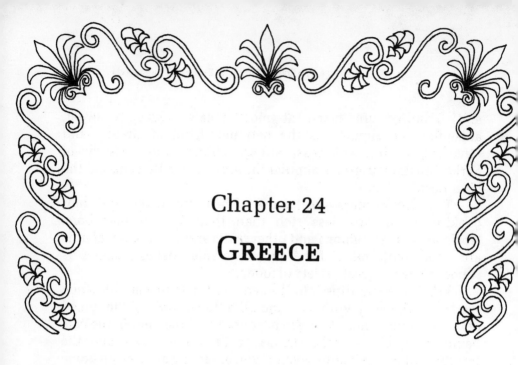

Chapter 24

GREECE

Pastel-colored fishing boats at Rhodes on white sand against the blue sea. The flood-lighted Acropolis on a full-moon midnight. The Temple of Zeus and the Olympic Stadium with their echoes of ages and battles past. The Agora and whispers in the wind of the voices of Socrates and Plato. The Temple of Poseidon, god of the sea, and the now-stilled victory cheers of the bull dancers.

Perhaps even more overwhelming than in Rome, the panoply of the ancient and modern world sweeps over you in Greece, the cradle of democracy, philosophy, medicine, law, drama, and epic poetry.

Despite political stresses since the king went into exile in 1967 and a constitutional monarchy was voted upon by plebiscite the following year, and wide coverage in the world press about patriots who have fled the country and refuse to return so long as the present government sits, Greece is not visibly that troubled. It is a nation that has learned to survive, with a history of war and political stresses that goes back 25,000 years.

A fisherman in a cafe on the idyllic island of Corfu told me that all Greeks are crazy. Like Zorba, who said that every man needs to have a little madness so he can be free of the torments of life, my fisherman friend meant it in a nice way, but he was firm in his belief. The Greeks I've met, including the fisherman, are only crazy with the love of life. Try to talk to a Greek for five minutes and you will hear him pour out his entire family's life history to you for hours, in such intimate detail you will flush. And between war and poverty, the Greeks have much to say that may sound wild or depressing. Yet you come away enriched, excited, that here as in few other countries, people will open their hearts to you and hope for nothing more in return than that you will do the same for them.

Greece itself is a most beautiful land, at the lower tip of the Balkan peninsula and with some 2,000 islands dotting the Aegean and Ionian seas. There are mountains such as Olympus, home of the Gods, and Parnassus, where Apollo and the Muses gathered. There are the ruins of Delphi where Greek heroes sought the wisdom of the Oracle, and at Olympia the Stadium where the first Olympic games were held in 776 B.C.

Today the citizens of Athens are a busy, urban people, while 60 percent of the Greek population farms or fishes for a living. Evenings and on Sundays and holidays, work is put aside and the Greeks do what they love best—gather together at home or in cafes and eat, drink, and dance. The *ouzo* flows and plates are piled with *moussaka*, a dish of meat and eggplant, and *souvlakia*, the Greek word for *shish kebab*.

Staples of Greek food include mutton and veal, olives, fresh fruits and vegetables, and varieties of nuts. Salads are popular and many foods are flavored with mint, bay leaves, and cinnamon. Fresh lemon juice is squeezed over many dishes, and olive oil is used extensively in cooking.

Fish naturally plays an important role in the food of Greece. The sea provides abundant supply of shrimps, bluefish, red snapper, crawfish, mackeral, and smelt. *Caccavia,* a delicious fish soup which contains fresh vegetables, is said to be the forerunner of French *bouillabaisse.*

Goat's milk provides a national cheese called *feta,* which is very strong and is grated for a variety of uses.

Pastries are often made with syrup, as they are in Turkey. Perhaps the most famous is *baklava,* layers of flaky pastry filled with honey and nuts.

Greek pine-scented wines and fruit-flavored brandies are widely drunk, but the most popular drink is *ouzo,* an anise-flavored liqueur which also is a before-meal drink.

Greece is rich in small, family-owned restaurants and cafes where you get a lot of hospitality with your meal. And it does not take luck to find a fisherman like my friend on Corfu sitting down with you. It merely takes a willingness to be talked to. For if there is one thought with which a Greek wants you to leave Greece, it is how great is the gift of life.

Appetizers

Kastana Psita
(roast chestnuts)

Skin off the outer shell of large chestnuts and put nuts in a flat pan. Sprinkle with a little water and place in a 375 degree oven. Sprinkle several times, at about 10 minute intervals, until the inner thin cover of the chestnut slips off.

Soups

Caccavia
(fish soup)

2 pounds whitefish	1 cup milk
1 onion, chopped	3 tablespoons tomato puree
1 clove garlic	1 glass white wine
4 sticks celery, chopped	1 teaspoon chopped fennel
1 leek, chopped	2 tablespoons chopped parsley
salt, pepper	1 strip chopped lemon peel
¼ cup flour	

Place the fish, onion, garlic, celery, and leek in a large pot, season with salt and pepper, and cover with cold water. Bring to a boil and simmer until fish is soft. When fish is cooked, take the fish out of the water, remove any bones, and break fish into large pieces. Simmer the fish broth for 20 more minutes, strain, and return to the pot. Mix the flour and milk to a smooth paste, add tomato puree and wine, and mix. Add mixture to the fish broth, simmer, and stir until it thickens. Return the cooked fish to the soup and add the herbs. Greeks serve a large piece of fish on a slice of toast and drink the soup from a bowl.

Soupa Avgolemono
(egg-lemon soup)

¼ cup rice
4½ cups chicken broth or
    bouillon

2 eggs
juice of 1 lemon

Add washed rice to the chicken broth, cook until done. Reduce heat to low and add beaten eggs to which the juice of one lemon has been gradually added. Keep over a low flame for about 2 minutes, then set aside, covered, for about 10 minutes to allow soup to set, and serve while still hot.

Salad

Salata
(mixed salad)

4 onions, chopped
3 tomatoes, peeled and
    chopped
2 green peppers, cut fine
1 bunch watercress, chopped
    fine

1 head lettuce, shredded
1 large cucumber, cut fine
3 tablespoons vinegar
1 teaspoon salt
12 black, ripe olives
⅓ cup olive oil

Toss all vegetables together with vinegar, salt, and olives. Pour olive oil over all and let stand ¼ hour before serving.

Vegetables

Dolmades
(stuffed vine or cabbage leaves)

12 vine or cabbage leaves	2 tablespoons olive oil
½ cup rice	3 tomatoes
¾ cup onions	½ teaspoon ground nutmeg
1 clove garlic	salt and pepper
¼ cup sultana raisins	

Blanch the leaves by putting them in boiling water for 2 to 3 minutes. Fry the washed rice, chopped onions and garlic and raisins in olive oil until they are a golden color. Add skinned and chopped tomatoes and nutmeg. Season liberally. Cut a little of the hard stem of each leaf, place a spoonful of the rice mixture in the center and roll up the leaf, tucking the ends in. Lay rolls in rows in a saucepan and cover with salted water. Cover and simmer for about 1 hour. Yield: 6 servings.

Dumplings

Keftepes
(croquettes)

6 or 8 slices of white bread, without crusts	salt and pepper
	3 teaspoons chopped parsley
3 onions	2 eggs
olive oil	flour
1½ pounds ground beef	

Soak bread in water. Divide finely chopped onions in half. Saute half in olive oil until almost brown. Put other half in a bowl with the minced meat. Pat the bread dry with paper towels and add to the meat and onions together with the sauted onions, stirring as each item is added. Add seasoning, parsley, and eggs. Knead and make into little balls or large flat pies. Dip in flour and fry in olive oil. Yield: 3 servings.

Fish

Plaki
(baked fish)

6 onions, chopped fine
olive oil
parsley, chopped
4 tomatoes

salt and pepper
2 pounds fish
tomato and lemon to garnish

Saute onions in olive oil and add parsley. When onions are golden yellow, add fried tomatoes and salt and pepper. Put over fish in a greased ovenproof casserole and bake at 450 degrees for 15 minutes. Garnish with slices of tomato and lemon. Yield: 2 servings.

Garides Pilaffi
(shrimp pilaf)

1½ pounds fresh shrimp
2 medium onions, chopped
    fine
½ cup olive oil
1½ cups rice
salt and pepper

2 tablespoons celery leaves,
    chopped
2 tablespoons parsley,
    chopped
oregano

Boil shrimp in salted water until they turn pink. Remove shrimp from cooking water, saving 3 cups of cooking water for future use. Rinse shrimp in cold water and peel them removing black strip with a knife. Saute onion in olive oil until golden. Add rice and cook another 5 minutes. Add shrimp and mix, then add 3 cups water in which shrimp was cooking, salt, pepper, celery leaves, parsley, and oregano. When mixture comes to a boil, reduce heat to low, cover, and cook until rice is tender and liquid has been absorbed, about 15 minutes. Yield: 4 servings.

Poultry

Kotopoulo Pilaffi
(chicken pilaf)

1 cup cooked chicken	1 cup rice
1 medium onion, chopped	4 cups chicken stock
4 tablespoons butter	2 large tomatoes, peeled and
salt and pepper	chopped
¼ teaspoon thyme	¼ cup walnuts, chopped

Cut chicken meat into strips and fry with onion in butter until brown. Add salt, pepper, thyme, rice, and stir over medium heat for 5 minutes. Pour in chicken stock, tomatoes, and walnuts. Cover and simmer about 20 minutes until liquid has been absorbed and rice is done. Stir mixture, leave covered in a warm place for 20 minutes, and serve. Yield: 3 servings.

Vrastos Kotopoulo
(boiled chicken with lemon)

1 stewing chicken, whole	½ pound mushrooms, sliced
1 lemon	1 cup chicken stock
salt and pepper	½ cup sherry wine
½ pound carrots, chopped	1 cup blanched almonds
3 sticks celery, chopped	4 tablespoons cream
3 onions, chopped	1 egg
4 tablespoons butter	

Rub the chicken with rind and juice of the lemon, salt and pepper liberally. Put half the lemon inside the chicken, place chicken in a deep pot. Cover the chicken with boiling water and add the vegetables. Simmer until tender, an hour or longer. When done, put chicken on a serving platter and keep warm. Saute mushrooms in butter. Pour chicken stock into a saucepan, add cooked mushrooms, sherry, almonds, and heat slowly. In a separate bowl, beat cream and eggs together and pour hot stock on gradually, stirring until mixture becomes thick. Pour over chicken and serve. Yield: 4 servings.

Meat

Atzem Pilaffi
(lamb pilaf)

2½ pounds stewing lamb	salt and pepper
6 tablespoons butter	tomato puree
1 onion, chopped fine	4 cups rice

Cut meat into small pieces and saute in butter, adding the onion. Season with salt and pepper, add tomato puree and simmer until browned. Add 7 cups water and cook about 45 minutes until tender. Add rice which has been washed in warm, salted water. When all water has been absorbed in the rice, stir mixture and put in a 350 degree oven for 5 minutes. Yield: 3 servings.

Moussaka
(meat and potato cake)

¾ pound ground beef	1 tablespoon margarine
½ cup sliced onions	2 tablespoons flour
chopped parsley	½ cup milk
4 tablespoons butter	salt and pepper
3 tomatoes, peeled and sliced	1 egg
3 potatoes, peeled and sliced thin	⅛ cup grated cheese

Simmer meat, onions, and parsley in ½ cup water in a skillet until all water is absorbed. Add butter and cook gently, then add tomatoes and season well. Cook slowly about 20 minutes more. Now grease a cake pan and place a layer of potatoes on the bottom, next a layer of meat mixture, and repeat, ending with potatoes. Make a white sauce with the butter, flour, milk, and seasonings. Remove from heat and beat egg and cheese in together. Pour over potatoes and bake at 350 degrees for 1 hour. Yield: 3 servings.

Stifado
(beef ragôut)

1½ pounds stewing beef
4 tablespoons olive oil
4 small onions
2 cups tomato puree
salt and pepper

2 bay leaves
2 or 3 cloves garlic
1 cup red wine
2 or 3 cloves

Cut meat into serving pieces and brown slightly in olive oil. Add other ingredients and cover in Dutch oven. Cook slowly for 4 to 5 hours until meat is tender. Pour gravy over meat and serve. Yield: 3 servings.

Souvlakia
(lamb on skewers)

2 pounds leg of lamb
1 teaspoon salt
¼ teaspoon pepper
1 large onion, grated

4 tablespoons olive oil
1 bay leaf
2 large onions, sliced

Rub lamb with salt, pepper, and grated onion, then cut into serving pieces. Place in a bowl and pour in olive oil add bay leaf. Let set for 2 hours, turning occasionally. Slice 2 large onions thinly and cut bay leaf into pieces. Put lamb on skewers with a slice of onion and bit of bay leaf between each two pieces. Grill under a hot fire, careful to turn so that all sides are done. Yield: 4 servings.

Sauces

Skordalia
(garlic sauce)

6 cloves garlic
2 egg yolks
½ cup grated almonds
¼ cup bread crumbs
¼ teaspoon salt

¼ teaspoon pepper
2 cups olive oil
1 tablespoon lemon juice
2 teaspoons chopped parsley

Crush garlic, add egg yolks, almonds, bread crumbs, and stir with a wooden spoon. Add salt and pepper and olive oil drop by drop, stirring constantly. Finally stir in lemon juice and parsley. Serve with fish, cold meats, vegetables, and on salads.

Desserts

Baklava
(walnut pastry)

2 pounds unshelled walnuts
¾ cup sugar
1 teaspoon allspice
2 teaspoons cinnamon
1 pound sweet butter, melted
1 pound Filo pastry sheets
    (bought from Greek pastry
    shop or made as below)
whole cloves

honey syrup

Filo
(pastry sheets)

3 cups flour
1 teaspoon salt
4 tablespoons butter
1 egg

To make Filo: Sift together flour and salt, fold in butter. When well blended, add egg, mixing well. Add enough water (about ¾ cup) gradually to make a soft dough. Knead dough for 20 minutes, place on a board sprinkled with a little flour, and cover with a warm cloth. Let rise in a warm place 45 minutes. Place half of dough in center of a table covered with a floured cloth. Roll dough thin. Stretch dough with your hands, taking it by the edges and careful not to split it. Stretch dough paper-thin, then let stand until it becomes stiff, about 30 minutes. Cut dough into sheets to fit 9 x 12-inch baking pan.

To make Baklava: Shell and chop walnuts. Mix with sugar, allspice, and cinnamon. Brush baking pan 9 x 12 x 1 ½-inches deep with butter. Place six Filo sheets on bottom of pan, brushing each layer with melted butter. Cover with a thin layer of the walnut mixture. Cover with a sheet of Filo, top with melted butter, and sprinkle nut mixture on top. Continue until six pastry sheets remain. Place these, one on top the other, to make a top for the baklava. Brush each sheet, including top sheet, with melted butter. Using a sharp knife dipped in hot butter, cut *baklava* into strips 1½ inches wide, then cut the strips diagonally to form small, diamond-shaped pastries. Place a clove in the center of each piece. Heat remaining butter and pour it into the knife cuts, between the strips. Bake in 300 degree oven about 1 hour. When lightly browned, pour some boiling hot syrup over it, return to oven, and bake at 400 degrees a few minutes more, until syrup has seeped in and top is golden brown. Remove and pour a little syrup on top. Let *baklava* cool at room temperature at least three hours.

Honey Syrup

1 cup sugar	2 teaspoons vanilla
1½ cups honey	

Mix sugar and 1 cup water, cook over low heat until syrupy, about 10 minutes. Add honey and vanilla and cook another 5 minutes.

Melachrino
(spice cake)

1⅔ cups sugar	1¼ teaspoon cinnamon
¾ cups butter	1½ teaspoon baking soda
1¾ cups flour	¼ teaspoon salt
¼ teaspoon mace	3 eggs
¼ teaspoon ground cloves	1½ tablespoons lemon juice

Blend sugar into butter and cream well. Sift flour twice. Sift flour again with spices, baking soda, and salt. Add eggs to creamed butter. Sift in flour mixture and stir in the milk. Stir in lemon juice shortly before baking. Bake cake in greased loaf pan in 350 degree oven for about 45 minutes. Top with icing:

Icing

1½ cups powdered sugar	½ teaspoon lemon juice

Stir 5 to 6 tablespoons water slowly into sugar, making a thick mixture. Add lemon juice. Pour over the cake while cake is hot and allow icing to harden before serving.

Tyropitakia
(cheese cookies)

1½ cups flour
½ cup butter
1 cup grated Romano cheese

3 tablespoons milk
1 egg, slightly beaten

Blend sifted flour, butter, and cheese. Add milk and mix. Shape into small round cookies about ⅛-inch thick. Brush tops with egg and bake on greased cookie sheet in 350 degree oven about 20 minutes until light brown on top.

Chapter 25

ALBANIA

Albania, long one of the most forgotten countries of Europe because of its physical remoteness and Communist-imposed isolation, is today making a start on the long road toward a joining with Western civilization.

Called the "eagle's country" because of its craggy mountains, it is still the only Iron Curtain country you are not allowed to drive in, though tourism has been encouraged in recent years.

Still to be dealt with is Albania's position in the family of Communist-controlled countries. Adopting the ideology of Mao-Tse-Tung rather than that of Lenin, Albania became a thorn in Russia's side and a bone of contention between the Soviets and the Communist Chinese. Russia cut off her aid, and what little assistance Red China could give Albania has not been enough to help the country develop. Increasing trade with Italy has been evidence that Albania's ties to Western Europe are being strengthened.

For 20,000 years, Albanians have been under control of one foreign power or another. Shortly after the division of the Roman Empire, when Albania became two Byzantine provinces, it was overrun by the Goths, then by the Serbians, the Bulgarians, Greeks, was occupied for 350 years by the Turks, then in World War II by the Italians and Germans, and now is under Communist rule. As if this history of domination, being torn from one foreign allegiance to another, was not enough to strain its national identity, the Albanians themselves have a long history for religious and cultural differences among the various national groups which keeps them further divided. Seventy percent of the population is Moslem. The remaining thirty percent is Catholic, in the north, and Protestant, in the south.

Albania's terrain is not unlike that of Scotland. It is a small country much of whose land is too barren for the growing of crops or raising of cattle. Some of its Adriatic coastline is too inaccessible for fishermen to fish off it. Only in the lowland plains are conditions right for growing. Rice, fruit, raisins, and nuts are among the crops.

Bread is not only a staple, it is a tradition. A bride carries a loaf of bread under each arm to her wedding party and breaks off a piece for each guest. Bread is also eaten symbolically at funerals.

The Moslem majority of Albanians never eat pork for religious reasons. Chicken and other fowl are plentiful, eaten with a stuffing of walnuts, raisins, and cinnamon. Lamb, mutton, and beef are served on the plain side, as is all Albanian food. Rich pastries make up for the otherwise simple fare.

Albanians long have been cursed with the custom of feuding. From generation to generation, male members of families have engaged in bloody vendettas with males of other families. The Montague and Capulet curse is not, however, extended to women, who are not only safe from vendetta, but a man in their company is safe as well.

Tourists are also safe, because Albanians regard few things as sacred as hospitality. Most tourists from the West visit Albania by bus from Yugoslavia, and then only in group tours. Turkish influences are felt in many parts of Albania where Moslem mosques and bazaars are found in the cities and villages.

It is not yet a thriving tourist mecca, this Albania that has been isolated from the rest of the world for so long. But the course for the future appears the most hopeful in years, and any country which has been around for 20,000 years is likely to ride out its present storm.

Vegetables

Dollma me Vaj
(stuffed green peppers)

1½ cups cooked rice
1 large onion, chopped
2 tablespoons oil
2 cups tomato pulp, drained
2 tablespoons lemon juice

3 tablespoons parsley,
   chopped
2 teaspoons salt
6 medium green peppers

Wash rice in cold water, then drain and dry. Saute onion in oil until golden, then add rice and saute until rice is golden. Add tomato, lemon juice, parsley, and salt. Stir for 3 or 4 minutes. Take off burner and cool. Prepare green peppers by washing them, cutting off the tops (retain the tops) and removing the seeds and the pulp. Stuff each pepper with rice and replace top. Stand each pepper up in a pan. Fill pan with enough water to reach about ½ inch from the tops of the peppers. Cover and cook over medium heat about 30 minutes, during which time the water should have evaporated. Before removing from heat, check to see if rice inside each pepper is tender. Cool before serving. Yield: 6 servings.

Kabuni
(rice with raisins)

1⅓ cups rice
¾ cup butter
3½ cups meat or chicken stock
   or bouillon

3 cups raisins
1½ cups sugar
¾ teaspoon cinnamon

Wash rice in cold water 4 times, drain and dry. Saute in butter until golden. Add beef or chicken stock or bouillon and cook slowly for 10 minutes. Add raisins, which have been washed and drained. Stir once, cover, and cook over low flame until everything is tender and all liquid has been absorbed by the rice. Mix sugar and cinnamon, and add to rice before serving. Yield: 4 servings.

Meats

Mish me Bamje
(lamb stew)

2 pounds shoulder of lamb
3 medium onions
3 tablespoons olive oil
3 medium tomatoes, sliced and

peeled
1 teaspoon salt
2 pounds small fresh okra

Cut lamb into serving pieces. Saute onions and meat in oil until brown. Add tomatoes and fry another 5 minutes. Add salt and 1½ cups water, then cook over a low fire until meat is tender. If using fresh okra, clean and wash it before adding to stew. You may substitute an 18-ounce can of okra for fresh okra. Add to stew and boil for about 25 minutes. (Less time if using canned okra.) Yield: 4 servings.

Quofte me Mente
(mint-flavored meat balls)

½ pound ground beef
2 cups bread crumbs
2 tablespoons fresh mint, chopped
1½ teaspoons salt

4 eggs
1½ teaspoon cornstarch
1 teaspoon cinnamon
olive oil for frying

Combine all ingredients and mix. Let stand for 10 minutes, then form into meat balls. Drop one at a time into deep hot oil or fat and cook until browned. Yield: 4 servings.

Desserts

Pelte
(almond molasses)

½ cup cornstarch
1 cup molasses
2 tablespoons sugar

¾ cup blanched almonds, slivered
3 tablespoons lemon juice

Mix cornstarch, molasses, sugar, and 4½ cups water together and boil about 30 minutes, stirring constantly. Add almonds and cook another 5 minutes. Take off burner, stir, and add lemon juice. Pour into dessert forms and bake in 350 degree oven about 10 minutes.

Revani
(sour milk cake)

1 cup sour milk	3 tablespoons butter
4 eggs	
1½ cups sugar	*To make syrup:*
2 cups flour	2 cups sugar
2 teaspoons baking soda	1 cup water

Mix sour milk with eggs and sugar, and beat thoroughly. Sift flour with soda and add gradually to batter and beat for 15 minutes. Add butter and blend. Bake in a flat greased baking pan in a 350 degree oven for about 30 minutes until done. Let cake cool. Make syrup by combining sugar and water and bringing mixture to a boil. Let boil about 8 minutes until it is rather thick. Cut cake in serving pieces and soak each piece in the hot syrup to serve.

Chapter 26

RUMANIA

Rumania (or Romania as it is also called), a romantic, ruggedly beautiful country, is unlike the other Balkan states in that it is the most Latinized. This comes logically from the fact that Roman colonists settled there as long ago as A.D. 106. They left a Roman spirit that has remained in the souls of the Rumanians to this day.

When most Americans think of Rumania they think of the Romany way of life: gypsies, dancing bears from out the Carpathian mountains, medieval towns in the Transylvanian Alps where Dracula and Frankenstein's monster lurk, and sort of a more Russianized version of wine, women, and song. All of this is true except for the monsters and vampires, of which none were recorded in the latest census.

On the contrary, Rumanians are not dark-thinking people but a happy breed who wouldn't think of going around driving a stake into even a monster's heart. That image is strictly from Hollywood. If Rumanians as they really are carry on at all, it is to thoroughly enjoy the varieties of pleasure in their republic. If they are not dining like royalty in their beautiful capital, Bucharest (which means "City of Pleasure"), exploring the wildlife or fishing along the Danube delta where it flows into the Black Sea, sunning there on the white sand beaches or searching out fox, wild boar, stag, wolf, or the elusive chamois in the Carpathians, they may be just gathering in their local cafe to eat, drink, and talk—three things the Rumanians love to do perhaps even more than their neighbors.

During the Middle Ages what is now Rumania became part of the Bulgarian Empire. The Turks overran the country in the sixteenth century and weren't driven out until 1859 when the several independent states united to establish the independent country of Rumania. Transylvania alone remained outside and fell to the Turks who were later driven out by the Austrians. After World War I, Transylvania, after a thousand years of Austro-Hungarian domination, finally was reunited with the mother country.

During World War II, Rumania first chose to be with the Nazis but later switched sides. Afterward, under Communist domination, Rumania became another Soviet satellite, though it has remained one of the most independent.

Rumanians are handsome and outgoing though tempermental—all you might expect of people with Latin and Hungarian-gypsy blood in them. Their villages are spotless, with white houses and thatched roofs, and they labor hard as farmers or fishermen, in expanding industry, or in the rich oil fields in the Transylvanian Alps. They are predominately Eastern Orthodox in religion.

Their food, as you might expect from a people who are a mixture of Greek, Roman, Slavic, Bulgarian, Hungarian, gypsy, Turk, Austrian, German, and French cultures, is both rich and varied.

Mamaliga, a cooked corn meal mush, is a national staple, eaten alone or combined with other foods. *Schnitzels* are made with lamb or veal, and there are Hungarian goulash-like stews. *Vacuta cu guitui,* beef with quince, and *Tocana,* beef and pork served with onion and tomato sauce, are gourmet dishes. *Mititei* (grilled meats) are very popular, consisting of ground beef with garlic and herbs, made into small sausage shapes which are broiled and eaten with hot peppers. Sour soups such as *Ciorba* show Russian influences.

Native wines and champagnes are excellent, and there also is the local *Tuica,* a delicious plum brandy.

In Bucharest, the capital, fine dining and gracious living is the rule rather than the exception. Its tree-lined boulevards, sidewalk cafes, and beautiful cultural buildings, its general atmosphere of opulence and gaiety, earn it its reputation as "the Paris of the Balkans."

The Danube winds its way lazily along the outskirts of Bucharest while every few blocks there are lovely gardens, peaceful grottos, magnificent fountains, and the food and wine in the lakeside cafes, especially when you are listening to a gypsy orchestra, will make you feel you are in a city like none other in Europe. A little Viennese, a little Parisian, a little Russian, all wrapped up in one unique experience: Bucharest.

Soups

Ciorba de Laptuca
(lettuce soup)

3 heads lettuce	⅓ cup mild vinegar
6 small onions, minced	2 egg yolks, beaten
1 clove garlic, minced	½ cup cream
1 teaspoon salt	1½ tablespoons parsley,
¼ teaspoon pepper	minced

Wash and clean lettuce, separating leaves and tearing each into tiny pieces. (Tear, do not cut.) Cook in 6 cups water, covered, and simmer. Add onion and garlic, salt and pepper. After 10 minutes, add vinegar and cook another 5 minutes. When lettuce is soft, beat egg yolks and add to cream, then add mixture to the boiling soup which has been taken off the burner. Do not boil after egg yolks are added. Garnish with parsley, adjust seasoning if necessary. Yield: 6 servings.

Vegetables

Ciuperci cu Marar
(mushrooms with fennel)

3 tablespoons butter
1½ tablespoons fennel root,
    chopped
3 tablespoons onion, chopped
1 tablespoon parsley
3¾ cups mushrooms, sliced
⅛ teaspoon nutmeg
½ teaspoon salt

⅛ teaspoon pepper
2 teaspoons butter
2 tablespoons flour
½ cup warm milk
2 teaspoons fennel leaves,
    chopped fine
1 egg yolk, beaten
2 tablespoons sour cream

In a skillet, heat 3 tablespoons butter and add fennel root, onion, parsley, mushrooms, nutmeg, salt, and pepper. Simmer slowly, covered, until mushrooms are tender. In another pan, mix 2 teaspoons butter and flour and add warm milk. Stir over low flame and make a smooth sauce. When thick, add fennel leaves and stir the sauce into the mushroom mixture. Cook all together until quite hot. Mix egg yolk with sour cream and stir into the cooking mushrooms, but remove from burner so egg does not cook. Serve hot. Yield: 4 servings.

Dumplings, Noodles

Mamaliga
(cornmeal mush)

2 cups coarse cornmeal   1 teaspoon salt

Sprinkle cornmeal into 8 cups boiling salted water very slowly, stirring with a wooden spoon over low heat. Cook gently until thickened, about 35 minutes, stirring frequently. When mush no longer sticks to the pan, remove to a bowl. Let cool, then cut with string into slices. Serve with grated cheese or a gravy or sauce.

Taetei cu Nuci
(noodles with nuts)

¾ pound wide noodles
¾ teaspoon salt
¼ cup sweet butter
½ cup sugar

½ cup toasted hazelnuts,
   chopped fine
2 tablespoons cherry preserves

Cook noodles in 6 cups salted, boiling water until tender, then drain. Pour cold water over them, then drain again. Mix hot noodles with softened butter in a heated bowl. Add sugar and hazlenuts. Fold in cherry preserves and serve hot.

Poultry

Kacsa Kukoricaval
(roast duck with corn)

1 or 2 slices white bread
   soaked in milk
1 can sweet corn
salt and pepper

3 slices bacon, chopped
duck liver
1 duck, 4 to 5 pounds

Soak bread in milk, then drain. Mix bread and corn together in a bowl. Add salt, generous sprinkling of pepper, and bacon. Chop liver finely. Add to the stuffing. Fill duck and sew up cavity. Rub outside of duck with coarse salt, place on a rack in a baking dish, and roast in 325 degree oven for 1 hour or until tender. Baste regularly with the duck's fat. Yield: 3 servings.

Fish

Peste al Bastru
(baked fish in foil)

1 fresh herring or red mullet
   per serving
salt and pepper
1 tablespoon cooking oil

3 slices lemon
1 tablespoon butter
2 tablespoons chives, chopped

Wash, scale, and clean out the fish but do not cut it up. Rub with salt, sprinkle with pepper, and brush with oil. Cut a sheet of aluminum foil into a rectangular shape, place fish in the center, cover with thin lemon slices, and dot with pieces of butter, garnish with chives. Fold foil over on two sides, tuck in at the edges to make certain juice does not flow out. Bake fish at 250 degrees for 20 minutes. Cut foil open carefully and serve fish on a heated plate. Pour juice over it. (Repeat above for each additional serving.)

Meats

Vacuta cu Gutui
(beef with quince)

4 large quinces	salt and pepper
3 pounds brisket of beef	2 onions, chopped
1 onion, sliced	2 tablespoons sugar
1 cup beef stock	½ tablespoon vinegar
3 tablespoons fat	1 tablespoon flour

Peel, core, and cut quinces into eighths. Cut beef into pieces 3 inches by 4 inches. Cover beef with cold water, add onion, and cook covered about 45 minutes until beef is half-cooked. Remove meat and cook broth to reduce it. Melt fat in skillet, saute drained beef until brown, adding salt, pepper, and onions, and stirring. Add quinces to meat. Continue cooking, covered, slowly. In another pan, brown sugar lightly. Sprinkle vinegar and water into pan and let carmelized sugar cook a short time, then pour over meat. Add flour which has been made into a smooth paste with a little cold water, and pour a cup of the reduced beef stock over the mixture. Simmer until fruit and meat are tender. Serve meat in center of hot platter, surrounded with fruit and covered by a small amount of gravy. Serve with rice. Yield: 4 to 6 servings.

Mititei
(grilled beef)

2 pounds ground beef
1½ teaspoons salt
½ teaspoon thyme
⅛ teaspoon nutmeg
⅔ cup beef stock or bouillon

2 large cloves garlic, minced
⅛ teaspoon pepper
¾ teaspoon allspice
¾ teaspoon baking soda

Combine all ingredients, adding beef stock gradually and stirring. Shape into small sausages about 1 inch thick and 3 inches long. Let sausages stand at room temperature about 30 minutes. Broil close to heat so meat browns quickly. Turn and brown other side.

Chifteluta
(hamburgers)

1 pound ground beef
salt and pepper
2 cloves garlic, crushed
2 teaspoons parsley, chopped

3 slices white bread soaked in
   milk
1 egg
oil

Place meat, salt, pepper, crushed garlic, and chopped parsley in a bowl. In another bowl, soak bread in milk, then drain and squeeze dry. Add bread to meat. Beat egg and add to meat. Work all into a paste. Form meat into golf balls, flatten into hamburger shapes, and broil or fry in oil until crisp and golden on both sides. Yield: 4 servings.

Tocana
(veal stew)

2 pounds stewing veal
6 large red onions
salt

3 tablespoons fat
½ cup beef bouillon

Cut veal into serving cubes, then slice onions finely. Heat meat, seasoned with salt, in a saucepan with the fat, and cover. Let cook slowly for 20 minutes, without adding any liquid but letting meat steam in its own juices. Pour half a cup of beef bouillon over meat, add finely sliced onions. Cover and slowly stew until all stock is absorbed and meat and onions are cooked and dry. Yield: 4 servings.

Miel
(lamb cutlets)

8 small lamb cutlets
1 cup milk
2 eggs
flour

bread crumbs
salt and pepper
oil

Let lamb soak in lukewarm milk diluted with ½ cup water for 2 hours. Drain and dry with paper towels. Beat eggs. Roll each cutlet in flour, dip into beaten egg, and cover with bread crumbs. Season with salt and pepper. Deep-fry veal until golden brown on both sides, drain excess oil, and serve hot. Yield: 4 servings.

Desserts

Minciunele
(fried bows)

5 tablespoons sweet cream
3 egg yolks
1 egg white
¼ teaspoon salt

2 tablespoons rum or whiskey
2¼ cups flour
fat for frying
powdered sugar

Beat cream and 4 egg yolks together and fold in 1 stiffly beaten egg white, salt, and rum or whiskey. Add 1 cup flour and stir. Add remaining flour and make a dough stiff enough to knead. Knead on floured board until it no longer sticks. Roll dough a little at a time into pieces about 1/16th of an inch thin. Cut into rectangles. Slit the center of a rectangle about 2 to 3 inches long and twist by folding one end of the rectangle through the slit. Deep fry in hot fat, turning so each side is golden brown. Drain on paper. When cool, sprinkle with powdered sugar. Yield: 6 dozen.

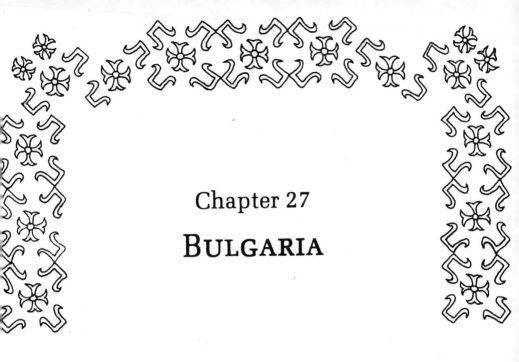

Chapter 27

BULGARIA

Bulgaria, one of Europe's lesser known but most fascinating and beautiful countries, is now considered the playground of the Communist bloc. Along the Black Sea coast are white beaches and luxury hotels attracting the international set on both sides of the Iron Curtain.

Yet the People's Republic of Bulgaria, like other Communist-dominated countries of the Balkans, suffers its privations and pays its dues. The difference here is that, mainly because of religious persuasion (90 percent of the population is Eastern Orthodox), Bulgaria by choice has for years been pro-Russian.

This is a heavily mountainous country with fish-laden rivers in valleys covered with gorgeous red and white Damask roses which have multiplied a hundredfold since the Turks, who dominated Bulgaria for 500 years, first planted them in the 1600s.

Bulgaria's history dates back to A.D. 44 when it was part of the Roman Empire. In the fifth century, Slavs migrated to that part of the Balkans and settled. In the seventh century, the Bulgars (a name which means "man with a plow," or peasant), a Finno-Tartar nomadic people, overran the Slavs. The marriage of the Bulgars and Slavs into a nation proved highly successful; Bulgaria became a power rivaling the Greek and Byzantine Empires.

Bulgaria remained strong until the fourteenth century when

it, like many of its neighboring countries, fell to the Turks. Five centuries later, after the Russo-Turkish War in 1877, Bulgaria finally gained its freedom from the Turks, while also recognizing its debt to the Russians for helping to free them.

Bulgaria joined the Axis in both world wars, but in World War II, out of admiration for Russia, did not declare war on her. In 1944, however, Russia declared war on Bulgaria and two years later Bulgaria became a People's Republic. Bulgarians are seemingly content to be under Communist domination.

Bulgarians are a hearty people with a history of longevity. Many believe they owe their great years to eating yogurt, the sour milk dieters all over the world know and eat religiously. Yogurt was brought there by the Bulgars and has become a national food, eaten on or in practically everything and, of course, alone. But Bulgarians also are heavy fish eaters, cook with either sunflower oil or olive oil rather than butter or fat, eat less meat than other Balkans, and consume large quantities of fresh vegetables, nuts, and whole grains, all of which apparently help them to live long, healthful lives. Others say their longevity is purely hereditary.

Bulgaria is heavily agrarian. Half of the land is used to grow cereal, and there are bountiful vineyards in the southern valleys. Farms are mostly collective, on the order of those in Russia.

Sofia, the capital, is a not-too-perfect blend of old Turkish-Moslem mosques and modern apartment and office buildings, yet a handsome city rich in both Eastern and Western history and art.

Rural Bulgaria remains much as it was centuries past, still a favorite place for mountain climbers and hunters. The Pirine mountains between Greece and Yugoslavia with myriad lakes and quaint hunting lodges are increasingly popular for those who like to hunt and fish. Near the Aegean Sea in the Rhodope mountains are Bulgaria's renowned mineral springs.

In May in Kazanluk, "The Valley of the Roses," millions of blooms and the soft scent of roses in the air intoxicate thousands who come for the joyous festivals. The Bulgars put on their colorful peasant costumes, lock arms and join in a circle and dance the spirited *Horo* while cooks in outdoor cafes bring out hot platters of *musaka*, fileted fish in layers of tomato-onion sauce and fried eggplant; a lamb stew called *guivetch*, named after the earthenware casserole it is baked in; and *sarmi*, stuffed cabbage rolls.

The locally-produced red wines flow, tea is drunk with rose water, or if you prefer, *slivovitza*, a plum brandy, or *mastika*, a grape brandy.

At rose festival time, harvest time, a wedding, or just on a Sunday in the mountain villages, Bulgaria still plays. Whether for the tourist or for themselves, is not quite discernable; for as in all festivals, those who do the singing and dancing have the most fun.

Appetizers

Zelen Haïver
(garlic-eggplant salad)

3 large eggplants	1 small hot green pepper
1 large clove garlic, minced	¾ teaspoon salt
1½ tablespoons parsley, chopped	¼ teaspoon pepper
	¾ cup olive oil
6 sweet green peppers, seeded and minced	¼ cup vinegar
	mayonnaise

Place eggplants in an ovenproof dish and bake or grill until it is soft and the dark skin can be removed. Chop and mince until eggplant is a very fine pulp. Chop garlic with eggplant, add parsley and sweet green peppers, and mix. Add a small, hot green pepper, chopped. Put in a bowl, add salt, pepper, and oil slowly, and enough mayonnaise to thicken. Add vinegar last. Stir with a wooden spoon. Place the mixture in a casserole dish and garnish with sliced tomatoes. Yield: 4 servings.

Soups

Sofia Corba
(lamb soup-stew)

1 pound stewing lamb	salt
4 onions	black pepper
2 carrots	2 teaspoons mint, chopped
1 turnip	½ cup uncooked rice
4 tablespoons vegetable oil	½ cup plain yogurt

Cut meat into serving cubes. Slice onions into small pieces; dice vegetables. Saute lamb cubes in oil in skillet until meat darkens, about 5 minutes. Add onions, vegetables, salt, pepper, and mint. Cover, lower heat, and simmer about 45 minutes. Add a few tablespoons of cold water when needed, to keep from sticking. Wash and dry rice, add to meat, and stir well. Pour on 6 cups lukewarm water, bring to a boil, then lower heat and let simmer until rice is done, about 12 minutes. Blend in yogurt just before serving, but do not let the soup boil with the yogurt. Yield: 4 to 6 servings.

Tarator
(yogurt and cucumber soup)

1½ cups cucumber, diced	1 teaspoon salt
1 teaspoon salt	2 cups plain yogurt
1 large clove garlic	2 tablespoons olive oil
⅔ cup ground walnuts	

Peel cucumber and slice lengthwise into ¼-inch strips, then slice crosswise into thin slices. Place in a bowl, sprinkle with 1 teaspoon salt, and refrigerate 1 hour. Mince a clove garlic and mash in a bowl with walnuts and another teaspoon salt. Blend in yogurt and 1½ cups water to walnuts, add cucumber with liquid it has been marinating in. Add olive oil, add more salt if needed. Serve chilled. Yield: 3 to 4 servings.

Vegetables

Fassoul Iahnia
(white beans in olive oil)

1 pound white beans
3 medium onions, chopped
1 cup olive oil
1 teaspoon paprika
2 tablespoons parsley,
    chopped fine

1 teaspoon salt
1 large carrot
¾ cup tomato juice (or 2
    medium tomatoes or 1
    small hot green pepper)

(White beans are available at Greek or Eastern food shops.) Wash beans, soak overnight, and drain. Put in casserole and cover with cold water, cook over low heat. Saute onions in oil until golden. Add paprika and a few tablespoons of the bean water and heat. When beans are tender, add onion mixture and stir. Before serving, add parsley and salt. (To enhance flavor, add carrot, sweet green pepper, and *one* of either hot green pepper, tomatoes, or tomato juice.) Yield: 4 servings.

Imam Bajaldo
(eggplant casserole)

5 large eggplants
flour
vegetable oil
3 red onions

5 tablespoons parsley,
    chopped
salt and pepper

Wash unpeeled eggplants and slice into finger-length strips. Roll in flour and deep fry in hot oil until crisp and golden. Line greased ovenproof casserole with eggplant slices, sprinkle with finely chopped onion and parsley. Season with salt and pepper. Cover with another layer of fried eggplant and sprinkle with another layer of onion, parsley, and seasoning. Repeat layers until you have used all the ingredients. Pour 1 cup hot water over mixture and bake in 350 degree oven until liquid is absorbed. Serve hot or cold. Yield: 5 servings.

Rice

Oriz
(boiled rice)

1 medium onion, chopped
1 cup butter
2½ cups rice

2 quarts boiling chicken broth
or chicken bouillon

Saute onion in ¼ cup butter until golden. Wash rice 3 times and fry with onion for a few minutes, mixing well. Gradually add chicken broth or bouillon, bring to a boil, and cook for about 15 minutes, until rice is tender and liquid is absorbed. Take off burner and mix ¾ cup butter in. Yield: 4 servings.

Fish

Riba Mussaka
(fish casserole)

1 large red onion
3 fresh tomatoes
4 tablespoons cooking
   oil
1 pound cod fillets
salt and pepper

3 large eggplants
flour
fat for deep frying
1 teaspoon paprika
3 eggs

Chop onion finely and peel and quarter tomatoes. Saute onion in cooking oil until golden, then add codfish cut into cubes, and tomatoes. Cover and stew about 15 minutes. Slice eggplants in ¼-inch pieces, sprinkle with salt and let stand in a covered bowl for 1 hour. Dry and coat with flour on both sides. Fry eggplants in hot fat in deep fryer until crisp and golden, then drain. Place a layer of fried eggplants in a deep, buttered, ovenproof casserole, then add a layer of fish stew and a layer of eggplant. Season with a little salt, more liberal amount of freshly ground black pepper, and a little sweet red paprika. Repeat, ending with a top layer of eggplant. Cook covered in 350 degree oven for 30 minutes. Beat eggs with a pinch of salt and pour over the top. Return to oven a few minutes until eggs puff and brown and serve either hot or cold. Yield: 4 servings.

Poultry

Pilaf
(chicken with rice)

1 medium-sized chicken
3 sets extra giblets
salt and pepper
6 small onions, diced
2 carrots, diced
1 stalk celery, diced

2 parsnips, diced
1 cup uncooked rice
2 teaspoons chopped parsley
1 cup sultana raisins
4 tablespoons bacon fat

Cover chicken (left whole) and cleaned giblets in water in a saucepan, add salt, pepper, and onions, cover and bring to a boil. Simmer 30 minutes. Add carrots, celery, and parsnips. Cook until meat is tender, about another hour. Remove chicken and strain the liquid (save it to use with rice). Discard the vegetables. In another saucepan, boil the rice with the chicken stock, about 12 minutes, until all liquid is absorbed and rice is fluffy. Sprinkle with chopped parsley. Cut chicken into small serving portions. Dice gizzards, cut up livers, leave necks whole. Mix in with rice, adding raisins and melted bacon fat, but do not cook the mixture. Yield: 2 to 3 servings.

Meats

Sarmi
(stuffed cabbage rolls)

2 large onions, chopped
⅔ cup fat
¾ cup rice
1 teaspoon paprika
2 tablespoons tomato juice
1 teaspoon mint, chopped

1 pound ground pork
½ pound ground veal
1 head cabbage
1½ teaspoons salt
slice of bacon
tomato juice

Saute onions in fat until golden. Add washed and dried rice, fry in pan until slightly golden. Add paprika, salt, 2 tablespoons tomato juice, and mint. Mix meat in pan, but do not cook. Cut out core of cabbage head, put head into large pan and cover with water. Bring to a boil and cook a few minutes. Drain and separate head, using whole leaves to make a bed for the meat. Cut heavy part of cabbage rib from leaf and fill each leaf with 1 spoonful of meat mixture. Roll up leaf tightly and tuck in ends to close the roll. Grease a baking dish or Dutch oven and put a thick layer of stuffed cabbage leaves close together in bottom of dish or oven. Place a slice of bacon over the rolls and pour tomato juice on top, but do not cover with juice. Place an inverted plate over the cabbage rolls to hold them down. Cook over a very low heat until well done, about 2 hours. Serve with rice. Yield: 4 servings.

Jachnia
(lamb with spinach)

1 pound stewing lamb	3 tablespoons oil
6 onions	salt and pepper
2 pounds fresh spinach	1 cup yogurt

Cut lamb into serving cubes, chop onions. Clean spinach and wash in several waters. Drain and chop. Fry meat in oil in deep pan until light golden. Add onions, salt and pepper, cover, reduce heat, and steam slowly about 45 minutes. Add a little water if necessary. Add spinach and cook together with meat until meat is tender, about 15 minutes longer. Before serving, pour on yogurt and heat but do not boil.

Turlu Guivetch
(mutton stew)

1¼ pounds breast of mutton	½ cup celery, sliced
2 tablespoons hot fat	¼ cup cauliflowerettes
⅓ cup carrots, sliced	⅓ cup green peas, shelled
⅓ cup green beans	2 tablespoons
¾ cup potatoes, diced	parsley, chopped
2 tablespoons green fennel	3 large tomatoes, peeled and
3 medium onions, sliced	sliced
⅓ cup turnips, sliced	1 teaspoon lemon juice

Scald meat twice to eliminate high mutton flavor. Braise on all sides in hot fat in pan for a few minutes, then put in pot with 2 cups water, cover, and cook slowly until tender. Remove meat and let stock reduce to about ¼ cup. Place layers of vegetables in a buttered casserole with a layer of meat, separated by a layer of tomatoes. Pour stock and fat from pan over the mixture and simmer about 15 minutes. Add lemon juice and bake in moderate 375 degree oven until tender. Yield: 4 servings.

Desserts

Banitza
(cheese dessert)

1 egg
2 tablespoons mild vinegar
⅛ teaspoon salt

1 cup water
1 tablespoon olive oil
3⅓ cups flour

Mix all ingredients together to make a soft dough. Roll out on floured board until thin. Mix filling ingredients:

2 cups cottage cheese
1 cup butter, melted
¼ teaspoon salt

3 eggs
3 tablespoons sugar

Pull off a small part of dough to use to make each layer of pastry. Make a ball, roll out on floured board until very thin and large enough to cover a 8- or 10-inch cake pan. Butter the pan, place a layer of dough down, then spread a layer of filling over it. Lay another layer of dough on top. Brush each layer of dough generously with melted butter and repeat layers of cheese between layers of dough, until you have about 8 layers of dough and filling. Top with layer of dough, brush with butter, and pour butter around sides of pan. Bake in 375 degree oven about ½ hour until golden brown and crisp on top.

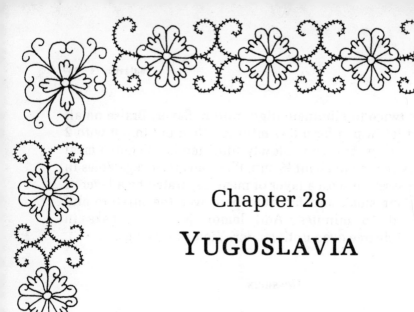

Chapter 28
YUGOSLAVIA

Yugoslavia means "land of the South Slavs," and it is without doubt one of the most beautiful and fascinating countries of Europe, yet most people know little about it.

Yugoslavia is actually six countries in one, a federation of the independent republics of Serbia, Croatia, Slovenia, Macedonia, Montenegro, and Bosnia-Hercegovina, plus some smaller republics. There are three languages (Serbo-Croat, Slovenian, and Macedonian); two alphabets (Cyrillic in the eastern section and Roman in the western); three major faiths (Orthodox, Catholic, and Moslem); and half a dozen basic cuisines.

What you might expect to be an impossible mixture of cultures has, since the end of World War II under the controversial Marshal Tito, merged into one country rapidly prospering and becoming more of a unified people. Citizens who until only recently would staunchly identify themselves as Serbs or Croats first and Yugoslavs second are coming to think of themselves as Yugoslavs first. The closest we have to compare with the identity crisis in America is Texas, and it appears that the Yugoslavs are getting the draw on Texans.

The Greeks were the first to land on the shores of what is now Yugoslavia, when their ships reached the Adriatic coast of Dalmatia in 500 B.C. Next came the Romans, some of whose culture still remains in Yugoslavia, including Diocletian's palace and an ancient amphitheatre where athletic contests were held. The Greeks and Romans planted vineyards, fruit trees, and olive groves, which still flourish in the warm regions.

The Turks invaded Yugoslavia in the fourteenth century and began their 500-year rule over most of the land, while Venetians held control of the coast for 400 years. Moslem mosques, minarets, bazaars, and many aspects of Turkish custom and culture remain in many parts of Yugoslavia, while the Latin influences of Venice are seen along the Adriatic.

Yugoslavia has for centuries been in the middle between the Latin world of the Western Empire and the Greek-Byzantine world of the Eastern Empire, making it an unique blend of the two. Further complicating matters, Slavs emigrated into Yugoslavia in the sixth century to add their various influences.

Just about every type of terrain and climate is found in Yugoslavia, from the spectacular Dalmatian coast and islands to the craggy Alps and verdant foothills to the Danube river basin. The coast can be just right for swimming while a blizzard is closing a mountain road.

Serbia, in the eastern part of Yugoslavia, was established as a kingdom in the twelfth century. Soon after it was the strongest of the Balkan states, but then late in the fourteenth century it fell under Turkish control, not regaining its independence until after World War II. Belgrade, its beautiful capital, was nearly totally destroyed in the war but has been restored and rebuilt into a most fascinating blend of Turkish, Roman, and modern architecture. The food of Serbia adapts some Turkish specialties: notably pork *kebabs*, vegetables stuffed with ground pork and rice, and cheese pastries.

Croatia to the north is a land of farms below the Alps bordering Austria, as well as Dalmatia, the popular resort coast. Influences of Venice are to be seen in the coastal villages. Zagreb, capital of Croatia, has through the years been strongly influenced by both Austria and Hungary and rivals Belgrade for beauty and culture. Croatian food has a strong Hungarian flavor with versions of goulash and chicken paprikash. Whipped cream tortes of both Austria and Hungary are favorites of the Croats.

Slovenia in the northwest, with Austria and Italy for

neighbors, has both mountain lake country and coastline where a Mediterranean-type climate is helpful for growing grapes, olives, and figs. The capital, Ljubljana, is dominated by its medieval hilltop castle, and there are churches and museums to visit which are full of eastern European history, but the main attraction in the fall is the year's vintage, for this is some of Yugoslavia's best wine-producing country. It is also the best ski resort area. Slovenia's Tyrolean villages are dead giveaways that the food here is heavily influenced by Austria, with variations of schnitzels, strudels, dumplings, as well as German-type sausages and beer.

Macedonia to the southeast felt the sandals of both the Greeks and Romans, whose culture remains behind. Here too, as in Serbia, are Byzantine monasteries built by the Turks. In food, the Turkish influences are strongest.

Montenegro, smallest and longest isolated of the republics, is surrounded by Serbia, Bosnia, and Albania, with a very short coastline on the Adriatic. Inland are the rugged Black Mountains and to the north, valleys and good farmland. Turkish food again dominates here, with lamb and mutton, cheeses, and yogurt, honey-rich desserts among the most popular.

Bosnia-Hercegovina in the east has cities and villages with minarets and domed churches as reminders of the Turks. The murder of Archduke Ferdinand in the capital city of Sarajevo became the opening shot fired in World War I. Turkish food again has the strongest influence.

Throughout Yugoslavia certain foods and methods of preparing them are enjoyed and practiced by all. *Raznichi,* skewered meat or *kebab,* is a national dish, as popular as *Djuvece,* a pork and vegetable dish with paprika and hot peppers eaten by all but Moslems. Chives, mint, and fennel are used extensively in cooking. Paprika, especially the sweet kind, is used in preparing meat and fowl. Hot peppers and raw onions are eaten as appetizers and used in dishes. Cheese is widely eaten, and Yugoslavia also grows enough prunes to supply all of Europe.

A kaleidoscope of cultures and fascinations, Yugoslavia is being discovered by the rest of the world only lately. What a treat the world has in store for itself!

Soup

Ostriga Supa
(oyster soup)

4 tablespoons olive oil
2 cloves garlic, chopped
2 teaspoons parsley
1 to 2 pounds small fish or
    parts of fish
salt

5 peppercorns
1 bay leaf
2 slices toast
½ cup dry white wine
juice of ½ lemon
1 to 2 dozen oysters

Heat oil and saute garlic and parsley for a few minutes. Add small fish or fish parts such as heads and fishbones, and cover with 8 cups cold water, season with salt, peppercorns, bay leaf. Bring to a boil uncovered and cook rapidly about 20 minutes. Strain, discard all bones and small fish, retaining the clear stock. Cut toast into strips, place in individual soup bowls. Reheat fish stock with white wine, remove from fire when hot, and add lemon juice and oysters. Pour soup over toasted bread strips. Yield: 4 servings.

Vegetables

Mushrooms and Eggs

1 small onion, sliced
2 tablespoons olive oil
1 green pepper, seeded and
    chopped
1 tomato, peeled and chopped

½ pound mushrooms
salt and pepper
4 eggs
2 tablespoons butter

Saute onion in olive oil until golden, then add green pepper, tomato, and mushrooms. Mix, cover, and stew slowly until tender. Season with salt and pepper and transfer into a serving dish. Beat eggs well and scramble them in butter, serve on top mixed vegetables.

Salads

Serbian Salad

2 small eggplants
6 green peppers
¼ cup olive oil

2 tablespoons vinegar
salt and pepper

Wash eggplant and green peppers and bake in 425 degree oven. When tender, remove skin and seeds, chop fine and add olive oil, vinegar, and season to taste. Serve chilled. Yield: 4 servings.

Dumplings

Gnocchi
(dumplings)

½ cup butter, melted
¼ cup flour
¼ cup cornstarch
½ teaspoon salt

2 cups milk, scalded
2 egg yolks
¾ cup grated cheese

Melt butter in top of a double boiler. Sift together flour, cornstarch, and salt. Stir flour mixture into butter when butter begins to bubble. Slowly add hot milk when mixture has blended, and cook 5 minutes, stirring constantly. Beat egg yolks and slowly add the hot sauce, then stir in ½ cup grated cheese. Pour mixture into a buttered shallow pan and cool. Turn dough out onto a lightly floured board and cut into squares or strips. Place on a cookie sheet, sprinkle with remaining ¼ cup of cheese, and brown in a 350 degree oven.

Fish

Som u Mileramu
(codfish in sour cream)

1 pound cod fillets
salt
4 peppercorns
½ red onion

peel of ½ lemon
½ cup dry white wine
6 anchovies
2 teaspoons flour

1 bay leaf   ¾ cup sour cream
parsley   1 tablespoon butter

Cover fish with water in a saucepan, add salt, peppercorns,
onion, bay leaf, parsley, and lemon peel; lastly add ½ cup of dry
white wine. Boil for 6 minutes, drain, but save the liquid. Clean
anchovies and chop finely. Place fillets in a buttered ovenproof
casserole, cover with chopped anchovies. Blend flour with sour
cream and dilute with the fish liquid that has been strained. Pour
over codfish fillets and dot with pieces of butter. Bake in 350
degree oven for about 15 minutes.

Poultry

Roast Goose and Cabbage

1 goose   3 onions, sliced
3 heads cabbage, chopped fine   salt and pepper

Clean and prepare goose for roasting. Cut into serving pieces,
place in roasting pan, and roast in 450 degree oven about 20
minutes, reducing heat to 350 degrees and continue roasting
until tender. Pour about 1 cup of the fat into a large saucepan,
saute onions in it until golden, then add finely chopped cabbage.
Cook several minutes, then place pieces of goose on top the
cabbage. Cover and simmer for 1 hour. Yield: 6 servings.

Poulet Sauté
(fried chicken)

2 onions, chopped fine   1 chicken, cut in pieces
2 tablespoons butter, melted   2 tomatoes
1 clove garlic   1 cup cream
1 teaspoon paprika

Saute onions in melted butter until brown. Add garlic, paprika,
and chicken parts and cook until chicken is nicely browned.
Add tomatoes, cover skillet and simmer until chicken is tender.
Strain gravy and add the cream, beating thoroughly. Pour over
chicken and serve with boiled potatoes. Yield: 2 servings.

Meats

Musaka sa Plavim
(eggplant and lamb)

1 eggplant
¼ cup flour
1 egg
4 cups milk
olive oil
3 tablespoons butter

1 onion, sliced
1 pound ground pork
¼ pound ground mutton
salt and pepper
6 egg yolks

Pare and slice eggplant, then dip in batter (flour, egg, and ⅛ cup milk), and saute in olive oil that is quite hot. Melt butter and saute onion in it, then add pork and mutton and season. Cook about 10 minutes. Place slices of fried eggplant in a buttered baking dish, then add meat. Beat egg yolks and add milk, pour over eggplant and meat and bake in 350 degree oven until golden brown. Yield: 4 servings.

Djuvetsch
(meat, rice, and vegetables)

½ pound each of pork, veal, and beef
¼ cup fat
¾ cup uncooked rice
4 onions, sliced
2 carrots, sliced
1 stick celery, chopped

4 tomatoes, peeled and quartered
1 green pepper, seeded and sliced
salt and pepper
1 teaspoon paprika

Cut meat into serving pieces. Brown in fat. Transfer into a casserole. Fry the rice in the fat, then add to casserole. Fry onions and add to casserole, then add other vegetables. Season with salt, pepper, and paprika. Pour enough hot water to cover contents and cook covered in 350 degree oven about 2 hours. Yield: 3 servings.

Raznjici
(skewered meats)

1 pound each beefsteak and
stewing lamb, cut in cubes
salt and pepper

5 tablespoons bacon fat
2 tablespoons olive oil
1 onion, chopped

Cut meat into cubes about 1-inch thick. Alternate beefsteak and lamb on a skewer and sprinkle with salt and pepper. Heat bacon fat and oil in small saucepan. When warm, brush over the meat and broil very slowly. Continue brushing meat with the fat and turn skewers so meat cooks evenly on all sides, about 20 minutes. Serve with chopped raw onion on each plate. Yield: 4 servings.

Desserts

Krofne
(fried cakes)

½ cake (½ ounce)
compressed yeast
½ cup warm milk
¼ cup butter
3 egg yolks

3 egg whites, beaten
2 cups flour
¼ teaspoon salt
powdered sugar

Mix yeast and warm milk and stir until dissolved. Let stand in warm place about 15 minutes. Cream butter, add egg yolks, then yeast. Fold in beaten whites of eggs. Add flour sifted with salt, one cup at a time, until mixture is smooth. Let stand about 1 hour, covered with a warm cloth. Roll dough out on floured board to about ½-inch thick, then cut into circles about 2 inches in diameter. Let rise another 30 minutes. Fry in deep fat until well-browned, turning once, then remove, drain on paper towels, and cool before sprinkling with powdered sugar. Yield: 3 dozen.

Potica

1 cup milk, scalded
1/2 cup butter
1/2 teaspoon salt
2 eggs
1/2 teaspoon vanilla
1/2 cake yeast
1/3 cup sugar

4 1/2 cups flour

Filling for *Potica:*
1 pound walnuts, ground
2 eggs
2 cups sugar
1/4 pound butter

Combine milk and butter, cool in refrigerator. Add salt, eggs, and vanilla. Dissolve yeast in sugar and add flour gradually. Place in greased bowl, cover, and let rise in warm place until doubled in bulk. Spread dough out on a floured cloth and pull until thin. Spread with filling and place in a 10 x 13-inch baking pan. Let rise for 30 minutes, then bake at 325 degrees for 1 hour.

8

Eastern Europe

Russia
(including Ukrainia, Byelorussia, Moldavia, Armenia, Ruthenia, Azerbaijan)

Growing up in Chicago of a Ukrainian-descended father and Austrian-born mother, but living in Polish or German neighborhoods bordering Jewish and Italian communities, I was never quite sure what nationality I was. But since my father had more relatives and they considered themselves to be Polish, I thought that I must be Polish too.

It was not until my late teens that I discovered I was certainly at least half Austrian, from my mother's side. On my father's side, I was every bit as much Russian as Polish, because the history of the Ukraine is a marriage of the two.

So must all the people of the Eastern European countries have a nationality identity crisis at one time or another, wondering whether they are Muscovite Russian, Ukrainian, Byelorussian (White Russian), Georgian, Azerbaijanian, Moldavian, Armenian, Uzbekistanian, Turkmenistanian, Karelian, Bessarabian, Ruthenian, or any of dozens of other smaller national groups, all now part of the Union of Soviet Socialist Republics. No matter what their origin, whether it be linked to Europe or the Near East, they all have one thing in common: they are from nations all straddling the globe between East and West. Historically, they have had to pay the price in wars, famine, and oppression. Only since World War II have these nations, united as the U.S.S.R., begun to throw off their yoke and pick themselves up by the bootstraps.

Throughout Russia, the people now eat reasonably well but not necessarily heartily. It is said they eat to keep working, not to enjoy the food. And though Russia is expanding as a destination for tourists, even most of the restaurants of Moscow and Leningrad can only fairly be described as mediocre. Most Russians are too busy working to prepare fine meals, even if they had the *rubles* to afford the ingredients. Instead they eat at factory-or-government-operated commissaries, saving up their money for an occasional Sunday dinner where they might escape the traditional food which has become routine to them and splurge on something French, Italian, or German at restaurants serving international dishes.

The national menu in Russia differs with the culture and climate of each area, not only influenced by local nationalities and their foods but by their neighbors, the Balkan and Baltic states, as well as Turkey, Persia, and India.

Peasant food, found throughout Russia, includes skewered and grilled meats such as lamb and veal; *Pierogs,* dough stuffed with cabbage, meat, or fish; a variety of fish dishes; vegetables either fresh or pickled; and soups both hot and cold but usually on the sour side. Sour cream is used on practically everything, and dill, green peppers, and sorrel are widely used to add spice to a dish. Russians like to mix contrasting flavors into one dish, creating many sweet-and-sour specialties.

Traditionally, most meals begin with *Zakouski*, a *smorgasbord*-like assortment of cold *hors d'oeuvres* such as cold meats, salted herring, cucumbers in sour cream, pickled beets, and mixed vegetables, all washed down with vodka, the clear, almost tasteless drink the Russians love.

How these foods are prepared may differ from region to region. In the south, by the Black Sea, rice is grown and incorporated into the foods, showing a Turkish influence. Caucasian *shashlik*, lamb or mutton with pepper, onion, mushrooms, and lemon, broiled on a skewer, originated with mountain shepherds who gathered around a campfire, stabbed a piece of lamb with their dagger, and broiled it in the fire.

In the north, where fish are plentiful, sturgeon, bream, carp, cod, crayfish, herring, salmon, haddock, pike, and trout are prepared in delicious ways. The roe of the sturgeon provides caviar, a favorite *hors d'oeuvre* the world around, while most Russians who can't afford it eat "red caviar," from the salmon rather than the sturgeon.

The staff of life for centuries has been black rye bread, and the staple dish cabbage soup. *Bliny* (pancakes), cherry and rose petal jams, with Chinese tea which may be sweetened with jam instead of sugar, are favorite desserts.

They say you can tell a country by its cooking. In Russia's union of Eastern European nations, the cooking is masculine, meant for both men and women who work much more than they play.

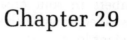

Chapter 29
RUSSIA

While Nicholas and Alexandra, splendid as they looked in their imperial robes, ate caviar, lamb *shashlik,* and beef Stroganoff, the peasants in their rags ate buckwheat groats. Not the only reason but certainly a strong contributing factor in Russia's bloody October Revolution of 1917.

The Union of Soviet Socialist Republics, the largest country on earth, covering more than eight million square miles, almost one-seventh of the land surface of the world, is a union of some fifteen republics and dozens of other allied regions and districts.

Russia's recorded beginnings date back to the third century A.D. with the first federation of eastern Slavonic tribes. These were later overrun by the nomadic Khazars who ruled until the tenth century when the Turks and Hungarians gained control of the steppe, the seemingly endless great plains of Eastern Europe.

About this time the northern Slavonic tribes who lived in the forests realized the need for allies against the Eastern invaders and invited the Rus, a Varangian tribe of Viking origin, to move down among them. The Rus settled at Novgorod, which means "new town," and founded what became modern Russia.

Mongol invaders swept through Russia and across Europe in the thirteenth century, were contained by Alexander Nevsky, the Prince of Novgorod, then finally defeated by Ivan the Great. He and his grandson, Ivan the Terrible, gained absolute control over the people and united them against their enemies. The crown was worn by the first Romanov, Michael, in 1613 and the dynasty marched on with one czar or empress after another who subjugated the people, while wars were fought with Napoleon and soon after Russia was drawn into the First World War.

The people finally had enough. Dying on the battlefield and starving at home, they revolted under Lenin and his Bolsheviks (now called Communists) and Nicholas II and his family were executed.

Wars, famine, serfdom, overlorded by the czars, virtually sealed off from the outside world, Russia is just lately emerging from the harsh self-imposed austerity their leaders hope may bring about a better life.

Throughout Russia today, at least in the 150 or so cities and towns the tourist is allowed to visit, evidence is positive that the hard years are starting to come to an end. But Moscow is still predominately the Kremlin fortress and Red Square, with stellar opera, ballet, and symphony but little else to amuse, relax, or uplift the resident or the visitor. Except for Leningrad, built by Peter the Great as the summer place for the czars, and the most westernized city, the tourist must content himself that while his senses may not be stimulated by a look at Russia, at least some of his curiosity will be satisfied.

The food of a nation sprawling from East to West is logically a blend of both. It is substantial, sometimes exotic, often unusual with conflicting tastes of sweet and sour. Black rye bread and cabbage or beet soup *(borscht)*, for centuries staples of the peasants, are still favorite foods and, depending on the region, you will be served a variety of pastry-filled meat and fish dishes, fresh or pickled vegetables, foods and sauces seasoned with dill and sorrel, smothered under heaps of sour cream.

Russian peasant food was enhanced in Imperial Russia by French cuisine introduced into the court of Empress Catherine II. Italian food found its its way into Russia when Ivan the Terrible brought Latin chefs along with architects in helping build the Kremlin. German vegetable dishes came to Russia when Peter the Great favored Dutchmen in his court. And from old wars and their neighbors, the culinary influences of Scandinavia, Europe, and the Near East crept into Russian ovens and cooking pots.

Westerners perhaps best know beef Stroganoff, finely cut

filet of beef fried with mushrooms and served with sour cream. Equally popular within Russia is *Shchi*, a cabbage and vegetable soup also made with sour cream; *Blini*, pancakes served with (you guessed it), sour cream; and *Kasha*, a peasant dish of porridge; *Kotlety*, chicken croquettes stuffed with melted butter; and Caucasian *Shashlik*, lamb or mutton skewered and grilled like Turkish *kebabs*.

The vineyards of the Caucasus provide wine for Russia, when the people aren't drinking *kvass*, a slightly alcoholic, cider-like drink made from rye, malt, yeast, sugar, and mint; and the inevitable vodka.

The ancient cities of Novgorod, Samarkand, Tashkent, and Bukhara; the spring wildflowers of Zhivago's Urals; the icy world of Siberia in winter; the fields of roses in the Caucasus; the tigers of Turkestan; the Black Sea resorts of Odessa; boatmen working along the Volga; the Transcarpathian villages with their onion-domed churches; the "Golden Gates" of Kiev. These are but a few of the fascinations of Russia, aside from the people themselves, who are less austere and more friendly than expected, and perhaps in the end Russia's greatest fascination.

Appetizers

Zakuski
(hors d'oeuvres)

What *smorgasbord* is to Scandinavians, *zakuski* is to Russians. It is a cold array of meats, fish (caviar and salted herring the favorites), pickled vegetables (especially beets), cucumbers in sour cream, salmon, and salted mushrooms. Either as a meal or as appetizers, *zakuski* is always served with vodka.

Ikra
(caviar)

Caviar, the salted roe of the sturgeon, is served on crackers or tiny pieces of toast.

Soups

Borscht
(beet soup)

3 pounds stewmeat
1 carrot, cut in strips
1½ cups canned tomatoes
salt and pepper
2 cups raw grated beets

3 cups shredded cabbage
8 cups cold water
dash of salt
sour cream

Mix all ingredients except sour cream into a large pot, bring to a boil and simmer slowly about 3 hours until meat is tender. Before serving, remove meat and serve soup accompanied by sour cream.

Shchi
(cabbage soup)

2 onions
2 tablespoons butter
flour
8 cups beef stock
1 pound rib of beef

1½ pounds cabbage
salt and pepper
2 sprigs fennel
sour cream

Chop onions and saute in butter, then sprinkle with flour. Add to stock and bring to a boil. Blanch the beef, cut in serving pieces, and add to stock. Blanch the cabbage, then chop it coarsely. Drain cabbage and add to soup. Season with salt, pepper, and fennel. Simmer slowly for 1½ hours. Just before serving, stir sour cream into the soup. Yield: 3 servings.

Salad

Svejie Ogourki so Smetanoi
(cucumber salad with sour cream)

Peel 1 cucumber, cut into dice, salt well, and let stand about 1 hour. Drain off water and mix with 1/2 cup sour cream. Sprinkle a little lemon juice on top and season with salt and pepper. Yield: 2 servings.

Vegetables

Nahit
(Russian peas)

1 pound peas	2 tablespoons butter
1 tablespoon salt	2 tablespoons flour
¼ teaspoon baking soda	2 tablespoons brown sugar
½ pound brisket of beef	

Soak salted peas in hot water for 12 hours. Drain and cover with fresh boiling water, cook 15 minutes, then add baking soda and meat. Cook over low heat for 3 hours until peas are tender. Melt butter, add flour, and blend, then add sugar. Add 1 cup of liquid from peas and cook until mixture is thick, stirring constantly. Mix with peas and bring to a boil, then bake in a casserole at 350 degrees for 30 minutes.

Dumplings, Potatoes

Piroshki
(stuffed pancakes)
Dough

1 cup flour, sifted	3 tablespoons sour cream
⅛ teaspoon salt	¼ pound butter

Sift flour and salt together into a bowl and mix in butter. Add sour cream and butter and work into a ball of dough. Wrap in waxed paper and refrigerate about 1 hour. Then divide dough in half and roll each half into a rectangle that will fit a shallow 9 x 12-inch baking pan. Cut each pan of dough into a dozen squares or circles about 3 inches in diameter. Prepare meat filling as on next page:

Meat filling

3 tablespoons onion, finely
   chopped
2 teaspoons butter
¼ pound ground beef

1 tablespoon minced parsley
1 hard-boiled egg, chopped
¼ teaspoon salt

Saute onion until golden, and then add beef. Cook until lightly browned, separating into small pieces with a fork. Add remaining ingredients. Mix and then cool. Place a teaspoonful of the filling in the center of each square or circle of dough and fold to make crescents, triangles, and the like. Moisten edges of dough with water before pinching to close. Chill 30 minutes before baking, then brush with beaten egg mixed with 1 teaspoon water. Bake 20 minutes until golden brown at 375 degrees. Yield: 2 dozen. Serve hot as either an *hors d'oeuvre* or with soup.

Kasha
(buckwheat groats)

4 cups buckwheat groats
1 teaspoon salt

1 tablespoon butter
sour cream

Sift buckwheat groats, spread into a skillet, and fry it slightly. Remove it to an earthenware container, add 1 teaspoon salt, 1 tablespoon butter, and enough water to cover. To prevent from sticking, place baking pot in a pan with a little water. Cook covered in a slow oven for 2 to 3 hours. Serve with sour cream. You may add cooked meats and slices of hard-boiled egg to the *Kasha* about 10 minutes before serving.)

Pechenaia Kartofel v Smetana
(baked potatoes with sour cream)

1 onion, chopped
2 tablespoons butter
4 potatoes
4 tablespoons grated cheese

bread crumbs
1 cup sour cream
2 eggs
salt and pepper

Saute onion in butter until golden. Cook potatoes with skins on. Peel and slice potatoes and place in an ovenproof dish with the onion. Sprinkle with grated cheese and bread crumbs. Mix sour cream with beaten eggs and pour on top of potatoes. Season with salt and pepper and brown in a 350 degree oven. Yield: 4 servings.

Fish

Zrazy Eze Ribi
(haddock fillet)

3 cups stale bread, diced	salt and pepper
¾ cup milk	2 pounds fillet of haddock
2 tablespoons butter	flour
4 onions, chopped	1 egg yolk
2 eggs	bread crumbs

Dice bread, pour milk over it in a bowl, and let soak 20 minutes. Melt 2 tablespoons butter and saute onions in skillet until golden. Drain, and add the bread to the onions and mix well. Beat 2 eggs and add to the bread mixture. Season with salt and pepper. Spread bread mixture on the filets and roll, securing each haddock roll with poultry pins. Dredge in flour, then beaten egg yolk, then in breadcrumbs. Fry in hot butter and serve with melted butter poured on top. Yield: 4 servings.

Marinovanie Korushki
(marinated smelts)

4 dozen smelts	1 teaspoon peppercorns
2 teaspoons salt	grated nutmeg
flour	1½ cups vinegar
oil	1 onion, sliced
1 tablespoon carrot, chopped	4 bay leaves
1 stick celery, chopped	a few cloves
1 teaspoon chopped parsley	

Clean and wash the smelts, then wipe dry. Sprinkle with salt, roll in flour, and brown in hot oil. Place in casserole. Combine other ingredients and simmer together in a pan until carrot and celery are tender. While still warm, pour over the fried smelts. Place in refrigerator for 12 to 24 hours. Yield: 4 to 6 servings.

Forelle s Vinom
(trout in wine)

6 small trout	peppercorns
1 cup white wine	mixed herbs
½ cup Madeira wine	salt
¼ cup rum	1 stick celery
fish stock or water	2 onions
1 bay leaf	1 small leek

Place trout in a casserole, add wines, rum and a little fish stock or water, add vegetables and seasoning. Let fish marinate for a few hours, then bring slowly to a boil and simmer a few minutes until tender, which may be as soon as liquid comes to a boil. Pour marinade over fish and serve hot or cold. Yield: 3 servings.

Poultry

Indieka s Vishniovim Sousom
(turkey with cherry sauce)

1 breast of turkey cut into thin slices	*For sauce:*
salt	2 pounds cherries
butter	2 tablespoons sugar
1 cup Madeira wine	2 tablespoons water
	mixed spices

Stone the cherries and, in a saucepan, add sugar, water, and spices. Cook slowly until they are pulpy, then sieve. Cut breast of turkey into thin slices, season with a little salt, and fry in butter and Madeira. Place cherry sauce in center of a hot serving dish and place turkey slices around the dish. (Recommended spices: blend of tarragon, basil, thyme, parsley, marjoram, celery root.) Yield: 2 servings.

Kotletki Kiev
(chicken, Kiev-style)

slices of liver sausage
cooked breast of chicken
salt and pepper

melted butter
artichoke hearts

Place layer of liver sausage in a fireproof dish or casserole, lay slices of cooked chicken on top, season with salt and pepper, pour melted butter over and heat through. Serve with artichoke hearts and cherry sauce (see above for sauce). Instead of spices, sauce may be made with 1 teaspoon cinnamon. Yield: 2 servings.

Meats

Boeuf Stroganoff
(beef stroganoff)

1½ pounds lean fillet of beef
3 tablespoons butter
½ pound mushrooms
1 tablespoon flour

salt and pepper
paprika
1 cup sour cream

Cut beef into serving cubes. Melt 2 tablespoons butter in a skillet and add the meat. Cover and cook slowly about 15 minutes. Add sliced mushrooms and cook another 10 minutes. Remove meat and mushrooms to top of a double boiler. Put remaining tablespoon butter in skillet; when melted, add flour and stir until blended. Add sour cream and cook until thick, stirring constantly. Season with salt, pepper, and paprika. Pour mixture over meat in double boiler and cook 10 minutes. Serve with rice. Yield: 3 servings.

Kavkaski Shasslik
(Caucasian skewered lamb)

4 pounds lamb
salt and pepper

2 onions, sliced
red wine or vinegar and water

Cut lamb into pieces about 1/2 inch thick and 1 1/2 inches in diameter. Place in earthenware container and sprinkle liberally with salt and pepper, cover with slices of onion. Add enough wine (or equal parts vinegar and water) to cover. Let marinate 5 or 6 hours. Drain and dry. Skewer alternate layers of lamb and onion and broil until tender, turning frequently. (A variation is to add slices of green pepper and/or mushrooms on the skewer.) Yield: 4 servings.

Solyanka
(steak in gherkin sauce)

4 slices fillet of beef, about 6 ounces each	1 tablespoon tomato puree
2 onions, chopped	¼ cup white wine
4 tablespoons butter	salt and pepper
2 gherkins, sliced	¼ cup beef stock

Cut steaks into 1-inch strips. Saute onion in 2 tablespoons butter, add the gherkins, tomato puree, wine, seasoning, and beef stock or bouillon. Melt the remaining butter. Fry the steak on both sides, then place in an ovenproof dish on top the tomato mixture. Cook at 325 degrees about 30 minutes. Yield: 2 servings.

Desserts, Pastries

Pasha op Paska
(Easter cheese dessert)

2 pounds dry cottage cheese	1 cup sour cream
½ pound unsalted butter	½ cup grated almonds
1 cup sugar	1 teaspoon vanilla
2 egg yolks	¼ cup white raisins

Put cottage cheese through a sieve. Blend together butter, sugar, and egg yolks. Add cottage cheese and blend. Add sour cream, almonds, and vanilla, and mix well. Pour mixture into gelatin mold lined with cheesecloth large enough to bring corners together tightly. Refrigerate overnight with a weight placed on top the cheese. (Mold should have a small hole in the bottom so moisture can be released.) When set, remove from mold and garnish with white raisins.

Cheese Blintzes
(cheese pancakes)

2 eggs
½ teaspoon salt
1 cup flour, sifted

½ pound cottage cheese
2 tablespoons butter
sour cream

Beat 1 egg until frothy, add salt, 1 cup water, and flour and beat until smooth. Heat a small frying pan and butter liberally. Pour on 2 tablespoons of the batter and heat over low flame on one side only. Remove each pancake to a clean white cloth, uncooked side up. Cool. Meanwhile make a filling by mixing remaining egg, cottage cheese, and 2 tablespoons butter. Spread a small portion of the mixture on each pancake and roll up, tucking edges in to hold the filling. Fry in hot oil or butter and serve hot with sour cream.

Kisyeli
(fruit compote)

1 pound red currants
1 cup raspberries
½ cup black currants

½ cup sugar
¼ cup ground rice or potato
 flour

Stew fruit with sugar and enough water to keep from burning. Strain off the juice, mix a little of the juice with the rice or potato flour, and cook for 5 minutes, stirring constantly. Chill and serve with whipped cream.

Malakoff Cake

¾ cup almonds
¾ cup sugar
¾ cup butter
2 glasses rum

2 egg yolks
1 sponge cake
1 cup milk
1 cup whipping cream

Chop almonds finely. Roast in skillet with a little sugar, stirring constantly, until light brown. Cream together the butter and sugar, then beat in the almonds, 1 glass rum, and egg yolks. Cut sponge cake into 3 flat layers, soak each in 1 glass rum and milk.

Alternate a layer of cake and a layer of almond filling in a cake tin, ending with a layer of cake. Let stand in cold place about 12 hours. Before serving, turn out and cover with whipped cream.

Drachona

3 egg yolks	2 cups milk
½ cup powdered sugar	pinch of salt
4 tablespoons butter	1 tablespoon butter
5 cups flour	

Beat egg yolks with powdered sugar. Cream the butter and add to egg yolk mixture. Blend flour and milk together and add a pinch of salt before adding to batter. Mix and beat together. Melt 1 tablespoon butter in a pan, pour mixture into it, and bake in 325 degree oven about 30 minutes.

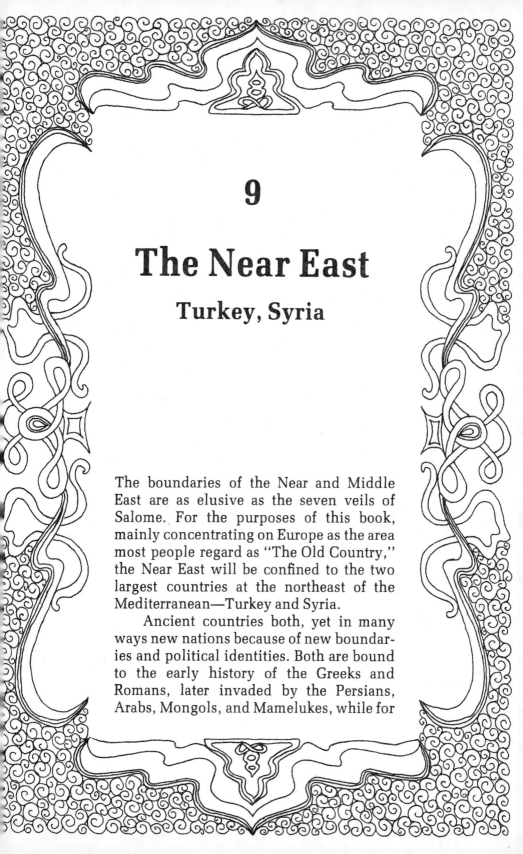

9

The Near East

Turkey, Syria

The boundaries of the Near and Middle East are as elusive as the seven veils of Salome. For the purposes of this book, mainly concentrating on Europe as the area most people regard as "The Old Country," the Near East will be confined to the two largest countries at the northeast of the Mediterranean—Turkey and Syria.

Ancient countries both, yet in many ways new nations because of new boundaries and political identities. Both are bound to the early history of the Greeks and Romans, later invaded by the Persians, Arabs, Mongols, and Mamelukes, while for centuries the Turkish Ottoman Empire dominated much of Eastern Europe.

Like their Middle Eastern neighbors—Lebanon, Iraq (formerly Mesopotamia), Iran (formerly Persia), Israel, and Jordan —Turkey and Syria are bound by similar foods both exotic and spicy.

Lamb is the staple meat of the Near and Middle East, since this is not good cattle grazing country. Eggplant is the most popular and versatile vegetable. The Turks alone claim forty ways to prepare eggplant. *Pila* (rice) accompanies many meat and fish dishes. Turkish *shish kabab* (skewered lamb) and yogurt have become world famous.

Turkish *Dolmas* are grape leaves stuffed with black currants, pine nuts, and rice, cooked in olive oil and served cold. Dough filled with meat, fish, rice, and nuts, called *Boreks* in Turkey have their counterpart in the Balkans. Eggplant and green peppers are also stuffed with meat and rice. Olives and their oil are used extensively as well as exported.

Fish is abundant throughout the Mediterranean and Black Seas, providing an almost endless variety of inexpensive foods for Eastern tables. Sturgeon, caviar, lobster, crab, mullet, anchovies, and swordfish are among the most popular.

Desserts are extra sweet, often made with honey and syrup (hence the name "Turkish Delight"), sometimes having suggestive names like *Kadin Gobegi* (lady's navel).

A visit to the bazaars of Istanbul and Damascus reveals many native vegetables and fruits, dried leaves and flowers, aromatic seeds, spices, varieties of rice and lentils that Eastern cooks conjur up into dishes Westerners never dreamed of, nor do they have the constitution for some of them.

Turkey and Syria are ageless lands, yet nearly brand new to us. Restaurants and kitchens of Near Eastern emigrants in America and elsewhere in the West offer us a dining table view into their fascinating pasts and a chance to share their exciting future.

Chapter 30

TURKEY

Turkey's 7,000-year history is one of the richest and most colorful of the East. Noah's Ark reputedly came to rest on Mount Ararat on the mountainous eastern frontier by Russia; Homer was born in Smyrna when it was part of Greece; and the Virgin Mary lived her last days at Ephesus. Cleopatra also spent some time in Ephesus, the tomb of St. John the Apostle lies there, and the world's first modern bank opened there. The cavern of St. Peter is in Antakya.

Greeks, Romans, Persians, and Mongols all marched across its mountains and valleys, and in the thirteenth century the Ottoman Empire (predecessor of Turkey) began a 500-year reign of supremacy over much of Eastern Europe.

Turkey became a republic in 1923, fiercely independent, especially of Russia, its neighbor to the north and east. In recent years Turkey's Mediterranean coastal beaches and resorts have earned it the title of an Eastern Riviera, though much less crowded.

The city of two million people now called Istanbul was founded in 658 B.C. by a Greek named Byzas, who gave his name to Byzantium. It became capital of the Eastern Roman Empire in A.D. 330 and was named Constantinople after the Roman Emperor Constantine, a name it kept until 1453 when the Turks captured it and changed its name to Istanbul, which means "Many Islams."

Today Istanbul shows many fascinating remnants of its Greek, Roman, and early Christian past, with triumphal arches, temples, mosques, minarets, churches, palaces, and museums containing priceless art objects of antiquity. The Seraglio, once the palace of the sultans, has the treasure-filled Topkapi Museum. Istanbul's Grand Bazaar, largest of its type in the world, has hundreds of small shops where every imaginable object can be bargained for. As if this wasn't enough to make the city memorable, the sarcophagus of Alexander the Great is located here.

Turkey's capital and more modern city is Ankara, which has half the population of Istanbul and is located in about the geographic center of the country. Here are the ancient temple of the Roman Emperor Augustus, the old fortress and white tower of Angora, and the renowned Archaeological Museum. But modern Ankara, more than Istanbul, is a symbol of Turkey's determination to look to the future. Yet while automobiles blare their horns and businessmen hurry to and from offices, the sound of the *Muezzin* calls the faithful to prayer and calm settles over the city.

Antakya, in southernmost Turkey near the Syrian border, was founded in 301 B.C. In ancient times the city was called Antioch. It was in Antioch that the disciples of Jesus, in the grotto of St. Peter, first called themselves Christians.

Straddling East and West, Turkey's cuisine is most strongly influenced by its immediate western neighbor, Greece. *Boreks* are dough balls filled with cheese and chopped nuts, similar to those eaten by the Greeks and to the *Pirogi* of the Russians. Sweetened versions of *Boreks* are made with honey, nuts, syrup, and cinnamon.

Halvah and *Baklava*, from both Greece and Arabia, are very sweet concoctions of honey and nuts adapted into "Turkish Delights."

Dolmas, popular throughout the East, are grape leaves stuffed with black currants, nuts, and rice. Rice, called *Pila*, is served many ways with many foods. Chicken is cooked with red pepper, topped with walnut sauce, and called *Cerkes Tavugu*.

Fish is plentiful in Turkey from both the Mediterranean and Black Seas. Lobster, red caviar, mullet, crab, and swordfish are most popular, the latter called *Kilic* when prepared with bay leaves and cooked on a spit.

Turkey's two major contributions to the tables of the world are *shish kebab* and yogurt. "Shish" is the Turkish word for sword. "Kebab" means lamb or mutton. The meat is marinated, then skewered with green pepper, onion, cherry tomatoes, and mushrooms and grilled.

Yogurt, the tangy curdled milk, is low in calories and high in claims for providing good health and long life. It is also used by some as a cosmetic and medicine. The Turks eat their yogurt much richer and less tart than in most Western countries.

Eggplant is the Turks' favorite vegetable, with okra a close second. Dates and figs are used extensively in desserts and pastries.

Turkish coffee, strong and black, is also world renowned. Favorite Turkish alcoholic drinks are *Raki*, a potent, anise-flavored beverage, and *Boza*, made of bread and water, like the Russian *Kvas*.

Turkey is called the new "in" spot of Europe or the Near East, wherever you choose to place it geographically. And the Turks are considered among the most friendly to tourists anywhere. An uncrowded, unhurried country with rich views into the distant past, Turkey stands on the brink of a most prosperous future, welcoming home those who once left it for political or economic reasons, and welcoming tourists who can't know the exciting visit in store for them.

Appetizers

Kadin Budu
(lady meatballs)

1 pound lean ground beef or lamb	1 tablespoon salt
	½ teaspoon pepper
½ cup onions, finely chopped	1 cup olive oil
¼ cup rice uncooked	2 eggs

Mix meat, onions, rice, salt and pepper together in a bowl. Roll the mixture into balls about 1 inch in diameter, then shape into ovals. Boil 2 cups of water in a skillet, add meatballs, and let water come to a boil again, then lower heat and simmer slowly, uncovered, about 30 minutes. Add water, if necessary, to keep meatballs covered. Remove balls to a warm plate. Pour out the water, add olive oil to the skillet, and heat slowly. Dip meatballs into the beaten eggs and drop them into the hot oil. Fry slowly for 5 to 8 minutes until brown on both sides. Drain and serve. Yield: 2 servings.

Soup

Cacik
(yogurt and cucumber soup)

1 medium cucumber
2 cups plain yogurt
2 teaspoons white vinegar
1 teaspoon olive oil

2 teaspoons fresh mint
¼ teaspoon dried dill
1 teaspoon salt

Peel and slice cucumber lengthwise in half. Remove and discard the seeds. Grate cucumber coarsely. (Recipe requires about 1 cup.) Stir yogurt in a bowl with a whisk or wooden spoon until it is smooth. Beat in cucumber, vinegar, olive oil, mint, dill, and salt. Season to taste and refrigerate 2 hours. Serve in chilled soup bowls. Yield: 2 servings.

Vegetables

Imam Baïldi
(stuffed eggplant)

eggplants
½ pound chopped onions
olive oil

1 pound tomatoes, quartered
1 clove garlic
salt and pepper

Remove stalks but do not peel eggplants. Blanch in boiling water about 8 minutes. Saute onions in oil until golden, then add tomatoes and garlic. Season and cook slowly until pulpy. Cut eggplant lengthwise in half, remove a little of the pulp and add the stuffing. Fill each half with tomato and onion, put in casserole, pour a little of the stuffing over them, and bake at 350 degrees for 1 hour. Yield: 4 servings.

Rice

Pilav
(tomato and rice)

2 cups uncooked rice	3½ cups beef or chicken
4 medium tomatoes	stock or broth
4 tablespoons butter	2 teaspoons salt

Wash and drain rice, then put aside. Peel and seed tomatoes, cut them into small chunks. Heat tomatoes with butter and make into a paste, then add stock or broth and salt and boil about 2 minutes. Add rice while liquid is boiling. Stir once, cover, and cook over medium heat without stirring again, until all liquid has been absorbed. Simmer over low heat another 20 minutes. Do not stir, remove from heat, and leave covered another 30 minutes. Gently transfer rice to a serving plate, keeping rice fluffy.

Fish

Ghyughej Balighi
(baked fish)

2 pounds striped bass or	salt
other fish	juice of ½ lemon
2 medium onions	3 stalks celery, chopped
½ cup olive oil	4 small carrots, peeled
¼ cup tomato paste	and diced
1½ cups water	½ teaspoon parsley, chopped
3 cloves garlic, crushed	lemon slices to garnish
paprika	

Clean and cut fish into 1-inch slices. Cut onions into rings and saute in skillet with ⅛ cup of olive oil until golden. Add tomato paste, water, garlic, paprika, salt, lemon juice, remaining olive oil, celery, and carrots. Cook covered over medium heat for 25 minutes. Remove fish to a baking casserole and cover with the sauce. Bake at 400 degrees for 25 minutes. Garnish with parsley and lemon slices. Yield: 2 servings.

Balighi Kebabi
(fish kebabs)

fresh mackerel	fennel
salt and pepper	bay leaves
parsley	

Cut off heads of mackeral; if large, divide into 3 slices; if small, cut into 2 pieces. Wash and dry them, sprinkle with salt and pepper and chopped parsley mixed with fennel. Let fish stand 1 hour. Skewer the fish with a bay leaf between each piece, and grill, turning so fish is done all over.

Poultry

Tawuk Circassian
(Circassian chicken)

1 broiling chicken	cinnamon
salt and pepper	chicken broth

Split chicken in half lengthwise and remove bones. Cut meat into 4 or 5 pieces and flatten thicker parts with a rolling pin. Salt and pepper each piece, sprinkle a little cinnamon on each, and let stand 1 or 2 hours. Charcoal broil them over a medium fire, turning frequently. When browned, place in a stewing pan and cover with chicken broth. Put pan over a moderate charcoal fire and simmer until tender. Yield: 2 servings.

Meat

Tomates Dolmasi
(baked stuffed tomatoes)

8 tomatoes
1 onion, chopped
½ clove garlic, crushed
4 tablespoons olive oil
½ pound ground lamb or pork
⅛ teaspoon pepper

½ teaspoon salt
½ teaspoon cinnamon
2 sprigs marjoram
⅓ cup cooked rice
1 egg

Cut off a little of the top of each tomato and scoop out the insides. Saute onion and garlic in olive oil, add meat, seasoning, spices, and tomato pulp. Cover and simmer a few minutes. Take from fire, add rice and beaten egg. Mix. Stuff tomatoes and place in buttered casserole. Bake at 375 degrees about 30 minutes until tender and brown. Add water to casserole if necessary. Yield: 8 servings.

Shish Kebab
(skewered lamb)

2-pound leg of lamb
1 tablespoon olive oil
juice of ½ lemon
salt and pepper
1 sliced onion

3 tomatoes, sliced
1 green pepper
eggplant
bay leaves

Cut lamb into 1-inch serving cubes. Mix olive oil with lemon juice and rub into the meat. Sprinkle with salt and pepper, cover with slices of onion and tomato and a few bay leaves. Marinate in refrigerator about 5 hours. Put meat on skewers, alternating with onion, tomatoes, green pepper, sliced eggplant, and 1 or 2 bay leaves. Broil over charcoal or under the grill until done, turning as needed. Yield: 4 servings.

Kizartma
(stewed mutton)

mutton cut in chunks
salt
butter

onions, sliced
flour

Put chunks of mutton in a pan, salt them, and cover with water. Let meat boil about 30 minutes. Skim off scum and remove meat. Saute onions in butter until golden brown. Fry meat chunks in butter until brown, then put in saucepan with sauted onions. Add liquid mutton was stewing in, cover the pan, and place over a moderate charcoal fire. Thicken gravy with flour and serve.

Desserts

Lalanga
(fried pastries)

Sprinkle 6 large tablespoons of flour into a bowl, make a hole in the middle, and put in 1 egg, a little salt, half a glass of water, and make a thick liquid. Fry by pouring it in spoonfuls into hot olive oil. Dip into cold maple syrup and place on a serving dish, pouring remaining syrup on top.

Kestane Sekeri
(chestnut dessert)

½ pound shelled chestnuts
⅛ teaspoon salt
1½ tablespoons butter
1½ tablespoons cream
2½ tablespoons sugar

4 egg yolks, beaten
1 tablespoon brandy
1 teaspoon vanilla
4 egg whites, beaten stiff

Boil the chestnuts, remove shells and skins. Cook in ¾ cup water until soft. Add salt, butter, cream, and sugar. Mix. Add egg yolks, brandy, and vanilla. Fold in egg whites. Bake in buttered baking dish at 350 degrees for 30 minutes.

Kaymakli Elma Kompostosu
(apple compote)

1 cup sugar
4 cooking apples, peeled and
  cored

16 whole cloves
½ cup whipped cream,
  chilled

Bring sugar and 1 cup water to a boil in a saucepan, stirring until sugar is dissolved. Set 4 cloves in a ring around top of each apple, place apples in the pan, pour syrup over each. Reduce heat and cover. Simmer 15 minutes, basting frequently, until apples are tender. Cool apples in the syrup. Serve apples in individual dishes, put whipped cream in center of each apple, and pour a little syrup over each. Yield: 4 servings.

Chapter 31

SYRIA

Syria long ago included the modern nations of Lebanon, Israel, and Jordan. Lying at the juncture of three continents, it had for centuries been dominated by the Hittites, Egyptians, Babylonians, Persians, Romans, Turks, Mongols, and Mamelukes. The Crusaders marched through Syria while it was incorporated into the Ottoman Empire from the eleventh to the sixteenth centuries.

After World War I, Syria, without Palestine and Trans-Jordan, was governed under French mandate. After World War II, Syria and Lebanon both gained their independence.

In its first 20 years of independence, Syria suffered under one political regime after another. At the same time Syria has been at odds with Israel since Israel's birth as a nation in 1948. Having anti-American feelings because of United States' ties with Israel, Syria turned to the U.S.S.R. for military and economic assistance.

After Israel's famous six-day war in 1967, Syria broke off diplomatic relations with the United States. But toward the end of 1972, a warming in Syria toward the United States became apparent, possibly because the people and government of Syria are currently enjoying their most serene period since the nation gained its independence.

Once completely government-dominated, businesses are

starting to be privately owned; relations are improving with Lebanon, Tunisia, and Morocco; and tourists are welcome, even from the United States.

Syria appears to be ending its western isolation, though in mid-1971 it joined with Egypt and Libya in forming a United Arab Republic. This was primarily to acquire financial aid from oil-rich Libya and for Egypt's help in recovering some territory lost to Israel. The federation is the latest in a long history of unsuccessful attempts at Arab political alliances, and the future will have to tell the results of this one. However the political winds blow in Syria these days, suffice to say that relations with the West are less tense.

Syria is a living museum of ancient history and culture. Some of its historic cities were lost by partitions to other nations. Still remaining within the boundaries of modern Syria are the ancient desert city of Palmyra, which reputedly was built by Solomon; the capital city of Damascus, said to be the oldest continuously existing city in the world; and the ancient seaport city of Latakia across the Mediterranean from Cyprus.

Syrian food is rather more simple than the food of Turkey or of other countries in the Near and Middle East, though many of the same ingredients are used. Lamb and rice, eggplant and olives are equally traditional foods. Chicken and bean or okra stews are popular, as well as the meat-and-fish-stuffed dough dishes. Fresh mint is a favorite spice. Green salads with olive oil dressing are very popular.

Syrians add garlic to their yogurt and enjoy it best with poached eggs. Their desserts are less rich than the desserts of Turkey. Syrians prefer stewed fruits mixed with nuts, or dried figs cooked with sugar and flavored with lemon juice or anise instead of the honey-soaked pastries of the Middle East.

Instead of making *shish kebab,* Syrians prefer their lamb baked in a casserole, called *Kibbi,* with cracked wheat, pine nuts, and onions.

The West is just beginning to learn about the wonders of Syria, an ancient land deservedly proud of its past and starting to come out of long years of isolation from the nations of the western world.

Soup

Shawrabat
(lentil soup)

1 pound lentils	1 teaspoon salt
2 medium onions, sliced	½ pound spinach, chopped
2 tablespoons olive oil	1 teaspoon lemon juice

Wash lentils. Saute onions in oil until light brown. Add lentils and salt, stir well, add 5 cups water. Bring to a boil, skim residue off top, and simmer slowly for 1 ¼ hours. Add spinach and cook another 15 minutes. Add lemon juice and serve. Yield: 4 servings.

Salads

Chozhaffe
(cold fruit salad)

½ cup dried apricots	¼ cup pine nuts
½ cup dried prunes	¼ cup pistachio nuts
½ cup dried figs	2 tablespoons rosewater
¼ cup raisins	sugar or fruit syrup
¼ cup almonds	ice

Wash all the dried fruit, cover with cold water, and soak in a cool place for 24 hours. Blanch the nuts and add to the fruit. Add rosewater and syrup to sweeten. Refrigerate until serving, then float ice cubes in the juice.

Khodar Salatat
(mixed salad)

½ head lettuce	½ teaspoon salt
1 medium cucumber, sliced	3 tablespoons olive oil
2 large tomatoes	2 tablespoons lemon juice
3 sprigs fresh mint	¼ clove garlic (optional)
4 sprigs parsley, chopped	

Wash lettuce, then tear into pieces for serving. Mix cucumber, tomatoes (cut into eighths), mint, and parsley. Add salt, oil, and lemon juice (and garlic, if desired).

Fish

Sayadiah
(Rice and fish casserole)

1½ pounds cod or haddock	3 cups rice
olive oil	1 teaspoon allspice
1 onion, sliced into rings	

Fry fish in olive oil; remove from oil and drain. Saute onion rings in same oil. Remove onions; strain and save oil. Wash the rice, cover with 3 cups boiling salted water, and add the strained oil. Simmer about 15 minutes, stirring often, until all liquid is absorbed. Add allspice and let rice steam a few minutes. Alternate rice and fish in layers in a greased casserole and bake at 350 degrees until brown.

Poultry

Dijaj
(roast chicken)

1 roasting chicken	2 tablespoons pine nuts
½ cup rice	1 teaspoon cinnamon
½ pound lamb, chopped	½ teaspoon salt
1 tablespoon butter	⅛ teaspoon pepper

Rub chicken inside and out with salt and pepper, then let stand. Wash rice 4 times, pour 2 cups boiling water over, and bring to a boil. Let cool about 7 minutes until half-cooked, then drain. Saute lamb in butter in skillet, add rice, pine nuts, cinnamon, pepper, and salt. Cover with water and cook slowly, covered, until water has evaporated. Stuff the chicken, secure with poultry pins or sew up the cavity, and roast until golden brown. Yield: 2 servings.

Meat

Kibbi
(lamb casserole)

1 cup cracked wheat
2 medium onions, chopped
1 pound lean lamb, ground
    twice
¼ pound butter

¼ cup pine nuts
1 pound lean and fat lamb,
    ground once
1½ teaspoons salt
¼ teaspoon pepper

Soak cracked wheat in cold water about 15 minutes, then drain and dry. Chill in refrigerator for 1 hour. Add 1 chopped onion to ground lean lamb and grind together. Saute remaining chopped onion in 2 tablespoons butter until golden, then mix with pine nuts. Add lean meat and stir. Let cool. Add cracked wheat to the mixture of lean and fat lamb. Add salt and pepper, knead until well blended, then separate into two equal portions. Place half of the wheat mixture in a buttered cake pan 9 inches square, add the ground meat and onion mixture, and cover with the rest of the wheat mixture. Press mixture down firmly in the pan, then cut into diamond shapes and lastly run knife around inside edges of pan. Put slices of butter on top and bake in 375 degree oven for about 1 hour. Separate the diamond-shaped pieces and serve with fluffy rice. Yield: 4 servings.

Desserts

Hrebah
(almond rings)

2 cups butter
1 cup sugar
3 cups flour, sifted

½ cup blanched, slivered
    almonds

Clarify butter by melting it, then removing from heat, and letting stand a few minutes, allowing solids to settle. Skim butterfat off the top and save. Let clarified butter cool, then beat with a wire whisk until it is white and creamy. Gradually beat in sugar, mix in flour, and knead until workable dough is formed. Roll into 4-inch lengths, curve into rings, and flatten just a little. Press almond slivers into the dough and bake at 300 degrees until done.

INDEX